DAVID
AND
GOLIATH

DAVID AND GOLIATH

UNDERDOGS, MISFITS, AND THE ART OF BATTLING GIANTS

MALCOLM GLADWELL

LITTLE, BROWN AND COMPANY

NEW YORK • BOSTON • LONDON

Little, Brown and Company
Hachette Book Group
237 Park Avenue, New York, NY 10017
littlebrown.com

First Edition: October 2013

Little, Brown and Company is a division of Hachette Book Group, Inc. The Little, Brown name and logo are trademarks of Hachette Book Group, Inc.

The publisher is not responsible for websites (or their content) that are not owned by the publisher.

The Hachette Speakers Bureau provides a wide range of authors for speaking events. To find out more, go to hachettespeakersbureau.com or call (866) 376-6591.

ISBN 978-0-316-20436-1 (hc) / 978-0-316-25178-5 (int'l pb) /
978-0-316-23985-1 (lp)
LCCN 2013941807

10 9 8 7 6 5 4 3

RRD-C

Printed in the United States of America

For A.L. and for S.F., a real underdog

Contents

But the Lord said to Samuel, "Do not look on his appearance or on the height of his stature, because I have rejected him; for the Lord does not see as mortals see; they look on the outward appearance, but the Lord looks on the heart."

1 Samuel 16:7

DAVID
AND
GOLIATH

Goliath

"AM I A DOG THAT YOU SHOULD
COME TO ME WITH STICKS?"

1.

At the heart of ancient Palestine is the region known as the Shephelah, a series of ridges and valleys connecting the Judaean Mountains to the east with the wide, flat expanse of the Mediterranean plain. It is an area of breathtaking beauty, home to vineyards and wheat fields and forests of sycamore and terebinth. It is also of great strategic importance.

Over the centuries, numerous battles have been fought for control of the region because the valleys rising from the Mediterranean plain offer those on the coast a clear path to the cities of Hebron, Bethlehem, and Jerusalem in the Judaean highlands. The most important valley is Aijalon, in the north. But the most storied is the Elah. The Elah was where Saladin faced off against the Knights of the Crusades in the twelfth century. It played a central role in the Maccabean wars with Syria more than a thousand years

3

before that, and, most famously, during the days of the Old Testament, it was where the fledgling Kingdom of Israel squared off against the armies of the Philistines.

The Philistines were from Crete. They were a seafaring people who had moved to Palestine and settled along the coast. The Israelites were clustered in the mountains, under the leadership of King Saul. In the second half of the eleventh century BCE, the Philistines began moving east, winding their way upstream along the floor of the Elah Valley. Their goal was to capture the mountain ridge near Bethlehem and split Saul's kingdom in two. The Philistines were battle-tested and dangerous, and the sworn enemies of the Israelites. Alarmed, Saul gathered his men and hastened down from the mountains to confront them.

The Philistines set up camp along the southern ridge of the Elah. The Israelites pitched their tents on the other side, along the northern ridge, which left the two armies looking across the ravine at each other. Neither dared to move. To attack meant descending down the hill and then making a suicidal climb up the enemy's ridge on the other side. Finally, the Philistines had enough. They sent their greatest warrior down into the valley to resolve the deadlock one on one.

He was a giant, six foot nine at least, wearing a bronze helmet and full body armor. He carried a javelin, a spear, and a sword. An attendant preceded him, carrying a large shield. The giant faced the Israelites and shouted out: "Choose you a man and let him come down to me! If he prevail in battle against me and strike me down, we shall be slaves to you. But if I prevail and strike him down, you will be slaves to us and serve us."

In the Israelite camp, no one moved. Who could win against such a terrifying opponent? Then, a shepherd boy who had come down from Bethlehem to bring food to his brothers stepped forward and volunteered. Saul objected: "You cannot go against this Philistine to do battle with him, for you are a lad and he is a man of war from his youth." But the shepherd was adamant. He had faced more ferocious opponents than this, he argued. "When the lion or the bear would come and carry off a sheep from the herd," he told Saul, "I would go after him and strike him down and rescue it from his clutches." Saul had no other options. He relented, and the shepherd boy ran down the hill toward the giant standing in the valley. "Come to me, that I may give your flesh to the birds of the heavens and the beasts of the field," the giant cried out when he saw his opponent approach. Thus began one of history's most famous battles. The giant's name was Goliath. The shepherd boy's name was David.

2.

David and Goliath is a book about what happens when ordinary people confront giants. By "giants," I mean powerful opponents of all kinds—from armies and mighty warriors to disability, misfortune, and oppression. Each chapter tells the story of a different person—famous or unknown, ordinary or brilliant—who has faced an outsize challenge and been forced to respond. Should I play by the rules or follow my own instincts? Shall I persevere or give up? Should I strike back or forgive?

Through these stories, I want to explore two ideas. The first is that much of what we consider valuable in our world arises out of these kinds of lopsided conflicts, because the act of facing overwhelming odds produces greatness and beauty. And second, that we consistently get these kinds of conflicts wrong. We misread them. We misinterpret them. Giants are not what we think they are. The same qualities that appear to give them strength are often the sources of great weakness. And the fact of being an underdog can *change* people in ways that we often fail to appreciate: it can open doors and create opportunities and educate and enlighten and make possible what might otherwise have seemed unthinkable. We need a better guide to facing giants—and there is no better place to start that journey than with the epic confrontation between David and Goliath three thousand years ago in the Valley of Elah.

When Goliath shouted out to the Israelites, he was asking for what was known as "single combat." This was a common practice in the ancient world. Two sides in a conflict would seek to avoid the heavy bloodshed of open battle by choosing one warrior to represent each in a duel. For example, the first-century BCE Roman historian Quintus Claudius Quadrigarius tells of an epic battle in which a Gaul warrior began mocking his Roman opponents. "This immediately aroused the great indignation of one Titus Manlius, a youth of the highest birth," Quadrigarius writes. Titus challenged the Gaul to a duel:

He stepped forward, and would not suffer Roman valour to be shamefully tarnished by a Gaul. Armed with a legionary's shield and a Spanish sword, he confronted the

Gaul. Their fight took place on the very bridge [over the Anio River] in the presence of both armies, amid great apprehension. Thus they confronted each other: the Gaul, according to his method of fighting, with shield advanced and awaiting an attack; Manlius, relying on courage rather than skill, struck shield against shield and threw the Gaul off balance. While the Gaul was trying to regain the same position, Manlius again struck shield against shield and again forced the man to change his ground. In this fashion he slipped under the Gaul's sword and stabbed him in the chest with his Spanish blade....After he had slain him, Manlius cut off the Gaul's head, tore off his tongue and put it, covered as it was with blood, around his own neck.

This is what Goliath was expecting—a warrior like himself to come forward for hand-to-hand combat. It never occurred to him that the battle would be fought on anything other than those terms, and he prepared accordingly. To protect himself against blows to the body, he wore an elaborate tunic made up of hundreds of overlapping bronze fishlike scales. It covered his arms and reached to his knees and probably weighed more than a hundred pounds. He had bronze shin guards protecting his legs, with attached bronze plates covering his feet. He wore a heavy metal helmet. He had three separate weapons, all optimized for close combat. He held a thrusting javelin made entirely of bronze, which was capable of penetrating a shield or even armor. He had a sword on his hip. And as his primary option, he carried a special kind of short-range spear with a metal shaft as "thick as a weaver's beam." It had a cord attached to it and an elaborate set of weights that allowed it to be released with extraordinary force and accuracy. As the historian Moshe Garsiel writes, "To the Israelites, this extraordinary spear, with its heavy shaft plus long and heavy iron blade, when hurled by Goliath's strong arm, seemed capable of piercing any bronze shield and bronze armor together." Can you see why no Israelite would come forward to fight Goliath?

Then David appears. Saul tries to give him his own sword and armor so at least he'll have a fighting chance. David refuses. "I cannot walk in these," he says, "for I am unused to it." Instead he reaches down and picks up five smooth stones, and puts them in his shoulder bag. Then he descends into the valley, carrying his shepherd's staff. Goliath looks at the boy coming toward him and is insulted. He was expecting to do battle with a seasoned warrior. Instead he sees a shepherd—a boy from one of the lowliest of all professions—who seems to want to use his shepherd's staff as a cudgel against Goliath's sword. "Am I a dog," Goliath says, gesturing at the staff, "that you should come to me with sticks?"

What happens next is a matter of legend. David puts one of his stones into the leather pouch of a sling, and he fires at Goliath's exposed forehead. Goliath falls, stunned. David runs toward him, seizes the giant's sword, and cuts off his head. "The Philistines saw that their warrior was dead," the biblical account reads, "and they fled."

The battle is won miraculously by an underdog who, by all expectations, should not have won at all. This is the way we have told one another the story over the many centuries since. It is how the phrase "David and Goliath" has come to be embedded in our language—as a metaphor for improbable victory. And the problem with that version of the events is that almost everything about it is wrong.

3.

Ancient armies had three kinds of warriors. The first was cavalry—armed men on horseback or in chariots. The second was infantry—foot soldiers wearing armor and carrying swords and shields. The third were projectile warriors, or what today would be called artillery: archers and, most important, slingers. Slingers had a leather pouch attached on two sides by a long strand of rope. They would put a rock or a lead ball into the pouch, swing it around in increasingly wider and faster circles, and then release one end of the rope, hurling the rock forward.

Slinging took an extraordinary amount of skill and practice. But in experienced hands, the sling was a devastating weapon. Paintings from medieval times show slingers hitting birds in midflight. Irish slingers were said to be able to hit a coin from as far away as they could see it, and in the Old Testament Book of Judges, slingers are described as being accurate within a "hair's breadth." An experienced slinger could kill or seriously injure a target at a distance of up to two hundred yards.[*] The Romans even had a special set of tongs made just to remove stones that had been embedded in some poor soldier's body by a sling. Imagine standing in front of a Major League Base-

---

[*] The modern world record for slinging a stone was set in 1981 by Larry Bray: 437 meters. Obviously, at that distance, accuracy suffers.

ball pitcher as he aims a baseball at your head. That's what facing a slinger was like—only what was being thrown was not a ball of cork and leather but a solid rock.

The historian Baruch Halpern argues that the sling was of such importance in ancient warfare that the three kinds of warriors balanced one another, like each gesture in the game of rock, paper, scissors. With their long pikes and armor, infantry could stand up to cavalry. Cavalry could, in turn, defeat projectile warriors, because the horses moved too quickly for artillery to take proper aim. And projectile warriors were deadly against infantry, because a big lumbering soldier, weighed down with armor, was a sitting duck for a slinger who was launching projectiles from a hundred yards away. "This is why the Athenian expedition to Sicily failed in the Peloponnesian War," Halpern writes. "Thucydides describes at length how Athens's heavy infantry was decimated in the mountains by local light infantry, principally using the sling."

Goliath is heavy infantry. He thinks that he is going to be engaged in a duel with another heavy-infantryman, in the same manner as Titus Manlius's fight with the Gaul. When he says, "Come to me, that I may give your flesh to the birds of the heavens and the beasts of the field," the key phrase is "come to me." He means come right up to me so that we can fight at close quarters. When Saul tries to dress David in armor and give him a sword, he is operating under the same assumption. He assumes David is going to fight Goliath hand to hand.

David, however, has no intention of honoring the rituals of single combat. When he tells Saul that he has killed bears and lions as a shepherd, he does so not just as testimony to his courage but to make another point as well: that he intends to fight Goliath the same way he has learned to fight wild animals—as a projectile warrior.

He *runs* toward Goliath, because without armor he has speed and maneuverability. He puts a rock into his sling, and whips it around and around, faster and faster at six or seven revolutions per second, aiming his projectile at Goliath's forehead—the giant's only point of vulnerability. Eitan Hirsch, a ballistics expert with the Israeli Defense Forces, recently did a series of calculations showing that a typical-size stone hurled by an expert slinger at a distance of thirty-five meters would have hit Goliath's head with a velocity of thirty-four meters per second—more than enough to penetrate his skull and render him unconscious or dead. In terms of stopping power, that is equivalent to a fair-size modern handgun. "We find," Hirsch writes, "that David could have slung and hit Goliath in little more than one second—a time so brief that Goliath would not have been able to protect himself and during which he would be stationary for all practical purposes."

What could Goliath do? He was carrying over a hundred pounds of armor. He was prepared for a battle at close range, where he could stand, immobile, warding off blows with his armor and delivering a mighty thrust of his spear. He watched David approach, first with scorn, then with surprise, and then with what can only have been horror—as it dawned on him that the battle he was expecting had suddenly changed shape.

"You come against me with sword and spear and javelin," David said to Goliath, "but I come against you in the name of the Lord Almighty, the God of the armies of

Israel, whom you have defied. This day the Lord will deliver you into my hands, and I'll strike you down and cut off your head....All those gathered here will know that it is not by sword or spear that the Lord saves; for the battle is the Lord, and he will give all of you into our hands."

Twice David mentions Goliath's sword and spear, as if to emphasize how profoundly different his intentions are. Then he reaches into his shepherd's bag for a stone, and at that point no one watching from the ridges on either side of the valley would have considered David's victory improbable. David was a slinger, and slingers beat infantry, hands down.

"Goliath had as much chance against David," the historian Robert Dohrenwend writes, "as any Bronze Age warrior with a sword would have had against an [opponent] armed with a .45 automatic pistol."*

4.

Why has there been so much misunderstanding around that day in the Valley of Elah? On one level, the duel reveals the folly of our assumptions about power. The reason King Saul is skeptical of David's chances is that David is small and Goliath is large. Saul thinks of power in terms

---

* The Israeli minister of defense Moshe Dayan — the architect of Israel's astonishing victory in the 1967 Six-Day War — also wrote an essay on the story of David and Goliath. According to Dayan, "David fought Goliath not with inferior but (on the contrary) with superior weaponry; and his greatness consisted not in his being willing to go out into battle against someone far stronger than he was. But in his knowing how to exploit a weapon by which a feeble person could seize the advantage and become stronger."

of physical might. He doesn't appreciate that power can come in other forms as well—in breaking rules, in substituting speed and surprise for strength. Saul is not alone in making this mistake. In the pages that follow, I'm going to argue that we continue to make that error today, in ways that have consequences for everything from how we educate our children to how we fight crime and disorder.

But there's a second, deeper issue here. Saul and the Israelites think they know who Goliath is. They size him up and jump to conclusions about what they think he is capable of. But they do not really *see* him. The truth is that Goliath's behavior is puzzling. He is supposed to be a mighty warrior. But he's not acting like one. He comes down to the valley floor accompanied by an attendant—a servant walking before him, carrying a shield. Shield bearers in ancient times often accompanied archers into battle because a soldier using a bow and arrow had no free hand to carry any kind of protection on his own. But why does Goliath, a man calling for sword-on-sword single combat, need to be assisted by a third party carrying an archer's shield?

What's more, why does he say to David, "Come to me"? Why can't Goliath go to David? The biblical account emphasizes how slowly Goliath moves, which is an odd thing to say about someone who is alleged to be a battle hero of infinite strength. In any case, why doesn't Goliath respond much sooner to the sight of David coming down the hillside without any sword or shield or armor? When he first sees David, his first reaction is to be insulted, when he should be terrified. He seems oblivious of what's happening around him. There is even that strange comment after he finally spots David with his shepherd's staff: "Am I a dog that you should come to me with sticks?" Sticks plural? David is holding only one stick.

What many medical experts now believe, in fact, is that Goliath had a serious medical condition. He looks and sounds like someone suffering from what is called acromegaly—a disease caused by a benign tumor of the pituitary gland. The tumor causes an overproduction of human growth hormone, which would explain Goliath's extraordinary size. (The tallest person in history, Robert Wadlow, suffered from acromegaly. At his death, he was eight foot eleven inches, and apparently still growing.)

And furthermore, one of the common side effects of acromegaly is vision problems. Pituitary tumors can grow to the point where they compress the nerves leading to the eyes, with the result that people with acromegaly often suffer from severely restricted sight and diplopia, or double vision. Why was Goliath led onto the valley floor by an attendant? Because the attendant was his visual guide. Why does he move so slowly? Because the world around him is a blur. Why does it take him so long to understand that David has changed the rules? Because he doesn't see David until David is up close. "Come to me, that I may give your flesh to the birds of the heavens and the beasts of the field," he shouts out, and in that request there is a hint of his vulnerability. *I need you to come to me because I cannot locate you otherwise.* And then there is the otherwise inexplicable "Am I a dog that you come to me with sticks?" David had only one stick. Goliath saw two.

What the Israelites saw, from high on the ridge, was an intimidating giant. In reality, the very thing that gave the giant his size was also the source of his greatest weakness. There is an important lesson in that for battles with all kinds of giants. The powerful and the strong are not always what they seem.

David came running toward Goliath, powered by courage and faith. Goliath was blind to his approach—and then he was down, too big and slow and blurry-eyed to comprehend the way the tables had been turned. All these years, we've been telling these kinds of stories wrong. *David and Goliath* is about getting them right.

PART ONE

THE ADVANTAGES OF DISADVANTAGES (AND THE DISADVANTAGES OF ADVANTAGES)

Some pretend to be rich, yet have nothing; others pretend to be poor, yet have great wealth.

Proverbs 13:7

CHAPTER ONE

Vivek Ranadivé

"IT WAS REALLY RANDOM. I
MEAN, MY FATHER HAD NEVER
PLAYED BASKETBALL BEFORE."

1.

When Vivek Ranadivé decided to coach his daughter Anjali's basketball team, he settled on two principles. The first was that he would never raise his voice. This was National Junior Basketball—the Little League of basketball. The team was made up mostly of twelve-year-olds, and twelve-year-olds, he knew from experience, did not respond well to shouting. He would conduct business on the basketball court, he decided, the same way he conducted business at his software firm. He would speak calmly and softly, and he would persuade the girls of the wisdom of his approach with appeals to reason and common sense.

The second principle was more important. Ranadivé was puzzled by the way Americans play basketball. He is from Mumbai. He grew up with cricket and soccer. He would never forget the first time he saw a basketball game. He thought it was mindless. Team A would score and then immediately retreat to its own end of the court. Team B would pass the ball in from the sidelines and dribble it into Team A's end, where Team A was patiently waiting. Then the process would reverse itself.

A regulation basketball court is ninety-four feet long. Most of the time, a team would defend only about twenty-four feet of that, conceding the other seventy feet. Occasionally teams played a full-court press—that is, they contested their opponent's attempt to advance the ball up the court. But they did it for only a few minutes at a time. It was as if there were a kind of conspiracy in the basketball world about the way the game ought to be played, Ranadivé thought, and that conspiracy had the effect of widening the gap between good teams and weak teams. Good teams, after all, had players who were tall and could dribble and shoot well; they could crisply execute their carefully prepared plays in their opponent's end. Why, then, did weak teams play in a way that made it easy for good teams to do the very things that they were so good at?

Ranadivé looked at his girls. Morgan and Julia were serious basketball players. But Nicky, Angela, Dani, Holly, Annika, and his own daughter, Anjali, had never played the game before. They weren't all that tall. They couldn't shoot. They weren't particularly adept at dribbling. They were not the sort who played pickup games at the playground every evening. Ranadivé lives in Menlo Park, in the heart of California's Silicon Valley. His team was made up of, as Ranadivé put it, "little blond girls." These were the daughters of nerds and computer programmers. They worked on science projects and read long and complicated books and dreamed about growing up to be marine biologists. Ranadivé knew that if they played the conventional way—if they let their opponents dribble the ball up the court without opposition—they would almost certainly lose to the girls for whom basketball was a passion. Ranadivé had come to America as a seventeen-year-old with fifty dollars in his pocket. He was not one to accept losing easily. His second principle, then, was that his team would play a real full-court press—every game, all the time. The team ended up at the national championships. "It was really random," Anjali Ranadivé said. "I mean, my father had never played basketball before."

2.

Suppose you were to total up all the wars over the past two hundred years that occurred between very large and very small countries. Let's say that one side has to be at least ten times larger in population and armed might than the other. How often do you think the bigger side wins? Most of us, I think, would put that number at close to 100 percent. A tenfold difference is *a lot.* But the actual answer may surprise you. When the political scientist Ivan Arreguín-Toft did the calculation a few years ago, what he came up with was 71.5 percent. Just under a third of the time, the weaker country wins.

Arreguín-Toft then asked the question slightly differently. What happens in wars between the strong and the weak when the weak side does as David did and refuses to

fight the way the bigger side wants to fight, using unconventional or guerrilla tactics? The answer: in those cases,
the weaker party's winning percentage climbs from 28.5
percent to 63.6 percent. To put that in perspective, the
United States' population is ten times the size of Canada's.
If the two countries went to war and Canada chose to fight
unconventionally, history would suggest that you ought to
put your money on Canada.

We think of underdog victories as improbable events:
that's why the story of David and Goliath has resonated so
strongly all these years. But Arreguín-Toft's point is that
they aren't at all. Underdogs win all the time. Why, then,
are we so shocked every time a David beats a Goliath? Why
do we automatically assume that someone who is smaller or
poorer or less skilled is *necessarily* at a disadvantage?

One of the winning underdogs on Arreguín-Toft's list,
for example, was T. E. Lawrence (or, as he is better known,
Lawrence of Arabia), who led the Arab revolt against the
Turkish army occupying Arabia near the end of the First
World War. The British were helping the Arabs in their up-
rising, and their goal was to destroy the long railroad the
Turks had built running from Damascus deep into the He-
jaz Desert.

It was a daunting task. The Turks had a formidable
modern army. Lawrence, by contrast, commanded an unruly band of Bedouin. They were not skilled troops. They
were nomads. Sir Reginald Wingate, one of the British
commanders in the region, called them "an untrained rabble, most of whom have never fired a rifle." But they were
tough and they were mobile. The typical Bedouin soldier
carried no more than a rifle, a hundred rounds of ammu-

nition, and forty-five pounds of flour, which meant that he could travel as much as 110 miles a day across the desert, even in summer. They carried no more than a pint of drinking water, since they were so good at finding water in the desert. "Our cards were speed and time, not hitting power," Lawrence wrote. "Our largest available resources were the tribesmen, men quite unused to formal warfare, whose assets were movement, endurance, individual intelligence, knowledge of the country, courage." The eighteenth-century general Maurice de Saxe famously said that the art of war was about legs, not arms, and Lawrence's troops were *all* legs. In one typical stretch in the spring of 1917, his men dynamited sixty rails and cut a telegraph line at Buair on March 24, sabotaged a train and twenty-five rails at Abu al-Naam on March 25, dynamited fifteen rails and cut a telegraph line at Istabl Antar on March 27, raided a Turkish garrison and derailed a train on March 29, returned to Buair and sabotaged the railway line again on March 31, dynamited eleven rails at Hedia on April 3, raided the train line in the area of Wadi Daiji on April 4 and 5, and attacked twice on April 6.

Lawrence's masterstroke was an assault on the port town of Aqaba. The Turks expected an attack from British ships patrolling the waters of the Gulf of Aqaba to the west. Lawrence decided to attack from the east instead, coming at the city from the unprotected desert, and to do that, he led his men on an audacious, six-hundred-mile loop—up from the Hejaz, north into the Syrian desert, and then back down toward Aqaba. This was in summer, through some of the most inhospitable land in the Middle East, and Lawrence tacked on a side trip to the outskirts

of Damascus in order to mislead the Turks about his intentions. "This year the valley seemed creeping with horned
vipers and puff-adders, cobras and black snakes,"
Lawrence writes in *Seven Pillars of Wisdom* about one
stage in the journey:

> We could not lightly draw water after dark, for there
> were snakes swimming in the pools or clustering in knots
> around their brinks. Twice puff-adders came twisting into
> the alert ring of our debating coffee-circle. Three of our
> men died of bites; four recovered after great fear and pain,
> and a swelling of the poisoned limb. Howeitat treatment
> was to bind up the part with snake-skin plaster, and read
> chapters of the Koran to the sufferer until he died.

When they finally arrived at Aqaba, Lawrence's band of
several hundred warriors killed or captured twelve hundred Turks and lost only two men. The Turks simply had
not thought that their opponent would be crazy enough to
come at them from the desert.

Sir Reginald Wingate called Lawrence's men an "untrained rabble." He saw the Turks as the overwhelming
favorites. But can you see how strange that was? Having
lots of soldiers and weapons and resources—as the Turks
did—is an advantage. But it makes you immobile and puts
you on the defensive. Meanwhile, movement, endurance,
individual intelligence, knowledge of the country, and
courage—which Lawrence's men had in abundance—
allowed them to do the impossible, namely, attack Aqaba
from the east, a strategy so audacious that the Turks never
saw it coming. There is a set of advantages that have to

do with material resources, and there is a set that have to do with the *absence* of material resources—and the reason underdogs win as often as they do is that the latter is sometimes every bit the equal of the former.

For some reason, this is a very difficult lesson for us to learn. We have, I think, a very rigid and limited definition of what an advantage is. We think of things as helpful that actually aren't and think of other things as unhelpful that in reality leave us stronger and wiser. Part One of *David and Goliath* is an attempt to explore the consequences of that error. When we see the giant, why do we automatically assume the battle is his for the winning? And what does it take to be that person who doesn't accept the conventional order of things as a given—like David, or Lawrence of Arabia, or, for that matter, Vivek Ranadivé and his band of nerdy Silicon Valley girls?

3.

Vivek Ranadivé's basketball team played in the National Junior Basketball seventh-and-eighth-grade division representing Redwood City. The girls practiced at Paye's Place, a gym in nearby San Carlos. Because Ranadivé had never played basketball, he recruited a couple of experts to help him. The first was Roger Craig, a former professional athlete who worked for Ranadivé's software company.*

---

* Roger Craig, it should be said, is more than simply a former professional athlete. Retired now, he was one of the greatest running backs in the history of the National Football League.

After Craig signed on, he recruited his daughter Rometra, who had played basketball in college. Rometra was the kind of person you assigned to guard your opponent's best player in order to render her useless. The girls on the team loved Rometra. "She has always been like my big sister," Anjali Ranadivé said. "It was so awesome to have her along."

Redwood City's strategy was built around the two deadlines that all basketball teams must meet in order to advance the ball. The first is the time allotted for the inbounds pass. When one team scores, a player from the other team takes the ball out-of-bounds and has five seconds to pass it to a teammate on the court. If that deadline is missed, the ball goes to the other team. Usually that's not an issue, because teams don't hang around to defend against the inbounds pass. They run back to their own end. Redwood City did not do that. Each girl on the team closely shadowed her counterpart. When some teams play the press, the defender plays behind the offensive player she's guarding in order to impede her once she catches the ball. The Redwood City girls, by contrast, played a more aggressive, high-risk strategy. They positioned themselves in front of their opponents to prevent them from catching the inbounds pass in the first place. And they didn't have anyone guard the player throwing the ball in. Why bother? Ranadivé used that extra player as a floater who could serve as a second defender against the other team's best player.

"Think about football," Ranadivé said. "The quarterback can run with the ball. He has the whole field to throw to, and it's still damned difficult to complete a pass." Basketball was harder. A smaller court. A five-second deadline. A heavier, bigger ball. As often as not, the teams Redwood City was playing against simply couldn't make the inbounds pass within the five-second limit. Or else the inbounding player, panicked by the thought that her five seconds were about to be up, would throw the ball away. Or her pass would be intercepted by one of the Redwood City players. Ranadivé's girls were maniacal.

The second deadline in basketball requires a team to advance the ball across midcourt into its opponent's end within ten seconds, and if Redwood City's opponents met the first deadline and were able to make the inbounds pass in time, the girls would turn their attention to the second deadline. They would descend on the girl who caught the inbounds pass and "trap" her. Anjali was the designated trapper. She'd sprint over and double-team the dribbler, stretching her long arms high and wide. Maybe she'd steal the ball. Maybe the other player would throw it away in a panic—or get bottled up and stalled, so that the ref would end up blowing the whistle.

"When we first started out, no one knew how to play defense or anything," Anjali said. "So my dad said the whole game long, 'Your job is to guard someone and make sure they never get the ball on inbounds plays.' It's the best feeling in the world to steal the ball from someone. We would press and steal, and do that over and over again. It made people so nervous. There were teams that were a lot better than us, that had been playing a long time, and we would beat them."

The Redwood City players would jump ahead 4–0, 6–0, 8–0, 12–0. One time they led 25–0. Because they typically got the ball underneath their opponent's basket, they rarely had to attempt the low-percentage, long-range shots that require skill and practice. They shot layups. In one of the few games that Redwood City lost that year, only four of the team's players showed up. They pressed anyway. Why not? They lost by only 3 points.

"What that defense did for us is that we could hide our weaknesses," Rometra Craig said. "We could hide the fact that we didn't have good outside shooters. We could hide the fact that we didn't have the tallest lineup. Because as long as we played hard on defense, we were getting steals and getting easy layups. I was honest with the girls. I told them, 'We're not the best basketball team out there.' But they understood their roles." A twelve-year-old girl would go to war for Rometra. "They were awesome," she said.

Lawrence attacked the Turks where they were weak—along the farthest, most deserted outposts of the railroad—and not where they were strong. Redwood City attacked the inbounds pass, the point in a game where a great team is as vulnerable as a weak one. David refused to engage Goliath in close quarters, where he would surely lose. He stood well back, using the full valley as his battlefield. The girls of Redwood City used the same tactic. They defended all ninety-four feet of the basketball court. The full-court press is legs, not arms. It supplants ability with effort. It is basketball for those who, like Lawrence's Bedouin, are "quite unused to formal warfare, whose assets [are] movement, endurance, individual intelligence…courage."

"It's an *exhausting* strategy," Roger Craig said. He and Ranadivé were in a conference room at Ranadivé's software company, reminiscing about their dream season.

Ranadivé was at the whiteboard, diagramming the intricacies of the Redwood City press. Craig was sitting at the table.

"My girls had to be more fit than the others," Ranadivé said.

"He used to make them run!" Craig said, nodding.

"We followed soccer strategy in practice," Ranadivé said. "I would make them run and run and run. I couldn't teach them skills in that short period of time, and so all we did was make sure they were fit and had some basic understanding of the game. That's why attitude plays such a big role in this, because you're going to get tired."

Ranadivé said "tired" with a note of approval in his voice. His father was a pilot who was jailed by the Indian government because he wouldn't stop challenging the safety of the country's planes. Ranadivé went to MIT after he saw a documentary on the school and decided that it was perfect for him. This was in the 1970s, when going abroad for undergraduate study required the Indian government to authorize the release of foreign currency, and Ranadivé camped outside the office of the governor of the Reserve Bank of India until he got his money. Ranadivé is slender and fine-boned, with a languorous walk and an air of imperturbability. But none of that should be mistaken for nonchalance. The Ranadivés are relentless.

He turned to Craig. "What was our cheer again?"

The two men thought for a moment, then shouted out happily, in unison: "One, two, three, *attitude!*"

The whole Redwood City philosophy was based on a willingness to try harder than anyone else.

"One time, some new girls joined the team," Ranadivé said, "and so in the first practice I had, I was telling them, 'Look, this is what we're going to do,' and I showed them. I said, 'It's all about attitude.' And there was this one new girl on the team, and I was worried that she wouldn't get the whole attitude thing. Then we did the cheer and she said, 'No, no, it's not one, two, three, *attitude*. It's one, two, three, attitude, *hah!*'" — at which point Ranadivé and Craig burst out laughing.

4.

In January of 1971, the Fordham University Rams played a basketball game against the University of Massachusetts Redmen. The game was in Amherst, at the legendary arena known as the Cage, where the Redmen hadn't lost since December of 1969. Their record was 11–1. The Redmen's star was none other than Julius Erving—Dr. J—one of the greatest athletes ever to play the game of basketball. The UMass team was very, very good. Fordham, on the other hand, was a team of scrappy kids from the Bronx and Brooklyn. Their center had torn up his knee the first week of practice and was out, which meant that their tallest player was six foot five. Their starting forward—and forwards are typically almost as tall as centers—was Charlie Yelverton, who was only six foot two. But from the opening buzzer, the Rams launched a full-court press, and they never let up. "We jumped out to a thirteen-to-six lead, and it was a war the rest of the way," Digger Phelps, the Fordham coach at the time, recalls. "These were tough city kids.

We played you ninety-four feet. We knew that sooner or later we were going to make you crack." Phelps sent in one indefatigable Irish or Italian kid from the Bronx after another to guard Erving, and, one by one, the indefatigable Irish and Italian kids fouled out. None of them were as good as Erving. It didn't matter. Fordham won 87–79.

In the world of basketball, there are countless stories like this about legendary games where David used the full-court press to beat Goliath. Yet the puzzle of the press is that it has never become popular. What did Digger Phelps do the season after his stunning upset of UMass? He never used the full-court press the same way again. And the UMass coach, Jack Leaman, who was humbled in his own gym by a bunch of street kids—did he learn from his defeat and use the press himself the next time he had a team of underdogs? He did not. Many people in the world of basketball don't really believe in the press because it's not perfect: it can be beaten by a well-coached team with adept ball handlers and astute passers. Even Ranadivé readily admitted as much. All an opposing team had to do to beat Redwood City was press back. The girls were not good enough to handle a taste of their own medicine. But all those objections miss the point. If Ranadivé's girls or Fordham's scrappy overachievers had played the conventional way, they would have lost by thirty points. The press was the best chance the underdog had of beating Goliath. Logically, *every* team that comes in as an underdog should play that way, shouldn't they? So why don't they?

Arreguín-Toft found the same puzzling pattern. When an underdog fought like David, he usually won. But most of the time, underdogs *didn't* fight like David. Of the 202 lopsided conflicts in Arreguín-Toft's database, the under-dog chose to go toe-to-toe with Goliath the conventional way 152 times—and lost 119 times. In 1809, the Peruvians fought the Spanish straight up and lost; in 1816, the Georgians fought the Russians straight up and lost; in 1817, the Pindaris fought the British straight up and lost; in the Kandyan rebellion of 1817, the Sri Lankans fought the British straight up and lost; in 1823, the Burmese chose to fight the British straight up and lost. The list of failures is endless. In the 1940s, the Communist insurgency in Vietnam bedeviled the French until, in 1951, the Viet Minh strategist Vo Nguyen Giap switched to conventional warfare—and promptly suffered a series of defeats. George Washington did the same in the American Revolution, abandoning the guerrilla tactics that had served the colonists so well in the conflict's early stages. "As quickly as he could," William Polk writes in *Violent Politics*, a history of unconventional warfare, Washington "devoted his energies to creating a British-type army, the Continental Line. As a result, he was defeated time after time and almost lost the war."

It makes no sense, unless you think back to Lawrence's long march across the desert to Aqaba. It is easier to dress soldiers in bright uniforms and have them march to the sound of a fife-and-drum corps than it is to have them ride six hundred miles through snake-infested desert on the back of camels. It is easier and far more satisfying to retreat and compose yourself after every score—and execute perfectly choreographed plays—than to swarm about, arms flailing, and contest every inch of the basketball court. Underdog strategies are *hard*.

The only person who seemed to have absorbed the lessons of that famous game between Fordham and the University of Massachusetts was a skinny little guard on the UMass freshman team named Rick Pitino. He didn't play that day. He watched, and his eyes grew wide. Even now, more than four decades later, he can name, from memory, nearly every player on the Fordham team: Yelverton, Sullivan, Mainor, Charles, Zambetti. "They came in with the most unbelievable pressing team I'd ever seen," Pitino said. "Five guys between six feet five and six feet. It was unbelievable how they covered ground. I studied it. There is no way they should have beaten us. Nobody beat us at the Cage."

Pitino became the head coach at Boston University in 1978, when he was twenty-five years old, and he used the press to take the school to its first NCAA tournament appearance in twenty-four years. At his next head-coaching stop, Providence College, Pitino took over a team that had gone 11–20 the year before. The players were short and almost entirely devoid of talent—a carbon copy of the Fordham Rams. They pressed, and ended up one game away from playing for the national championship. Again and again, in his career, Pitino has achieved extraordinary things with a fraction of the talent of his competitors.

"I have so many coaches come in every year to learn the press," Pitino said. He is now the head basketball coach at the University of Louisville, and Louisville has become the Mecca for all those Davids trying to learn how to beat Goliaths. "Then they e-mail me. They tell me they can't do it. They don't know if their players can last." Pitino shook his head. "We practice every day for two hours," he went on. "The players are moving almost ninety-eight percent of the practice. We spend very little time talking. When we make our corrections"—that is, when Pitino and his coaches stop play to give instructions—"they are seven-second corrections, so that our heart rate never rests. We are always working." Seven seconds! The coaches who come to Louisville sit in the stands and watch that ceaseless activity and despair. To play by David's rules you have to be desperate. You have to be so *bad* that you have no choice. Their teams are just good enough that they know it could never work. Their players could never be convinced to play that hard. They were not desperate enough. But Ranadivé? Oh, he was desperate. You would think, looking at his girls, that their complete inability to pass and dribble and shoot was their greatest disadvantage. But it wasn't, was it? It was what made their winning strategy possible.

5.

One of the things that happened to Redwood City the minute the team started winning basketball games was that opposing coaches began to get angry. There was a sense that Redwood City wasn't playing fair—that it wasn't right to use the full-court press against twelve-year-old girls who were just beginning to grasp the rudiments of the game. The point of youth basketball, the dissenting chorus said, was to learn basketball skills. Ranadivé's girls, they felt, were not really playing *basketball*. Of course, you could as easily argue that in playing the press, a twelve-year-old girl learned much more valuable lessons—that effort can trump ability and that conventions are made to be challenged. But the coaches on the other side of Redwood City's lopsided scores were disinclined to be so philosophical.

"There was one guy who wanted to have a fight with me in the parking lot," Ranadivé said. "He was this big guy. He obviously played football and basketball himself, and he saw that skinny, foreign guy beating him at his own game. He wanted to beat me up."

Roger Craig said that he was sometimes startled by what he saw. "The other coaches would be screaming at their girls, humiliating them, shouting at them. They would say to the refs, 'That's a foul! That's a foul!' But we weren't fouling. We were just playing aggressive defense."

"One time, we were playing this team from East San Jose," Ranadivé said. "They had been playing for years. These were born-with-a-basketball girls. We were just crushing them. We were up something like twenty to zero. We wouldn't even let them inbound the ball, and the coach got so mad that he took a chair and threw it. He started screaming at his girls, and of course the more you scream at girls that age, the more nervous they get." Ranadivé shook his head. You should never, ever raise your voice. "Finally, the ref physically threw the guy out of the building. I was afraid. I think he couldn't stand it because here were all these blond-haired girls who were clearly inferior players, and we were killing them."

All the qualities that distinguish the ideal basketball player are acts of skill and finely calibrated execution. When the game becomes about effort over ability, it be-

35

comes unrecognizable: a shocking mixture of broken plays and flailing limbs and usually competent players panicking and throwing the ball out-of-bounds. You have to be outside the establishment—a foreigner new to the game or a skinny kid from New York at the end of the bench—to have the audacity to play it that way.

T. E. Lawrence could triumph because he was the farthest thing from a proper British Army officer. He did not graduate with honors from the top English military academy. He was an archaeologist by trade who wrote dreamy prose. He wore sandals and full Bedouin dress when he went to see his military superiors. He spoke Arabic like a native, and handled a camel as if he had been riding one all his life. He didn't care what people in the military establishment thought about his "untrained rabble" because he had little invested in the military establishment. And then there's David. He must have known that duels with Philistines were supposed to proceed formally, with the crossing of swords. But he was a shepherd, which in ancient times was one of the lowliest of all professions. He had no stake in the finer points of military ritual.

We spend a lot of time thinking about the ways that prestige and resources and belonging to elite institutions make us better off. We don't spend enough time thinking about the ways in which those kinds of material advantages limit our options. Vivek Ranadivé stood on the sidelines as the opposing teams' parents and coaches heaped abuse on him. Most people would have shrunk in the face of that kind of criticism. Not Ranadivé. *It was really random. I mean, my father had never played basketball before.* Why should he care what the world of basketball thought of him? Ranadivé coached a team of girls who had no talent in a sport he knew nothing about. He was an underdog and a misfit, and that gave him the freedom to try things no one else even dreamt of.

6.

At the nationals, the Redwood City girls won their first two games. In the third round, their opponents were from somewhere deep in Orange County. Redwood City had to play them on their own court, and the opponents supplied their own referee as well. The game was at eight o'clock in the morning. The Redwood City players left their hotel at six to beat the traffic. It went downhill from there. The referee did not believe in "one, two, three, attitude, *hah!*" He didn't think that playing to deny the inbounds pass was basketball. He began calling one foul after another.

"They were touch fouls," Craig said. Ticky-tacky stuff. The memory was painful.

"My girls didn't understand," Ranadivé said. "The ref called something like four times as many fouls on us as on the other team."

"People were booing," Craig said. "It was bad."

"A two-to-one ratio is understandable, but a ratio of four to one?" Ranadivé shook his head.

"One girl fouled out."

"We didn't get blown out. There was still a chance to win. But…"

Ranadivé called the press off. He had to. The Redwood City players retreated to their own end and passively watched as their opponents advanced down the court. The Redwood City girls did not run. They paused and deliberated between each possession. They played basketball the way basketball is supposed to be played, and in the end they lost—but not before proving that Goliath is not quite the giant he thinks he is.

CHAPTER TWO

Teresa DeBrito

"MY LARGEST CLASS WAS TWENTY-NINE KIDS. OH, IT WAS FUN."

1.

When Shepaug Valley Middle School was built, to serve the children of the baby boom, three hundred students spilled out of school buses every morning. The building had a line of double doors at the entrance to handle the crush, and the corridors inside seemed as busy as a highway.

But that was long ago. The baby boom came and went. The bucolic corner of Connecticut where Shepaug is located—with its charming Colonial-era villages and winding country lanes—was discovered by wealthy couples from New York City. Real-estate prices rose. Younger families could no longer afford to live in the area. Enrollment dropped to 245 students, then to just over 200. There are now eighty children in the school's sixth grade. Based on the number of students coming up through the region's elementary schools, that number may soon be cut in half, which means that the average class size in the school will soon fall well below the national average. A once-crowded school has become an intimate one.

Would you send your child to Shepaug Valley Middle School?

2.

The story of Vivek Ranadivé and the Redwood City girls' basketball team suggests that what we think of as an advantage and as a disadvantage is not always correct, that we mix the categories up. In this chapter and the next, I want to apply that idea to two seemingly simple questions about education. I say "seemingly" because they seem simple— although, as we will discover, they are really anything but.

The Shepaug Valley Middle School question is the first of the two simple questions. My guess is that you'd be delighted to have your child in one of those intimate classrooms. Virtually everywhere in the world, parents and policymakers take it for granted that smaller classes are better classes. In the past few years, the governments of the United States, Britain, Holland, Canada, Hong Kong, Singapore, Korea, and China—to name just a few—have all taken major steps to reduce the size of their classes. When the governor of California announced sweeping plans to reduce the size of his state's classes, his popularity *doubled* within three weeks. Inside of a month, twenty other governors had announced plans to follow suit, and within a month and a half, the White House announced class-size reduction plans of its own. To this day, 77 percent of Americans think that it makes more sense to use taxpayer money to lower class sizes than to raise teachers' salaries. Do you know how few things 77 percent of Americans agree on?

There used to be as many as twenty-five students in a classroom at Shepaug Valley. Now that number is sometimes as low as fifteen. That means students at Shepaug get far more individual attention from their teacher than before, and common sense says that the more attention children get from their teacher, the better their learning experience will be. Students at the new, intimate Shepaug Valley ought to be doing better at school than students at the old crowded Shepaug—right?

It turns out that there is a very elegant way to test whether this is true. Connecticut has a lot of schools like Shepaug. It's a state with many small towns with small elementary schools, and small schools in small towns are subject to the natural ebbs and flows of birthrates and real-estate prices—which means that a grade can be all but empty one year and crowded the next. Here are the enrollment records, for example, for the fifth grade in another Connecticut middle school:

1993	18	2000	21
1994	11	2001	23
1995	17	2002	10
1996	14	2003	18
1997	13	2004	21
1998	16	2005	18
1999	15		

In 2001, there were twenty-three fifth graders. The next year there were ten! Between 2001 and 2002, everything else in that school remained the same. It had the same teachers, the same principal, the same textbooks. It was in the same building in the same town. The local economy and the local population were virtually identical. The only thing that changed was the number of students in fifth grade. If the students in the year with a larger enrollment did better than the students in the year with a smaller one, then we can be pretty sure that it was because of the size of the class, right?

This is what is called a "natural experiment." Sometimes scientists set up formal experiments to try and test hypotheses. But on rare occasions the real world provides a natural way of testing the same theory—and natural experiments have many advantages over formal experiments. So what happens if you use the natural experiment of Connecticut—and compare the year-to-year results of every child who happens to have been in a small class with the results of those who happened to have come along in years with lots of kids? The economist Caroline Hoxby has done just that, looking at every elementary school in the state of Connecticut, and here's what she found: Nothing! "There are many studies that say they can't find a statistically significant effect of some policy change," Hoxby says. "That doesn't mean that there wasn't an effect. It just means that they couldn't find it in the data. In this study, I found estimates that are very precisely estimated around the point zero. I got a precise zero. In other words, *there is no effect.*"

This is just one study, of course. But the picture doesn't get any clearer if you look at all the studies of class size—and there have been hundreds done over the years. Fifteen percent find statistically significant evidence that students do better in smaller classes. Roughly the same number find that students do worse in smaller classes. Twenty percent are like Hoxby's and find no effect at all—and the balance find a little bit of evidence in either direction that isn't strong enough to draw any real conclusions. The typical class-size study concluded with a paragraph like this:

> In four countries—Australia, Hong Kong, Scotland, and the United States—our identification strategy leads to extremely imprecise estimates that do not allow for any confident assertion about class-size effects. In two countries—Greece and Iceland—there seem to be nontrivial beneficial effects of reduced class sizes. France is the only country where there seem to be noteworthy differences between mathematics and science teaching: While there is a statistically significant and sizable class-size effect in mathematics, a class-size effect of comparable magnitude can be ruled out in science. The nine school systems for which we can rule out large-scale class-size effects in both mathematics and science are the two Belgian schools, Canada, the Czech Republic, Korea, Portugal, Romania, Slovenia, and Spain. Finally, we can rule out any noteworthy causal effect of class size on student performance in two countries, Japan and Singapore.

Did you follow that? After sorting through thousands of pages of data on student performance from eighteen separate countries, the economists concluded that there were only two places in the world—Greece and Iceland—where there were "nontrivial beneficial effects of reduced class sizes." *Greece and Iceland?* The push to lower class sizes in the United States resulted in something like a quarter million new teachers being hired between 1996 and 2004. Over that same period, per-pupil spending in the United States soared 21 percent—with nearly all of those many tens of billions of new dollars spent on hiring those extra teachers. It's safe to say that there isn't a single profession in the world that has increased its numbers over the past two decades by as much or as quickly or at such expense as teaching has. One country after another has spent that kind of money because we look at a school like Shepaug Valley—where every teacher has a chance to get to know every student—and we think, "There's the place to send my child." But the evidence suggests that the thing we are convinced is such a big advantage might not be such an advantage at all.[*]

3.

Not long ago, I sat down with one of the most powerful people in Hollywood. He began by talking about his childhood in Minneapolis. He would go up and down the streets of his neighborhood at the beginning of every win-

---

[*] The definitive analysis of the many hundreds of class-size studies was done by the educational economist Eric Hanushek, *The Evidence on Class Size*. Hanushek says, "Probably no aspect of schools has been studied as much as class size. This work has been going on for years, and there is no reason to believe that there is any consistent relationship with achievement."

ter, he said, getting commitments from people who wanted their driveways and sidewalks cleared of snow. Then he would contract out each job to other children in the neighborhood. He paid his workers the moment the job was done, with cash on hand, and collected from the families later because he learned that was the surest way to get his crew to work hard. He had eight, sometimes nine, kids on the payroll. In the fall, he would switch to raking leaves.

"I would go and check their work so I could tell the customer that their driveway would be done the way they wanted it done," he remembered. "There would always be one or two kids who didn't do it well, and I would have to fire them." He was ten years old. By the age of eleven, he had six hundred dollars in the bank, all earned by himself. This was in the 1950s. That would be the equivalent today of five thousand dollars. "I didn't have money for where I wanted to go," he said with a shrug, as if it was obvious that an eleven-year-old would have a sense of where he wanted to go. "Any fool can spend money. But to earn it and save it and defer gratification—then you learn to value it differently."

His family lived in what people euphemistically called a "mixed neighborhood." He went to public schools and wore hand-me-downs. His father was a product of the Depression, and talked plainly about money. The man from Hollywood said that if he wanted something—a new pair of running shoes, say, or a bicycle—his father would tell him he had to pay half. If he left the lights on, his father would show him the electric bill. "He'd say, 'Look, this is what we pay for electricity. You're just being lazy, not turning the lights off. We're paying for you being lazy.

But if you need lights for working—twenty-four hours a day—no problem.'"

The summer of his sixteenth year, he went to work at his father's scrap-metal business. It was hard, physical labor. He was treated like any other employee. "It made me not want to live in Minneapolis," he said. "It made me never want to depend on working for my father. It was awful. It was dirty. It was hard. It was boring. It was putting scrap metal in barrels. I worked there from May fifteenth through Labor Day. I couldn't get the dirt off me. I think, looking back, my father wanted me to work there because he knew that if I worked there, I would want to escape. I would be motivated to do something more."

In college he ran a laundry service, picking up and delivering dry cleaning for his wealthy classmates. He organized student charter flights to Europe. He went to see basketball games with his friend and sat in terrible seats—obstructed by a pillar—and wondered what it would be like to sit in the premium seats courtside. He went to business school and law school in New York, and lived in a bad neighborhood in Brooklyn to save money. After graduation, he got a job in Hollywood, which led to a bigger job, and then to an even bigger job, and side deals and prizes and a string of extraordinary successes—to the point where he now has a house in Beverly Hills the size of an airplane hangar, his own jet, a Ferrari in the garage, and a gate in front of his seemingly never-ending driveway that looks like it was shipped over from some medieval castle in Europe. He understood money. And he understood money because he felt he had been given a thorough education in its value and function back home on the streets of Minneapolis.

"I wanted to have more freedom. I wanted to aspire to have different things. Money was a tool that I could use for my aspiration and my desires and my drive," he said. "Nobody taught me that. I learned it. It was kind of like trial and error. I liked the juice of it. I got some self-esteem from it. I felt more control over my life."

He was sitting in his home office as he said that—a room easily the size of most people's houses—and then he finally came to the point. He had children that he loved very dearly. Like any parent, he wanted to provide for them, to give them more than he had. But he had created a giant contradiction, and he knew it. He was successful because he had learned the long and hard way about the value of money and the meaning of work and the joy and fulfillment that come from making your own way in the world. But because of his success, it would be difficult for his children to learn those same lessons. Children of multimillionaires in Hollywood do not rake the leaves of their neighbors in Beverly Hills. Their fathers do not wave the electricity bill angrily at them if they leave the lights on. They do not sit in a basketball arena behind a pillar and wonder what it would be like to sit courtside. They *live* courtside.

"My own instinct is that it's much harder than anybody believes to bring up kids in a wealthy environment," he said. "People are ruined by challenged economic lives. But they're ruined by wealth as well because they lose their ambition and they lose their pride and they lose their sense of self-worth. It's difficult at both ends of the spectrum. There's some place in the middle which probably works best of all."

There are few things that inspire less sympathy than a multimillionaire crying the blues for his children, of course.

The man from Hollywood's children will never live in anything but the finest of houses and sit anywhere but in first class. But he wasn't talking about material comforts. He was a man who had made a great name for himself. One of his brothers had taken over the family scrap-metal business and prospered. Another of his brothers had become a doctor and built a thriving medical practice. His father had produced three sons who were fulfilled and motivated and who had accomplished something for themselves in the world. And his point was that it was going to be harder for him, as a man with hundreds of millions of dollars, to be as successful in raising his children as his father had been back in a mixed neighborhood of Minneapolis.

4.

The man from Hollywood is not the first person to have had this revelation. It is something, I think, that most of us understand intuitively. There is an important principle that guides our thinking about the relationship between parenting and money—and that principle is that more is not always better.

It is hard to be a good parent if you have too little money. That much is obvious. Poverty is exhausting and stressful. If you have to work two jobs to make ends meet, it's hard to have the energy in the evening to read to your children before they go to bed. If you are a working single parent, trying to pay your rent and feed and clothe your family and manage a long and difficult commute to a physically demanding job, it is hard to provide your children with the kind of consistent love and attention and discipline that makes for a healthy home.

But no one would ever say that it is *always* true that the more money you have, the better parent you can be. If you were asked to draw a graph about the relationship between parenting and money, you wouldn't draw this:

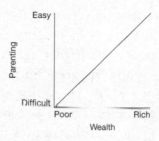

Money makes parenting easier until a certain point—when it stops making much of a difference. What is that point? The scholars who research happiness suggest that more money stops making people happier at a family income of around seventy-five thousand dollars a year. After that, what economists call "diminishing marginal returns" sets in. If your family makes seventy-five thousand and your neighbor makes a hundred thousand, that extra twenty-five thousand a year means that your neighbor can drive a nicer car and go out to eat slightly more often. But it doesn't make your neighbor happier than you, or better equipped to do the thousands of small and large things that make for being a good parent. A better version of the parenting-income graph looks like this:

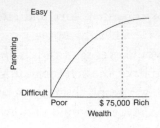

But that curve tells only part of the story, doesn't it? Because when the income of parents gets high enough, then parenting starts to be *harder* again. For most of us, the values of the world we grew up in are not that different from the world we create for our children. But that's not true for someone who becomes very wealthy. The psychologist James Grubman uses the wonderful expression "immigrants to wealth" to describe first-generation millionaires—by which he means that they face the same kinds of challenges in relating to their children that immigrants to any new country face. Someone like the Hollywood mogul grew up in the Old Country of the middle class, where scarcity was a great motivator and teacher. His father taught him the meaning of money and the virtues of independence and hard work. But his children live in the New World of riches, where the rules are different and baffling. How do you teach "work hard, be independent, learn the meaning of money" to children who look around themselves and realize that they never have to work hard, be independent, or learn the meaning of money? That's why so many cultures around the world have a proverb to describe the difficulty of raising children in an atmosphere of wealth. In English, the saying is "Shirtsleeves to shirtsleeves in three generations." The

Italians say, *"Dalle stelle alle stalle"* ("from stars to sta-
bles"). In Spain it's *"Quien no lo tiene, lo hance; y quien lo
tiene, lo deshance"* ("he who doesn't have it, does it, and
he who has it, misuses it"). Wealth contains the seeds of
its own destruction.

"A parent has to set limits. But that's one of the most
difficult things for immigrants to wealth, because they
don't know what to say when having the excuse of 'We
can't afford it' is gone," Grubman said. "They don't want
to lie and say, 'We don't have the money,' because if you
have a teenager, the teenager says, 'Excuse me. You have
a Porsche, and Mom has a Maserati.' The parents have to
learn to switch from 'No we can't' to 'No we won't.'"

But "no we won't," Grubman said, is much harder.
"No we can't" is simple. Sometimes, as a parent, you have
to say it only once or twice. It doesn't take long for the
child of a middle class family to realize that it is pointless
to ask for a pony, because a pony simply can't happen.

"No we won't" get a pony requires a *conversation,* and
the honesty and skill to explain that what is possible is not
always what is right. "I'll walk wealthy parents through
the scenario, and they have no idea what to say," Grubman
said. "I have to teach them: 'Yes, I can buy that for you.
But I choose not to. It's not consistent with our values.'"
But then that, of course, requires that you have a set of values, and know how to articulate them, and know how to
make them plausible to your child—all of which are really
difficult things for anyone to do, under any circumstances,
and especially if you have a Ferrari in the driveway, a private jet, and a house in Beverly Hills the size of an airplane
hangar.

The man from Hollywood had *too much* money. That was his problem as a parent. He was well past the point where money made things better, and well past the point where money stopped mattering all that much. He was at the point where money starts to make the job of raising normal and well-adjusted children more difficult. What the parenting graph really looks like is this:

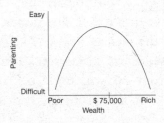

That's what is called an inverted-U curve. Inverted-U curves are hard to understand. They almost never fail to take us by surprise, and one of the reasons we are so often confused about advantages and disadvantages is that we forget when we are operating in a U-shaped world.*

Which brings us back to the puzzle of class size: What if the relationship between the number of children in a classroom and academic performance is not this:

---

* The psychologists Barry Schwartz and Adam Grant argue, in a brilliant paper, that, in fact, nearly everything of consequence follows the inverted U: "Across many domains of psychology, one finds that X increases Y to a point, and then it decreases Y....There is no such thing as an unmitigated good. All positive traits, states, and experiences have costs that at high levels may begin to outweigh their benefits."

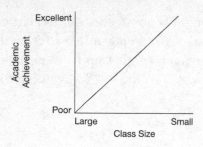

or even this:

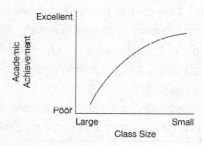

What if it's this?

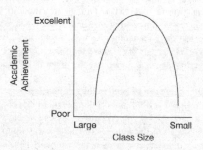

The principal of Shepaug Valley Middle School is a woman named Teresa DeBrito. In her five-year tenure at the school, she has watched the incoming class dwindle year by year. To a parent, that might seem like good news. But when she thought about it, she had that last curve in mind. "In a few years we're going to have fewer than fifty kids for the whole grade coming up from elementary school," she said. She was dreading it: "We're going to struggle."

5.

Inverted-U curves have three parts, and each part follows a different logic.* There's the left side, where doing more or having more makes things better. There's the flat middle, where doing more doesn't make much of a difference. And there's the right side, where doing more or having more makes things *worse*.†

If you think about the class-size puzzle this way, then what seems baffling starts to make a little more sense. The

---

* My father, a mathematician and stickler on these matters, begs to differ. I am oversimplifying things, he points out. Inverted-U curves actually have four parts. Stage one, where the curve is linear. Stage two, where "the initial linear relation has flagged." This is the area of diminishing marginal returns. Stage three, where extra resources have no effect on the outcome. And stage four, in which more resources are counterproductive. He writes: "We take a term in house construction— footing—to label the first stage, and then use the mnemonic 'footing, flagging, flat, and falling.'"

† A classic inverted-U curve can be seen in the relationship between alcohol consumption and health. If you go from not drinking at all to drinking one glass of wine a week, you'll live longer. And if you drink two glasses a week, you'll live a little bit longer, and three glasses a little bit longer still—all the way up to about seven glasses a week. (These numbers are for men, not women.) That's the upslope: the more, the merrier. Then there's the stretch from, say, seven to fourteen glasses of wine a week. You're not helping yourself by drinking more in that range. But you're not particularly hurting yourself either. That's the middle part of the curve. Finally, there's the right side of the curve: the downslope. That's when you get past fourteen glasses of wine a week and drinking more starts to leave you with a *shorter* life. Alcohol is not inherently good or bad or neutral. It starts out good, becomes neutral, and ends up bad.

number of students in a class is like the amount of money a parent has. It all depends on where you are on the curve. Israel, for example, has historically had quite large elementary school classes. The country's educational system uses the "Maimonides Rule," named after the twelfth-century rabbi who decreed that classes should not exceed forty children. That means elementary school classes can often have as many as thirty-eight or thirty-nine students. Where there are forty students in a grade, though, the same school could suddenly have two classes of twenty. If you do a Hoxby-style analysis and compare the academic performance of one of those big classes with a class of twenty, the small class will do better. That shouldn't be surprising. Thirty-six or thirty-seven students is a lot for any teacher to handle. Israel is on the left side of the inverted-U curve.

Now think back to Connecticut. In the schools Hoxby looked at, most of the variation was between class sizes in the mid- to low twenties and those in the high teens. When Hoxby says that her study found nothing, what she means is that she could find no real benefit to making classes smaller *in that medium range.* Somewhere between Israel and Connecticut, in other words, the effects of class size move along the curve to the flat middle—where adding resources to the classroom stops translating into a better experience for children.

Why isn't there much of a difference between a class of twenty-five students and a class of eighteen students? There's no question that the latter is easier for the teacher: fewer papers to grade, fewer children to know and follow. But a smaller classroom translates to a better outcome only if teachers change their teaching style when given a lower workload. And what the evidence suggests is that in this midrange, teachers don't necessarily do that. They just work less. This is only human nature. Imagine that you are a doctor and you suddenly learn that you'll see twenty patients on a Friday afternoon instead of twenty-five, while getting paid the same. Would you respond by spending more time with each patient? Or would you simply leave at six-thirty instead of seven-thirty and have dinner with your kids?

Now for the crucial question. Can a class be *too* small, the same way a parent can make *too* much money? I polled a large number of teachers in the United States and Canada and asked them that question, and teacher after teacher agreed that it can.

Here's a typical response:

My perfect number is eighteen: that's enough bodies in the room that no one person needs to feel vulnerable, but everyone can feel important. Eighteen divides handily into groups of two or three or six—all varying degrees of intimacy in and of themselves. With eighteen students, I can always get to each one of them when I need to. Twenty-four is my second favorite number—the extra six bodies make it even more likely that there will be a dissident among them, a rebel or two to challenge the status quo. But the trade-off with twenty-four is that it verges on having the energetic mass of an audience instead of a team. Add six more of them to hit thirty bodies and we've weakened the energetic connections so far that even the most charismatic of teachers can't maintain the magic all the time.

And what about the other direction? Drop down six from the perfect eighteen bodies and we have the Last Supper. And that's the problem. Twelve is small enough to fit around the holiday dinner table—too intimate for many high schoolers to protect their autonomy on the days they need to, and too easily dominated by the bombast or bully, either of whom could be the teacher herself. By the time we shrink to six bodies, there is no place to hide at all, and not enough diversity in thought and experience to add the richness that can come from numbers.

The small class is, in other words, potentially as difficult for a teacher to manage as the very large class. In one case, the problem is the number of potential interactions to manage. In the other case, it is the intensity of the potential interactions. As another teacher memorably put it, when a class gets too small, the students start acting "like siblings in the backseat of a car. There is simply no way for the cantankerous kids to get away from one another."

Here's another comment from a high school teacher. He had recently had a class of thirty-two and hated it. "When I face a class that large, the first thought that I have is 'Damn it, every time I collect something to mark, I am going to spend *hours* of time here at the school when I could be with my own kids.'" But he didn't want to teach a class of fewer than twenty either:

> The life source of any class is discussion, and that tends to need a certain critical mass to get going. I teach classes right now with students who simply don't discuss anything, and it is brutal at times. If the numbers get too low, discussion suffers. That seems counterintuitive because I

would think that the quiet kids who would hesitate to speak in a class of thirty-two would do so more readily in a class of sixteen. But that hasn't really been my experience. The quiet ones tend to be quiet regardless. And if the class is too small, among the speakers, you don't have enough breadth of opinion perhaps to get things really going. There is also something hard to pin down about energy level. A very small group tends to lack the sort of energy that comes from the friction between people.

And a really, *really* small class? Beware.

I had a class of nine students in grade-twelve Academic French. Sounds like a dream, doesn't it? It was a nightmare! You can't get any kind of conversation or discussion going in the target language. It's difficult to play games to reinforce vocabulary, grammar skills, et cetera. The momentum just isn't there.

The economist Jesse Levin has done some fascinating work along these same lines, looking at Dutch schoolchildren. He counted how many peers children had in their class—that is, students at a similar level of academic ability—and found that the number of peers had a surprising correlation with academic performance, particularly for struggling students.[*] In other words, if you are a student—particularly a poor student—what you need is to have people around you asking the same questions,

---

[*] The clear exception: children with serious behavioral or learning disabilities. For special-needs students, the inverted-U curve is shifted far to the right.

wrestling with the same issues, and worrying about the same things as you are, so that you feel a little less isolated and a little more normal.

This is the problem with really small classes, Levin argues. When there are too few students in a room, the chances that children are surrounded by a critical mass of other people like them start to get really low. Taken too far, Levin says, class-size reduction "steals away the peers that struggling students learn from."

Can you see why Teresa DeBrito was so worried about Shepaug Valley? She is the principal of a middle school, teaching children at precisely the age when they begin to make the difficult transition to adolescence. They are awkward and self-conscious and anxious about seeming too smart. Getting them to engage, to move beyond simple question-and-answer sessions with their teacher, she said, can be "like pulling teeth." She wanted lots of interesting and diverse voices in her classrooms, and the kind of excitement that comes from a critical mass of students grappling with the same problem. How do you do that in a half-empty room? "The more students you have," she continued, "the more variety you can have in those discussions. If it's too small with kids this age, it's like they have a muzzle on." She didn't say it, but you could imagine her thinking that if someone went and built a massive subdivision on the gently rolling meadow next to the school, she wouldn't be that unhappy.

"I started in Meriden as a middle-school math teacher," DeBrito went on. Meriden is a middle- and lower-income city in another part of the state. "My largest class was twenty-nine kids." She talked about how hard that was, how much work it took to follow and know and respond to that many students. "You've got to be able to have eyes in the back of your head. You've got to be able to hear what's happening when you're working with a particular group. You have to really be on top of your game when you have that many kids in a classroom so that over there in a corner, they're not just talking about something that has nothing to do with what they're supposed to be working on."

But then she made a confession. She *liked* teaching that class. It was one of the best years of her career. The great struggle for someone teaching math to twelve- and thirteen-year-olds is to make it seem exciting—and twenty-nine kids was exciting. "There were so many more peers to interact with," she said. "They weren't always relating with just this one group. There was more opportunity to vary your experiences. And that's the real issue—what can be done to enliven, enrich, and engage the child, so they aren't just being passive."

Did she want twenty-nine children in every classroom at Shepaug? Of course not. DeBrito knew that she was a bit unusual and that the ideal number for most teachers was lower than that. Her point was simply that on the question of class size, we have become obsessed with what is good about small classrooms and oblivious of what can also be good about large classes. It is a strange thing, isn't it, to have an educational philosophy that thinks of the other students in the classroom with your child as competitors for the attention of the teacher and not allies in the adventure of learning? When she thought back to that year in Meriden, DeBrito got a faraway look in her eyes. "I like the noise. I like to hear them interact. Oh, it was fun."

6.

A half-hour drive up the road from Shepaug Valley, in the town of Lakeville, Connecticut, is a school called Hotchkiss. It is considered one of the premier private boarding schools in the United States. Tuition is almost $50,000 a year. The school has two lakes, two hockey rinks, four telescopes, a golf course, and twelve pianos. And not just any pianos, but, as the school takes pains to point out, *Steinway* pianos, the most prestigious piano money can buy.* Hotchkiss is the kind of place that spares no expense in the education of its students. The school's average class size? Twelve students. The same condition that Teresa DeBrito dreads, Hotchkiss—just up the road—advertises as its greatest asset. "[Our] learning environment," the school proudly declares, "is intimate, interactive, and inclusive."

Why does a school like Hotchkiss do something that so plainly makes its students worse off? One answer is that the school isn't thinking of its students. It is thinking of the parents of its students, who see things like golf courses and Steinway pianos and small classes as evidence that their $50,000 is well spent. But the better answer is that Hotchkiss has simply fallen into the trap that wealthy people and wealthy institutions and wealthy countries—all Goliaths—too often fall into: the school assumes that the

---

* Although the Hotchkiss website claims to have twelve Steinway pianos, the school's music director has said elsewhere that they actually have twenty—plus a Fazioli, which is the Rolls-Royce of performance grand pianos. That's more than a million dollars' worth of pianos. If you are playing "Chopsticks" in a Hotchkiss practice room, it's going to sound *really* good.

kinds of things that wealth can buy always translate into real-world advantages. They don't, of course. That's the lesson of the inverted-U curve. It is good to be bigger and stronger than your opponent. It is not so good to be so big and strong that you are a sitting duck for a rock fired at 150 miles per hour. Goliath didn't get what he wanted, because he was *too* big. The man from Hollywood was not the parent he wanted to be, because he was *too* rich. Hotchkiss is not the school it wants to be, because its classes are *too* small. We all assume that being bigger and stronger and richer is always in our best interest. Vivek Ranadivé, a shepherd boy named David, and the principal of Shepaug Valley Middle School will tell you that it isn't.

CHAPTER THREE

Caroline Sacks

"IF I'D GONE TO THE UNIVERSITY OF MARYLAND, I'D STILL BE IN SCIENCE."

1.

One hundred and fifty years ago, when Paris was at the center of the art world, a group of painters used to gather every evening at Café Guerbois, in the neighborhood of Batignolles. The ringleader of the group was Édouard Manet. He was one of the oldest and most established members of the group, a handsome and gregarious man in his early thirties who dressed in the height of fashion and charmed all those around him with his energy and humor. Manet's great friend was Edgar Degas. He was among the few who could match wits with Manet; the two shared a fiery spirit and a sharp tongue and would sometimes descend into bitter argument. Paul Cézanne, tall and gruff, would come and sit moodily in the corner, his trousers held up with string. "I am not offering you my hand,"

Cézanne said to Manet once before slumping down by himself. "I haven't washed for eight days." Claude Monet, self-absorbed and strong willed, was a grocer's son who lacked the education of some of the others. His best friend was the "easygoing urchin" Pierre-Auguste Renoir, who, over the course of their friendship, would paint eleven portraits of Monet. The moral compass of the group was Camille Pissarro: fiercely political, loyal, and principled. Even Cézanne—the most ornery and alienated of men—loved Pissarro. Years later, he would identify himself as "Cézanne, pupil of Pissarro."

Together this group of remarkable painters would go on to invent modern art with the movement known as Impressionism. They painted one another and painted next to one another and supported one another emotionally and financially, and today their paintings hang in every major art museum in the world. But in the 1860s, they were struggling. Monet was broke. Renoir once had to bring him bread so that he wouldn't starve. Not that Renoir was in any better shape. He didn't have enough money to buy stamps for his letters. There were virtually no dealers interested in their paintings. When the art critics mentioned the Impressionists—and there was a small army of art critics in Paris in the 1860s—it was usually to belittle them. Manet and his friends sat in the dark-paneled Café Guerbois with its marble-topped tables and flimsy metal chairs and drank and ate and argued about politics and literature and art and most specifically about their careers—because the Impressionists all wrestled with one crucial question: What should they do about the Salon?

Art played an enormous role in the cultural life of

France in the nineteenth century. Painting was regulated by a government department called the Ministry of the Imperial House and the Fine Arts, and it was considered a profession in the same way that medicine or the law is a profession today. A promising painter would start at the École Nationale Supérieure des Beaux-Arts in Paris, where he would receive a rigorous and formal education, progressing from the copying of drawings to the painting of live models. At each stage of his education, there would be competitions. Those who did poorly would be weeded out. Those who did well would win awards and prestigious fellowships, and at the pinnacle of the profession was the Salon, the most important art exhibition in all of Europe.

Every year each of the painters of France submitted two or three of his finest canvases to a jury of experts. The deadline was the first of April. Artists from around the world pushed handcarts loaded with canvases through Paris's cobblestoned streets, bringing their work to the Palais de l'Industrie, an exhibition hall built for the Paris World Fair between the Champs-Élysées and the Seine. Throughout the next few weeks, the jury would vote on each painting in turn. Those deemed unacceptable would be stamped with the red letter "R" for *rejected*. Those accepted would be hung on the walls of the Palais, and over the course of six weeks beginning in early May, as many as a million people would throng the exhibition, jostling for position in front of the biggest and best-known artists' works and jeering at the works they did not like. The best paintings were given medals. The winners were celebrated and saw the value of their paintings soar. The losers limped home and went back to work.

"There are in Paris scarcely fifteen art-lovers capable of liking a painting without Salon approval," Renoir once said. "There are 80,000 who won't buy so much as a nose from a painter who is not hung at the Salon." The Salon made Renoir so anxious that one year he went down to the Palais during jury deliberations and waited outside, hoping to find out early whether he got in or not. But then becoming shy, he introduced himself as a friend of Renoir's. Another of the Guerbois regulars, Frédéric Bazille, once confessed, "I have an appalling fear of getting rejected." When the artist Jules Holtzapffel didn't make it into the Salon of 1866, he shot himself in the head. "The members of the jury have rejected me. Therefore I have no talent," read his suicide note. "I must die." For a painter in nineteenth-century France, the Salon was everything, and the reason that the Salon was such an issue for the group of Impressionists was that time and again, the Salon jury turned them down.

The Salon's attitude was traditional. "Works were expected to be microscopically accurate, properly 'finished' and formally framed, with proper perspective and all the familiar artistic conventions," the art historian Sue Roe writes. "Light denoted high drama, darkness suggested gravitas. In narrative painting, the scene should not only be 'accurate,' but should also set a morally acceptable tone. An afternoon at the Salon was like a night at the Paris Opéra: audiences expected to be uplifted and entertained. For the most part, they knew what they liked, and expected to see what they knew." The kinds of paintings that won medals, Roe says, were huge, meticulously painted canvases showing scenes from French history or mythology, with horses and armies or beautiful women, with titles like *Soldier's Departure*, *Young Woman Weeping over a Letter*, and *Abandoned Innocence*.

The Impressionists had an entirely different idea about what constituted art. They painted everyday life. Their brushstrokes were visible. Their figures were indistinct. To the Salon jury and the crowds thronging the Palais, their work looked amateurish, even shocking. In 1865, the Salon, surprisingly, accepted a painting by Manet of a prostitute, called *Olympia,* and the painting sent all of Paris into an uproar. Guards had to be placed around the painting to keep the crowds of spectators at bay. "An atmosphere of hysteria and even fear predominated," the historian Ross King writes. "Some spectators collapsed in 'epidemics of crazed laughter' while others, mainly women, turned their heads from the picture in fright." In 1868, Renoir, Bazille, and Monet managed to get paintings accepted by the Salon. But halfway through the Salon's six-week run, their works were removed from the main exhibition space and exiled to the *dépotoir*—the rubbish dump—a small, dark room in the back of the building, where paintings considered to be failures were relocated. It was almost as bad as not being accepted at all.

The Salon was the most important art show in the world. Everyone at the Café Guerbois agreed on that. But the acceptance by the Salon came with a cost: it required creating the kind of art that they did not find meaningful, and they risked being lost in the clutter of other artists' work. Was it worth it? Night after night, the Impressionists argued over whether they should keep knocking on the Salon door or strike out on their own and stage a show just for themselves. Did they want to be a Little Fish in the Big Pond of the Salon or a Big Fish in a Little Pond of their own choosing?

In the end, the Impressionists made the right choice, which is one of the reasons that their paintings hang in every major art museum in the world. But this same dilemma comes up again and again in our own lives, and often we don't choose so wisely. The inverted-U curve reminds us that there is a point at which money and resources stop making our lives better and start making them worse. The story of the Impressionists suggests a second, parallel problem. We strive for the best and attach great importance to getting into the finest institutions we can. But rarely do we stop and consider—as the Impressionists did—whether the most prestigious of institutions is always in our best interest. There are many examples of this, but few more telling than the way we think about where to attend university.

2.

Caroline Sacks[*] grew up on the farthest fringes of the Washington, DC, metropolitan area. She went to public schools through high school. Her mother is an accountant and her father works for a technology company. As a child she sang in the church choir and loved to write and draw. But what really excited her was science.

"I did a lot of crawling around in the grass with a mag-

---

* I've changed her name and identifying details.

nifying glass and a sketchbook, following bugs and drawing them," Sacks says. She is a thoughtful and articulate young woman, with a refreshing honesty and directness. "I was really, really into bugs. And sharks. So for a while I thought I was going to be a veterinarian or an ichthyologist. Eugenie Clark was my hero. She was the first woman diver. She grew up in New York City in a family of immigrants and ended up rising to the top of her field, despite having a lot of 'Oh, you're a woman, you can't go under the ocean' setbacks. I just thought she was great. My dad met her and was able to give me a signed photo and I was really excited. Science was always a really big part of what I did."

Sacks sailed through high school at the top of her class. She took a political science course at a nearby college while she was still in high school, as well as a multivariant calculus course at the local community college. She got As in both, as well as an A in every class she took in high school. She got perfect scores on every one of her Advanced Placement pre-college courses.

The summer after her junior year in high school, her father took her on a whirlwind tour of American universities. "I think we looked at five schools in three days," she says. "It was Wesleyan, Brown, Providence College, Boston College, and Yale. Wesleyan was fun but very small. Yale was cool, but I definitely didn't fit the vibe." But Brown University, in Providence, Rhode Island, won her heart. It is small and exclusive, situated in the middle of a nineteenth-century neighborhood of redbrick Georgian and Colonial buildings on the top of a gently sloping hill. It might be the most beautiful college campus in the

United States. She applied to Brown, with the University of Maryland as her backup. A few months later, she got a letter in the mail. She was in.

"I expected that everyone at Brown would be really rich and worldly and knowledgeable," she says. "Then I got there, and everybody seemed to be just like me—intellectually curious and kind of nervous and excited and not sure whether they'd be able to make friends. It was very reassuring." The hardest part was choosing which courses to take, because she loved the sound of everything. She ended up in Introductory Chemistry, Spanish, a class called the Evolution of Language, and Botanical Roots of Modern Medicine, which she describes as "sort of half botany class, half looking at uses of indigenous plants as medicine and what kind of chemical theories they are based on." She was in heaven.

3.

Did Caroline Sacks make the right choice? Most of us would say that she did. When she went on that whirlwind tour with her father, she ranked the colleges she saw, from best to worst. Brown University was number one. The University of Maryland was her backup because it was not in any way as good a school as Brown. Brown is a member of the Ivy League. It has more resources, more academically able students, more prestige, and more accomplished faculty than the University of Maryland. In the rankings of American colleges published every year by the magazine *U.S. News & World Report*, Brown routinely places among the top ten or twenty colleges in the United States. The University of Maryland finishes much farther back in the pack.

But let's think about Caroline's decision in the same way the Impressionists thought about the Salon. What the Impressionists understood, in their endless debates at the Café Guerbois, was that the choice between the Salon and a solo show wasn't a simple case of a best option and a second-best option. It was a choice between two very *different* options, each with its own strengths and drawbacks.

The Salon was a lot like an Ivy League school. It was the place where reputations were made. And what made it special was how selective it was. There were roughly three thousand painters of "national reputation" in France in the 1860s, and each submitted two or three of his best works to the Salon, which meant the jury was picking from a small mountain of canvases. Rejection was the norm. Getting in was a feat. "The Salon is the real field of battle," Manet said. "It's there that one must take one's measure." Of all the Impressionists, he was the one most convinced of the value of the Salon. The art critic Théodore Duret, another of the Guerbois circle, agreed. "You have still one step to take," Duret wrote to Pissarro in 1874. "That is to succeed in becoming known to the public and accepted by all the dealers and art lovers....I urge you to exhibit; you must succeed in making a noise, in defying and attracting criticism, coming face-to-face with the big public."

But the very things that made the Salon so attractive—how selective and prestigious it was—also made it problematic. The Palais was an enormous barn of a building three hundred yards long with a central aisle that was two stories high. A typical Salon might accept three or four thousand paintings, and they were hung in four tiers, starting at ground level and stretching up to the ceiling. Only paintings that met with the unanimous approval of the jury were hung "on the line," at eye level. If you were "skyed"—that is, hung closest to the ceiling—it was all but impossible for your painting to be seen. (One of Renoir's paintings was once skyed in the *dépotoir.*) No painter could submit more than three works. The crowds were often overwhelming. The Salon was the Big Pond. But it was very hard to be anything at the Salon but a Little Fish.

Pissarro and Monet disagreed with Manet. They thought it made more sense to be a Big Fish in a Little Pond. If they were off by themselves and held their own show, they said, they wouldn't be bound by the restrictive rules of the Salon, where *Olympia* was considered an outrage and where the medals were won by paintings of soldiers and weeping women. They could paint whatever they wanted. And they wouldn't get lost in the crowd, because there wouldn't be a crowd. In 1873, Pissarro and Monet proposed that the Impressionists set up a collective called the Société Anonyme Coopérative des Artistes Peintres, Sculpteurs, Graveurs. There would be no competition, no juries, and no medals. Every artist would be treated as an equal. Everyone but Manet was in.

The group found space on the Boulevard des Capucines on the top floor of a building that had just been vacated by a photographer. It was a series of small rooms with red-brown walls. The Impressionists' exhibition opened on April 15, 1874, and lasted one month. The entrance fee was one franc. There were 165 works of art on display, including three Cézannes, ten paintings by Degas, nine Monets, five Pissarros, six Renoirs, and five by Alfred Sisley—a tiny fraction of what was on the walls of the Salon across town. In their show, the Impressionists could exhibit as many canvases as they wished and hang them in a way that allowed people to actually see them. "The Impressionists were lost in the mass of Salon paintings, even when accepted," the art historians Harrison White and Cynthia White write. "With...the independent group show, they could gain the public's eye."

Thirty-five hundred people attended the show—175 on the first day alone, which was enough to bring the artists critical attention. Not all of that attention was positive: one joke told was that what the Impressionists were doing was loading a pistol with paint and firing at the canvas. But that was the second part of the Big Fish–Little Pond bargain. The Big Fish–Little Pond option might be scorned by some on the outside, but Small Ponds are welcoming places for those on the inside. They have all of the support that comes from community and friendship—and they are places where innovation and individuality are not frowned upon. "We are beginning to make ourselves a niche," a hopeful Pissarro wrote to a friend. "We have succeeded as intruders in setting up our little banner in the midst of the crowd." Their challenge was "to advance without worrying about opinion." He was right. Off by themselves, the Impressionists found a new identity. They felt a new creative freedom, and before long, the outside world began to sit up and take notice. In the history of modern art, there has never been a more important or more famous exhibition. If you tried to buy the paintings in that warren of top-floor rooms today, it would cost you more than a billion dollars.

The lesson of the Impressionists is that there are times and places where it is better to be a Big Fish in a Little Pond than a Little Fish in a Big Pond, where the apparent disadvantage of being an outsider in a marginal world turns out not to be a disadvantage at all. Pissarro, Monet, Renoir, and Cézanne weighed prestige against visibility, selectivity against freedom, and decided the costs of the Big Pond were too great. Caroline Sacks faced the same choice. She could be a Big Fish at the University of Maryland, or a Little Fish at one of the most prestigious universities in the world. She chose the Salon over the three rooms on Boulevard des Capucines—and she ended up paying a high price.

4.

The trouble for Caroline Sacks began in the spring of her freshman year, when she enrolled in chemistry. She was probably taking too many courses, she realizes now, and doing too many extracurricular activities. She got her grade on her third midterm exam, and her heart sank. She went to talk to the professor. "He ran me through some exercises, and he said, 'Well, you have a fundamental deficiency in some of these concepts, so what I would actually recommend is that you drop the class, not bother with the final exam, and take the course again next fall.'" So she did what the professor suggested. She retook the course in the fall of her sophomore year. But she barely did any better. She got a low B. She was in shock. "I had never gotten a B in an academic context before," she said. "I had never *not* excelled. And I was taking the class for the second time, this time as a sophomore, and most of the kids in the class were first-semester freshmen. It was pretty disheartening."

She had known when she was accepted to Brown that it wasn't going to be like high school. It couldn't be. She wasn't going to be the smartest girl in the class any-more—and she'd accepted that fact. "I figured, regardless of how much I prepared, there would be kids who had been exposed to stuff I had never even heard of. So I was trying not to be naive about that." But chemistry was beyond what she had imagined. The students in her class were *competitive*. "I had a lot of trouble even talking with people from those classes," she went on. "They didn't want to share their study habits with me. They didn't want to talk about ways to better understand the stuff that we were learning, because that might give me a leg up."

In spring of her sophomore year, she enrolled in organic chemistry—and things only got worse. She couldn't do it: "You memorize how a concept works, and then they give you a molecule you've never seen before, and they ask you to make another one you've never seen before, and you have to get from this thing to that thing. There are people who just think that way and in five minutes are done. They're the curve busters. Then there are people who through an amazing amount of hard work trained themselves to think that way. I worked *so* hard and I never got it down." The teacher would ask a question, and around her, hands would go up, and Sacks would sit in silence and listen to everyone else's brilliant answers. "It was just this feeling of overwhelming inadequacy."

One night she stayed up late, preparing for a review session in organic chemistry. She was miserable and angry. She didn't want to be working on organic chemistry at three in the morning, when all of that work didn't seem to be getting her anywhere. "I guess that was when I started thinking that maybe I shouldn't pursue this any further," she said. She'd had enough.

The tragic part was that Sacks *loved* science. As she talked about her abandonment of her first love, she mourned all the courses she would have loved to take but now never would—physiology, infectious disease, biology, math. In the summer after her sophomore year, she agonized over her decision: "When I was growing up, it was a subject of much pride to be able to say that, you know, 'I'm a seven-year-old girl, and I love bugs! And I want to study them, and I read up on them all the time, and I draw them in my sketchbook and label all the different parts of them and talk about where they live and what they do.' Later it was 'I am so interested in people and how the human body works, and isn't this amazing?' There is definitely a sort of pride that goes along with 'I am a science girl,' and it's almost shameful for me to leave that behind and say, 'Oh, well, I am going to do something easier because I can't take the heat.' For a while, that is the only way I was looking at it, like I have completely failed. This has been my goal and I can't do it."

And it shouldn't have mattered how Sacks did in organic chemistry, should it? She never wanted to be an organic chemist. It was just a course. Lots of people find organic chemistry impossible. It's not uncommon for premed students to take organic chemistry over the sum-

mer at another college just to give themselves a full se-
mester of practice. What's more, Sacks was taking organic
chemistry at an extraordinarily competitive and academically rigorous university. If you were to rank all the students in the world who are taking organic chemistry, Sacks
would probably be in the 99th percentile.

But the problem was, Sacks wasn't comparing herself
to all the students in the world taking Organic Chemistry.
She was comparing herself to her fellow students at
Brown. She was a Little Fish in one of the deepest and
most competitive ponds in the country—and the experience of comparing herself to all the other brilliant fish
shattered her confidence. It made her feel stupid, even
though she isn't stupid at all. "Wow, other people are mastering this, even people who were as clueless as I was in
the beginning, and I just can't seem to learn to think in this
manner."

5.

Caroline Sacks was experiencing what is called "relative
deprivation," a term coined by the sociologist Samuel
Stouffer during the Second World War. Stouffer was com-
missioned by the U.S. Army to examine the attitudes and
morale of American soldiers, and he ended up studying
half a million men and women, looking at everything from
how soldiers viewed their commanding officers to how
black soldiers felt they were being treated to how difficult
soldiers found it to serve in isolated outposts.

But one set of questions Stouffer asked stood out. He

quizzed both soldiers serving in the Military Police and those serving in the Air Corps (the forerunner of the Air Force) about how good a job they thought their service did in recognizing and promoting people of ability. The answer was clear. Military Policemen had a far more positive view of their organization than did enlisted men in the Air Corps.

On the face of it, that made no sense. The Military Police had one of the worst rates of promotion in all of the armed forces. The Air Corps had one of the best. The chance of an enlisted man rising to officer status in the Air Corps was *twice* that of a soldier in the Military Police. So, why on earth would the Military Policemen be more satisfied? The answer, Stouffer famously explained, is that Military Policemen compared themselves only to other Military Policemen. And if you got a promotion in the Military Police, that was such a rare event that you were very happy. And if you didn't get promoted, you were in the same boat as most of your peers—so you weren't *that* unhappy.

"Contrast him with the Air Corps man of the same education and longevity," Stouffer wrote. His chance of getting promoted to officer was greater than 50 percent. "If he had earned a [promotion], so had the majority of his fellows in the branch, and his achievement was less conspicuous than in the MP's. If he had failed to earn a rating while the majority had succeeded, he had more reason to feel a sense of personal frustration, which could be expressed as criticism of the promotion system."

Stouffer's point is that we form our impressions not globally, by placing ourselves in the broadest possible context, but locally—by comparing ourselves to people "in the same boat as ourselves." Our sense of how deprived we are is *relative*. This is one of those observations that is both obvious and (upon exploration) deeply profound, and it explains all kinds of otherwise puzzling observations. Which do you think, for example, has a higher suicide rate: countries whose citizens declare themselves to be very happy, such as Switzerland, Denmark, Iceland, the Netherlands, and Canada? or countries like Greece, Italy, Portugal, and Spain, whose citizens describe themselves as not very happy at all? Answer: the so-called happy countries. It's the same phenomenon as in the Military Police and the Air Corps. If you are depressed in a place where most people are pretty unhappy, you compare yourself to those around you and you don't feel all that bad. But can you imagine how difficult it must be to be depressed in a country where everyone else has a big smile on their face?[*]

Caroline Sacks's decision to evaluate herself, then, by looking around her organic chemistry classroom was not some strange and irrational behavior. It is what human beings do. We compare ourselves to those in the same

---

[*] This example is from the work of the economist Mary Daly, who has written widely on this phenomenon. Here's another example, this one from Carol Graham's *Happiness Around the World: The Paradox of Happy Peasants and Miserable Millionaires*. Who do you think is happier: a poor person in Chile or a poor person in Honduras? Logic would say Chile. Chile is a modern developed economy. The poor in Chile make somewhere close to twice the amount of money that the poor in Honduras do, which means that they can live in nicer homes and eat better food and afford more material comforts. But if you compare the happiness scores of the poor in both countries, Hondurans trump Chileans handily. Why? Because Hondurans care only about how other Hondurans are doing. Graham states, "Because average country income levels do not matter to happiness, but relative distances from the average do, the poor Honduran is happier because their distance from mean income is smaller." And in Honduras, the poor are much closer in wealth to the middle class than the poor are in Chile, so they *feel* better off.

situation as ourselves, which means that students in an elite school—except, perhaps, those at the very top of the class—are going to face a burden that they would not face in a less competitive atmosphere. Citizens of happy countries have higher suicide rates than citizens of unhappy countries, because they look at the smiling faces around them and the contrast is too great. Students at "great" schools look at the brilliant students around them, and how do you think they feel?

The phenomenon of relative deprivation applied to education is called—appropriately enough—the "Big Fish–Little Pond Effect." The more elite an educational institution is, the worse students feel about their own academic abilities. Students who would be at the top of their class at a good school can easily fall to the bottom of a really good school. Students who would feel that they have mastered a subject at a good school can have the feeling that they are falling farther and farther behind in a *really* good school. And that feeling—as subjective and ridiculous and irrational as it may be—*matters.* How you feel about your abilities—your academic "self-concept"—in the context of your classroom shapes your willingness to tackle challenges and finish difficult tasks. It's a crucial element in your motivation and confidence.

The Big Fish–Little Pond theory was pioneered by the psychologist Herbert Marsh, and to Marsh, most parents and students make their school choices for the wrong reasons. "A lot of people think that going to an academically selective school is going to be good," he said. "That's just not true. The reality is that it is going to be *mixed.*" He went on: "When I was living in Sydney, there were a small number of selective public schools that were even more prestigious than the elite private schools. The tests to get into them were incredibly competitive. So the *Sydney Morning Herald*—the big newspaper there—would always call me up whenever they were holding their entrance examinations. It would happen every year, and there was always this pressure to say something new. So finally I just said—and maybe I shouldn't have—well, if you want to see the positive effects of elite schools on self-concept, you are measuring the wrong person. You should be measuring the parents."

6.

What happened to Caroline Sacks is all too common. More than half of all American students who start out in science, technology, and math programs (or STEM, as they are known) drop out after their first or second year. Even though a science degree is just about the most valuable asset a young person can have in the modern economy, large numbers of would-be STEM majors end up switching into the arts, where academic standards are less demanding and the coursework less competitive. That's the major reason that there is such a shortage of qualified American-educated scientists and engineers in the United States.

To get a sense of who is dropping out—and why—let's take a look at the science enrollment of a school in upstate New York called Hartwick College. It's a small liberal arts college of the sort that is common in the American Northeast. Here are all the Hartwick STEM majors divided into three groups—top third, middle third, and bottom third—according to their test scores in mathematics. The scores are from the SAT, the exam used by many American colleges as an admissions test. The mathematics section of the test is out of 800 points.*

STEM majors	Top Third	Middle Third	Bottom Third
Math SAT	569	472	407

If we take the SAT as a guide, there's a pretty big difference in raw math ability between the best and the poorest students at Hartwick.

Now let's look at the portion of all science degrees at Hartwick that are earned by each of those three groups.

STEM degrees	Top Third	Middle Third	Bottom Third
Percent	55.0	27.1	17.8

The students in the top third at Hartwick earn well over half of the school's science degrees. The bottom third end up earning only 17.8 percent of Hartwick's science degrees. The students who come into Hartwick with the poorest levels of math ability are dropping out of math and science in droves. This much seems like common sense. Learning the advanced mathematics and physics necessary to become an engineer or scientist is really hard—and only a

*These statistics are derived from a paper entitled "The Role of Ethnicity in Choosing and Leaving Science in Highly Selective Institutions" by the sociologists Rogers Elliott and A. Christopher Strenta et al. The SAT scores are from the early 1990s, and may be somewhat different today.

small number of students clustered at the top of the class are smart enough to handle the material.

Now let's do the same analysis for Harvard, one of the most prestigious universities in the world.

STEM majors	Top Third	Middle Third	Bottom Third
Math SAT	753	674	581

Harvard students, not surprisingly, score far higher on the math SAT than their counterparts at Hartwick. In fact, the students in Harvard's bottom third have higher scores than the *best* students at Hartwick. If getting a science degree is about how smart you are, then virtually everyone at Harvard should end up with a degree—right? At least on paper, there is no one at Harvard who lacks the intellectual firepower to master the coursework. Well, let's take a look at the portion of degrees that are earned by each group.

STEM degrees	Top Third	Middle Third	Bottom Third
Percent	53.4	31.2	15.4

Isn't that strange? The students in the bottom third of the Harvard class drop out of math and science just as much as their counterparts in upstate New York. *Harvard has the same distribution of science degrees as Hartwick.*

Think about this for a moment. We have a group of high achievers at Hartwick. Let's call them the Hartwick All-Stars. And we've got another group of lower achievers at Harvard. Let's call them the Harvard Dregs. Each is studying the same textbooks and wrestling with the same concepts and trying to master the same problem sets in courses like advanced calculus and organic chemistry, and according to test scores, they are of roughly equal academic ability. But the overwhelming majority of Hartwick All-Stars get what they want and end up as engineers or biologists. Meanwhile, the Harvard Dregs—who go to the far more prestigious school—are so demoralized by their experience that many of them drop out of science entirely and transfer to some nonscience major. The Harvard Dregs are Little Fish in a Very Big and Scary Pond. The Hartwick All-Stars are Big Fish in a Very Welcoming Small Pond. What matters, in determining the likelihood of getting a science degree, is not just how smart you are. It's how smart you *feel* relative to the other people in your classroom.

By the way, this pattern holds true for virtually any school you look at—regardless of its academic quality. The sociologists Rogers Elliott and Christopher Strenta ran these same numbers for eleven different liberal arts colleges across the United States. Take a look for yourself:

School	Top Third	Math SAT	Middle Third	Math SAT	Bottom Third	Math SAT
1. Harvard University	53.4%	753	31.2%	674	15.4%	581
2. Dartmouth College	57.3%	729	29.8%	656	12.9%	546
3. Williams College	45.6%	697	34.7%	631	19.7%	547
4. Colgate University	53.6%	697	31.4%	626	15.0%	534
5. University of Richmond	51.0%	696	34.7%	624	14.4%	534
6. Bucknell University	57.3%	688	24.0%	601	18.8%	494
7. Kenyon College	62.1%	678	22.6%	583	15.4%	485
8. Occidental College	49.0%	663	32.4%	573	18.6%	492

School	Top Third	Math SAT	Middle Third	Math SAT	Bottom Third	Math SAT
9. Kalamazoo College	51.8%	633	27.3%	551	20.8%	479
10. Ohio Wesleyan	54.9%	591	33.9%	514	11.2%	431
11. Hartwick College	55.0%	569	27.1%	472	17.8%	407

Let's go back, then, and reconstruct what Caroline Sacks's thinking should have been when faced with the choice between Brown and the University of Maryland. By going to Brown, she would benefit from the prestige of the university. She might have more interesting and wealthier peers. The connections she made at school and the brand value of Brown on her diploma might give her a leg up on the job market. These are all classic Big Pond advantages. Brown is the Salon.

But she would be taking a risk. She would dramatically increase her chances of dropping out of science entirely. How large was that risk? According to research done by Mitchell Chang of the University of California, the likelihood of someone completing a STEM degree—all things being equal—rises by 2 percentage points for every 10-point decrease in the university's average SAT score.[*] The smarter

---

[*] This is a crucial enough point that it is worth spelling out in more detail. Chang and his coauthors looked at a sample of several thousand first-year college students and measured which factors played the biggest role in a student's likelihood of dropping out of science. The most important factor? How academically able the university's students were. "For every 10-point increase in the average SAT score of an entering cohort of freshmen at a given institution, the likelihood of retention decreased by two percentage points," the authors write. Interestingly, if you look just at students who are members of ethnic minorities, the numbers are even higher. Every 10-point increase in SAT score causes retention to fall by *three* percentage points. "Students who attend what they considered to be their first-choice school were less likely to persist in a biomedical or behavioral science major," they write. You think you want to go to the fanciest school you can. You don't.

your peers, the dumber you feel; the dumber you feel, the more likely you are to drop out of science. Since there is roughly a 150-point gap between the average SAT scores of students attending the University of Maryland and Brown, the "penalty" Sacks paid by choosing a great school over a good school is that she reduced her chances of graduating with a science degree by 30 percent. *Thirty percent!* At a time when students with liberal arts degrees struggle to find jobs, students with STEM degrees are almost assured of good careers. Jobs for people with science and engineering degrees are plentiful and highly paid. That's a very large risk to take for the prestige of an Ivy League school.

Let me give you one more example of the Big Pond in action. It might be even more striking. Suppose you are a university looking to hire the best young academics coming out of graduate school. What should your hiring strategy be? Should you hire only graduates from the most elite graduate schools? Or should you hire students who finished at the top of their class, regardless of what school they went to?

Most universities follow the first strategy. They even make a boast out of it: *We hire only graduates of the very top schools.* But I hope that by this point you are at least a little bit skeptical of that position. Shouldn't a Big Fish at a Little Pond be worth at least a second look before a Little Fish at a Big Pond is chosen?

Luckily there is a very simple way to compare those two strategies. It comes from the work of John Conley and Ali Sina Önder on the graduates of PhD programs in economics. In academic economics, there are a handful of economics journals that everyone in the field reads and respects. The top journals accept only the best and most creative research and economists rate one another according to—for the most part—how many research articles they have published in those elite journals. To figure out the best hiring strategy, then, Conley and Önder argue that all we have to do is compare the number of papers published by Big Fish in Little Ponds with the number published by Little Fish in Big Ponds. So what did they find? *That the best students from mediocre schools were almost always a better bet than good students from the very best schools.*

I realize that this is a deeply counterintuitive fact. The idea that it might not be a good idea for universities to hire from Harvard and MIT seems crazy. But Conley and Önder's analysis is hard to refute.

Let's start with the top economics PhD programs in North America—all of which are among the very top programs in the world: Harvard, MIT, Yale, Princeton, Columbia, Stanford, and the University of Chicago. Conley and Önder divided up the graduates of each of those programs according to where they ranked in their class, and then counted up the number of times each PhD graduate was published in the first six years of his or her academic career.

	99th	95th	90th	85th	80th	75th	70th	65th	60th	55th
Harvard	4.31	2.36	1.47	1.04	0.71	0.41	0.30	0.21	0.12	0.07
MIT	4.73	2.87	1.66	1.24	0.83	0.64	0.48	0.33	0.20	0.12
Yale	3.78	2.15	1.22	0.83	0.57	0.39	0.19	0.12	0.08	0.05
Princeton	4.10	2.17	1.79	1.23	1.01	0.82	0.60	0.45	0.36	0.28
Columbia	2.90	1.15	0.62	0.34	0.17	0.10	0.06	0.02	0.01	0.01

	99th	95th	90th	85th	80th	75th	70th	65th	60th	55th
Stanford	3.43	1.58	1.02	0.67	0.50	0.33	0.23	0.14	0.08	0.05
Chicago	2.88	1.71	1.04	0.72	0.51	0.33	0.19	0.10	0.06	0.03

I realize that this is a lot of numbers. But just look at the left-hand side—the students who finish in the 99th percentile of their class. To publish three or four papers in the most prestigious journals at the beginning of your career is quite an accomplishment. These people are really good. That much makes sense. To be the top economics graduate student at MIT or Stanford is an extraordinary achievement.

But then the puzzles start. Look at the 80th percentile column. Schools like MIT and Stanford and Harvard accept somewhere around two dozen PhD students a year, so if you are in the 80th percentile, you are roughly fifth or sixth in your class. These are also extraordinary students. But look at how few papers the 80th percentile publishes! A fraction of the number of the very best students. And by the way, look at the last column—the 55th percentile, the students who are just above average. They are brilliant enough to make it into one of the most competitive graduate programs in the world, and to finish their studies in the top half of their class. And yet they barely publish anything at all. As professional economists, they can only be considered disappointments.

Next let's look at the graduates of mediocre schools. I say "mediocre" only because that's what someone from one of those seven elite schools would call them. In the annual *U.S. News & World Report* rankings of graduate schools, these are the institutions that are buried somewhere near the bottom of the list. I've selected three for comparison purposes. The first is my own alma mater, the University of Toronto (out of a sense of school spirit!). The second is Boston University. The third is what Conley and Önder call "non–top 30," which is simply an average of all the schools at the very, *very* bottom of the list.

	99th	95th	90th	85th	80th	75th	70th	65th	60th	55th
Univ. of Toronto	3.13	1.85	0.80	0.61	0.29	0.19	0.15	0.10	0.07	0.05
Boston Univ.	1.59	0.49	0.21	0.08	0.05	0.02	0.02	0.01	0.00	0.00
Non–top 30	1.05	0.31	0.12	0.06	0.04	0.02	0.01	0.01	0.00	0.00

Do you see what is so fascinating? The very best students at a non–top 30 school—that is, a school so far down the list that someone from the Ivy League would grimace at the thought of even setting foot there—have a publication number of 1.05, substantially better than everyone except the very best students at Harvard, MIT, Yale, Princeton, Columbia, Stanford, and Chicago. Are you better off hiring a Big Fish from a Tiny, Tiny Pond than even a Middle-Sized Fish from a Big Pond? *Absolutely.*

Conley and Önder struggle to explain their own findings.[*] "To get to Harvard," they write,

---

[*] A small point of clarification: Conley and Önder's chart isn't a list of the total number of publications by each economist. Rather, it is a weighted number—getting a paper accepted by one of the most prestigious journals (*The American Economic Review* or *Econometrica*) counts more than getting a paper published in a less competitive journal. In other words, their numbers aren't measuring just how many articles an academic can turn out. They are measuring how many *high-quality* articles an academic can get published.

an applicant has to have great grades, perfect test scores, strong and credible recommendations, and know how to package all this to stand out to the admissions committee. Thus, successful candidates must be hardworking, intelligent, well-trained as undergraduates, savvy and ambitious. Why is it that the majority of these successful applicants, who were winners and did all the right things up to the time they applied to graduate school, become so unimpressive after they are trained? Are we failing the students, or are the students failing us?

The answer, of course, is neither. No one is *failing* anyone. It's just that the very thing that makes elite schools such wonderful places for those at the top makes them very difficult places for everyone else. This is just another version of what happened to Caroline Sacks. The Big Pond takes really bright students and demoralizes them.

By the way, do you know what elite institution has recognized this very fact about the dangers of the Big Pond for nearly fifty years? Harvard! In the 1960s, Fred Glimp took over as director of admissions and instituted what was known as the "happy-bottom-quarter" policy. In one of his first memos after taking office, he wrote: "Any class, no matter how able, will always have a bottom quarter. What are the effects of the psychology of feeling average, even in a very able group? Are there identifiable types with the psychological or what-not tolerance to be 'happy' or to make the most of education while in the bottom quarter?" He knew exactly how demoralizing the Big Pond was to everyone but the best. To Glimp's mind, his job was to find students who were tough enough and had enough achievements outside the classroom to be able to survive the stress of being Very Small Fish in Harvard's Very Large Pond. Thus did Harvard begin the practice (which continues to this day) of letting in substantial numbers of gifted athletes who have academic qualifications well below the rest of their classmates. If someone is going to be cannon fodder in the classroom, the theory goes, it's probably best if that person has an alternative avenue of fulfillment on the football field.

Exactly the same logic applies to the debate over affirmative action. In the United States, there is an enormous controversy over whether colleges and professional schools should have lower admissions standards for disadvantaged minorities. Supporters of affirmative action say helping minorities get into selective schools is justified given the long history of discrimination. Opponents say that access to selective schools is so important that it ought to be done purely on academic merit. A group in the middle says that using race as the basis for preference is a mistake—and what we really should be doing is giving preference to people who are poor. What all three groups take for granted is that being able to get into a great school is such an important advantage that the small number of spaces at the top are worth fighting over. But why on earth are people convinced that places at the top are so valuable that they are worth fighting over?

Affirmative action is practiced most aggressively in law schools, where black students are routinely offered positions in schools one tier higher than they would otherwise be able to attend. The result? According to the law professor Richard Sander, more than half of all African-American law students in the United States—51.6 percent—are in the bottom 10 percent of their law school class and almost three-quarters fall in the bottom 20 percent.* After reading about how hard it is to get a science degree if you're at the bottom of your class, you'll probably agree that those statistics are terrifying. Remember what Caroline Sacks said? *Wow, other people are mastering this, even people who were as clueless as I was in the beginning, and I just can't seem to learn to think in this manner.* Sacks isn't stupid. She's really, really smart. But Brown University made her feel stupid—and if she truly wanted to graduate

---

* The law professor Richard Sander is the leading proponent of the Big Pond case against affirmative action. He has written with Stuart Taylor a fascinating book on the subject called *Mismatch: How Affirmative Action Hurts Students It's Intended to Help, and Why Universities Won't Admit It.* I've provided a summary of some of Sander's argument in the notes at the back of this book.

For example, one of the questions Sander looks at is this. It is harder for a minority student to become a lawyer if he or she goes to a better school. That's clear. But what if that difficulty is offset by the fact that a degree from a better school is worth more? Not true, Sander and Taylor argue. Getting great grades at a good school is about the same—and maybe even better—than getting good grades at a great school. They write:

> A student who went to thirtieth-ranked Fordham and ended up in the top fifth of her class had jobs and earnings very similar to a student who went to fifth-ranked, much more competitive Columbia and earned grades that put her slightly below the middle of the class. I found that in most cases like this, the Fordham student had the edge in the job market.

This should not be surprising. Why should black students behave any differently from anyone else who is forced to learn from the least advantageous position in the classroom?

Sander's arguments are controversial. Some of his findings have been disputed by other social scientists who interpret the data differently. On a general level, though, what he says about the perils of the Big Pond is something that many psychologists, going back as far as Stouffer's work in the Second World War, would consider to be common sense.

with a science degree, the best thing for her to do would have been to go *down* a notch to Maryland. No sane person would say that the solution to her problems would be for her to go to an even more competitive school like Stanford or MIT. Yet when it comes to affirmative action, that's exactly what we do. We take promising students like Caroline Sacks—but who happen to be black—and offer to bump them *up* a notch. And why do we do that? *Because we think we're helping them.*

That doesn't mean affirmative action is wrong. It is something done with the best of intentions, and elite schools often have resources available to help poor students that other schools do not. But this does not change the fact that—as Herbert Marsh says—the blessings of the Big Pond are mixed, and it is strange how rarely the Big Pond's downsides are mentioned. Parents still tell their children to go to the best schools they possibly can, on the grounds that the best schools will allow them to do whatever they wish. We take it for granted that the Big Pond expands opportunities, just as we take it for granted that a smaller class is always a better class. We have a definition in our heads of what an advantage is—and the definition isn't right. And what happens as a result? It means that we make mistakes. It means that we misread battles between underdogs and giants. It means that we underestimate how much freedom there can be in what looks like a disadvantage. It's the Little Pond that maximizes your chances to do whatever you want.

At the time she was applying to college, Caroline Sacks had no idea she was taking that kind of chance with the thing she loved. Now she does. At the end of our talk, I asked her what would have happened if she had chosen instead to go to the University of Maryland—to be, instead, a Big Fish in a Little Pond. She answered without hesitation: "I'd still be in science."

7.

"I was a very enthusiastic student growing up, and I really liked learning and I liked school, and I was good at it," Stephen Randolph began.[*] He is a tall young man with carefully combed dark brown hair and neatly pressed khakis. "I took high school algebra starting in fourth grade. Then I did algebra two in fifth grade and geometry in sixth grade. By the time I got to middle school, I was going to high school for math and for biology, chemistry, and Advanced Placement U.S. history. I also went to a local college starting in fifth grade, taking some math, but I did other science in fifth grade as well. I actually think by the time I graduated high school, I had more than enough credits to immediately get a bachelor's degree from the University of Georgia. I'm pretty certain of that."

Every day from first grade until the end of high school, Randolph wore a tie to school. "It's kind of embarrassing," he said, "kind of crazy. But I did it. I forget how it started. I just wanted to wear a tie one day in first grade and then I just kept doing it. I was a nerd, I guess."

Randolph was valedictorian of his high school class. His college admission-test scores were nearly perfect. He was

---

* "Stephen Randolph" is a pseudonym.

accepted by both Harvard and MIT and chose Harvard. In the first week of school, he walked through Harvard Yard and marveled at his good fortune. "It occurred to me that everyone here was a student who got into Harvard. Which was a crazy thought, but it was like, oh, yeah, all these people are interesting and smart and amazing and this is going to be a great experience. I was so enthusiastic."

His story was almost word for word the same as Caroline Sacks's, and hearing it a second time made it plain how remarkable the achievement of the Impressionists really was. They were artistic geniuses. But they were also possessed of a rare wisdom about the world. They were capable of looking at what the rest of us thought of as a great advantage, and seeing it for what it really was. Monet, Degas, Cézanne, Renoir, and Pissarro would have gone to their second choice.

So what happened to Stephen Randolph at Harvard? I think you can guess the answer. In his third year, he took quantum mechanics. "I didn't do well," he admitted. "I think I might have gotten a B-minus." It was the lowest grade he'd ever received. "My perception was that either I wasn't good at it or I wasn't good enough at it. Maybe I felt that I had to be the best at it or be a genius at it for it to make sense for me to continue. Some people seemed to get it more quickly than I did—and you tend to focus on those people and not the ones who are just as lost as you are.

"I was excited by the material," he continued. "But I was humbled by the experience—humbled as in, you sit in the class and you don't understand and you feel like, 'I will never be able to understand this!' And you do problem sets and you understand a little bit of this and a little bit of that, but you always think that the other people in your class understand it a lot better. I think one of the things about Harvard is that there's just so many smart people there that it's hard to feel smart there." He decided he couldn't go on.

"You know, there's something about solving a math problem that's very satisfying," Randolph said at one point, and an almost wistful look came over his face. "You start with a problem that you may not know how to solve, but you know there are certain rules you can follow and certain approaches you can take, and often during this process, the intermediate result is more complex than what you started with, and then the final result is simple. And there's a certain joy in making that journey." Randolph went to the school he wanted. But did he get the education he wanted? "I think I'm generally pleased with the way things turned out," he said. Then he laughed, a little rue-fully. "At least that's what I tell myself."

At the end of his third year in college, Randolph decided to take the entrance exam for law school. After graduating, he took a job with a law firm in Manhattan. Harvard cost the world a physicist and gave the world another lawyer. "I do tax law," Randolph said. "It's funny. There are a fair number of math and physics majors who end up in tax law."

Part Two

The Theory of Desirable Difficulty

I was given a thorn in my flesh, a messenger of Satan, to torment me. Three times I pleaded with the Lord to take it away from me. But he said to me, "My grace is sufficient for you, for my power is made perfect in weakness." Therefore I will boast all the more gladly about my weaknesses, so that Christ's power may rest on me. That is why, for Christ's sake, I delight in weaknesses, in insults, in hardships, in persecutions, in difficulties. For when I am weak, then I am strong.

2 Corinthians 12:7–10

CHAPTER FOUR

David Boies

YOU WOULDN'T WISH DYSLEXIA
ON YOUR CHILD. OR WOULD YOU?

1.

If you do a brain scan on a person with dyslexia, the images that are produced seem strange. In certain critical parts of the brain—those that deal with reading and processing words—dyslexics have less gray matter. They don't have as many brain cells in those regions as they should. As the fetus develops inside the womb, neurons are supposed to travel to the appropriate areas of the brain, taking their places like pieces on a chessboard. But for some reason, the neurons of dyslexics sometimes get lost along the way. They end up in the wrong place. The brain has something called the ventricular system, which functions as the brain's entry and exit point. Some people with reading disorders have neurons lining their ventricles, like passengers stranded in an airport.

While an image of the brain is being made, a patient

performs a task, and then a neuroscientist looks to see what parts of the brain have been activated in response to that task. If you ask a dyslexic to read when he or she is having a brain scan, the parts that are supposed to light up might not light up at all. The scan looks like an aerial photo of a city during a blackout. Dyslexics use a lot more of the right hemisphere of their brains during reading than normal readers do. The right hemisphere is the conceptual side. That's the wrong half of the brain for a precise and rigorous task like reading. Sometimes when a dyslexic reads, every step will be delayed, as if the different parts of the brain responsible for reading were communicating via a weak connection. One of the ways to test for the presence of dyslexia in a small child is to have him engage in "rapid automatized naming." Show him one color after another—a red dot, then a green dot, then a blue dot, then a yellow dot—and check his response. *See the color. Recognize the color. Attach a name to the color. Say the name.* That's automatic in most of us. It's not in someone with a reading disorder; somewhere along the way, the links between those four steps start to break down. Ask a four-year-old: Can you say the word "banana" without the *buh*? Or say, Listen to the following three sounds: *cuh, ah,* and *tuh.* Can you combine them into "cat"? Or take "cat," "hat," and "dark." Which one of those words doesn't rhyme? Easy questions for most four-year-olds. Really hard questions for dyslexics. Many people used to think that what defines dyslexics is that they get words backwards—"cat" would be "tac," or something like that—making it sound like dyslexia is a problem in the way the words are seen. But it is much more profound than that. Dyslexia is a problem in the way people hear and manipulate sounds. The difference between *bah* and *dah* is a subtlety in the first 40 milliseconds of the syllable. Human language is based on the assumption that we can pick up that 40-millisecond difference, and the difference between the *bah* sound and the *dah* sound can be the difference between getting something right and getting something catastrophically wrong. Can you imagine the consequences of having a brain so sluggish that when it comes to putting together the building blocks of words, those crucial 40 milliseconds simply go by too quickly?

"If you have no concept of the sounds of language—if you take away a letter, if you take away a sound, and you don't know what to do, then it's really hard to map the sounds to the written counterparts," Nadine Gaab, a dyslexia researcher at Harvard, explained. "It may take you a while to learn to read. You read really slowly, which then impairs your reading fluency, which then impairs your reading comprehension, because you're so slow that by the time you're at the end of the sentence, you've forgotten what the beginning of the sentence was. So it leads to all these problems in middle school or high school. Then it starts affecting all other subjects in school. You can't read. How are you going to do on math tests that have a lot of writing in them? Or how do you take an exam in social studies if it takes you two hours to read what they want from you?

"Usually you get a diagnosis at eight or nine," she went on. "And we find that by that point, there are already a lot of serious psychological implications, because by that time, you've been struggling for three years.

Maybe you were the cool kid on the playground when you were four. Then you entered kindergarten and all your peers suddenly started reading, and you can't figure it out. So you get frustrated. Your peers may think you're stupid. Your parents may think you're lazy. You have very low self-esteem, which leads to an increased rate of depression. Kids with dyslexia are more likely to end up in the juvenile system, because they act up. It's because they can't figure things out. It's *so* important in our society to read."

You wouldn't wish dyslexia on your child. Or would you?

2.

So far in *David and Goliath,* we've looked at the ways in which we are often misled about the nature of advantages. Now it is time to turn our attention to the other side of the ledger. What do we mean when we call something a *dis*advantage? Conventional wisdom holds that a disadvantage is something that ought to be avoided—that it is a setback or a difficulty that leaves you worse off than you would be otherwise. But that is not always the case. In the next few chapters, I want to explore the idea that there are such things as "*desirable* difficulties." That concept was conceived by Robert Bjork and Elizabeth Bjork, two psychologists at the University of California, Los Angeles, and it is a beautiful and haunting way of understanding how underdogs come to excel.

Consider, for example, the following puzzle.

1. A bat and a ball cost $1.10 in total. The bat costs $1.00 more than the ball. How much does the ball cost?

What's your instinctive response? I'm guessing that it is that the ball must cost 10 cents. That can't be right, though, can it? The bat is supposed to cost $1.00 *more than* the ball. So if the ball costs 10 cents, the bat must cost $1.10, and we've exceeded our total. The right answer must be that the ball costs 5 cents.

Here's another question:

2. If it takes 5 machines 5 minutes to make 5 widgets, how long would it take 100 machines to make 100 widgets?

The setup of the question tempts you to answer 100. But it's a trick. One hundred machines take exactly the same amount of time to make 100 widgets as 5 machines take to make 5 widgets. The right answer is 5 minutes.

These puzzles are two of the three questions that make up the world's shortest intelligence test.* It's called the Cognitive Reflection Test (CRT). It was invented by the Yale professor Shane Frederick, and it measures your ability to understand when something is more complex than it appears—to move past impulsive answers to deeper, analytic judgments.

Frederick argues that if you want a quick way to sort people according to their level of basic cognitive ability, his little test is almost as useful as tests that have hundreds of items and take several hours to finish. To prove his

---

* Actually, there's an even shorter test. One of the most brilliant modern psychologists was a man named Amos Tversky. Tversky was so smart that his fellow psychologists devised the "Tversky Intelligence Test": The faster you realized Tversky was smarter than you, the smarter you were. Adam Alter told me about the Tversky test. He would score very highly on it.

point, Frederick gave the CRT to students at nine American colleges, and the results track pretty closely with how students from those colleges would rank on more traditional intelligence tests.* Students from the Massachusetts Institute of Technology—perhaps the brainiest college in the world—averaged 2.18 correct answers out of three. Students at Carnegie Mellon University in Pittsburgh, another extraordinarily elite institution, averaged 1.51 right answers out of three. Harvard students scored 1.43; the University of Michigan, Ann Arbor, 1.18; and the University of Toledo 0.57.

The CRT is really hard. But here's the strange thing. Do you know the easiest way to raise people's scores on the test? Make it just a little bit *harder*. The psychologists Adam Alter and Daniel Oppenheimer tried this a few years ago with a group of undergraduates at Princeton University. First they gave the CRT the normal way, and the students averaged 1.9 correct answers out of three. That's pretty good, though it is well short of the 2.18 that MIT students averaged. Then Alter and Oppenheimer printed out the test questions in a font that was really hard to read—a 10 percent gray, *10-point* italics Myriad Pro font—so that it looked like this:

---

* To make sure he was measuring intelligence and not something else, Frederick also correlated CRT scores with other factors. "An analysis of these responses shows that CRT scores are unrelated to preferences between apples and oranges, Pepsi and Coke, beer and wine or rap concerts and ballet," he writes. "However, CRT scores are strongly predictive of the choice between *People* magazine and *The New Yorker*. Among the low CRT group, 67 percent preferred *People*. Among the high CRT group, 64 percent preferred *The New Yorker*." (I'm a writer for *The New Yorker*, so there was no way I wasn't going to mention this, right?)

1. A bat and a ball cost $1.10 in total. The bat costs $1.00 more than the ball. How much does the ball cost?

The average score this time around? 2.45. Suddenly, the students were doing much better than their counterparts at MIT.

That's strange, isn't it? Normally we think that we are better at solving problems when they are presented clearly and simply. But here the opposite happened. A 10 percent gray, 10-point italics Myriad Pro font makes reading really frustrating. You have to squint a little bit and maybe read the sentence twice, and you probably wonder halfway through who on earth thought it was a good idea to print out the test this way. Suddenly you have to work to read the question.

Yet all that extra effort pays off. As Alter says, making the questions "disfluent" causes people to "think more deeply about whatever they come across. They'll use more resources on it. They'll process more deeply or think more carefully about what's going on. If they have to overcome a hurdle, they'll overcome it better when you force them to think a little harder." Alter and Oppenheimer made the CRT more difficult. But that difficulty turned out to be *desirable*.

Not all difficulties have a silver lining, of course. What Caroline Sacks went through, in her organic chemistry class at Brown was an undesirable difficulty. She is a curious, hardworking, talented student who loves science—and there was no advantage to putting her in a situation where she felt demoralized and inadequate. The struggle did not give her a new appreciation of science.

It scared her away from science. But there are times and places where struggles have the opposite effect—where what seems like the kind of obstacle that ought to cripple an underdog's chances is actually like Alter and Oppenheimer's Myriad Pro 10 percent gray, *10-point* italics font.

Can dyslexia turn out to be a desirable difficulty? It is hard to believe that it can, given how many people struggle with the disorder throughout their lives—except for a strange fact. An extraordinarily high number of successful entrepreneurs are dyslexic. A recent study by Julie Logan at City University London puts the number somewhere around a third. The list includes many of the most famous innovators of the past few decades. Richard Branson, the British billionaire entrepreneur, is dyslexic. Charles Schwab, the founder of the discount brokerage that bears his name, is dyslexic, as are the cell phone pioneer Craig McCaw; David Neeleman, the founder of JetBlue; John Chambers, the CEO of the technology giant Cisco; Paul Orfalea, the founder of Kinko's—to name just a few. The neuroscientist Sharon Thompson-Schill remembers speaking at a meeting of prominent university donors—virtually all of them successful businesspeople—and on a whim asking how many of them had ever been diagnosed with a learning disorder. "Half the hands went up," she said. "It was unbelievable."

There are two possible interpretations for this fact. One is that this remarkable group of people triumphed in spite of their disability: they are so smart and so creative that nothing—not even a lifetime of struggling with reading— could stop them. The second, more intriguing, possibility is that they succeeded, in part, *because* of their disorder—

that they learned something in their struggle that proved to be of enormous advantage. Would you wish dyslexia on your child? If the second of these possibilities is true, you just might.

3.

David Boies grew up in farming country in rural Illinois. He was the eldest of five. His parents were public school teachers. His mother would read to him when he was young. He would memorize what she said because he couldn't follow what was on the page. He didn't begin to read until the third grade, and then did so only slowly and with great difficulty. Many years later, he would realize that he had dyslexia. But at the time, he didn't think he had a problem. His little town in rural Illinois wasn't a place that regarded reading well as some crucial badge of achievement. Many of his schoolmates quit school to work on the farm the first chance they got. Boies read comic books, which were easy to follow and had lots of pictures. He never read for fun. Even today, he might read one book a year, if that. He watches television—anything, he says with a laugh, "that moves and is in color." His speaking vocabulary is limited. He uses small words and short sentences. Sometimes if he's reading something out loud and runs into a word he doesn't know, he will stop and spell it out slowly. "My wife gave me an iPad a year and a half ago, which was my first computer-like device, and one of the things that was interesting is that my attempt to spell many words is not close enough for spell-check to find the correct spelling," Boics says. "I can't tell you how many times I get the little message that says, 'No spelling suggestions.'"

When Boies graduated from high school, he didn't have any great ambitions. His grades had been "ragged." His family had moved to Southern California by then, and the local economy was booming. He got a job in construction. "It was outside work, with older guys," Boies remembers. "I was making more money than I could ever have imagined. It was a lot of fun." After that, he worked for a while as a bookkeeper in a bank while playing a lot of bridge on the side. "It was a great life. I could have gone on like that for a while. But after our first child was born, my wife became increasingly serious-minded about my future." She brought home brochures and pamphlets from local colleges and universities. He remembered a childhood fascination with the law and decided that he would go to law school. Today David Boies is one of the most famous trial lawyers in the world.

How Boies went from a construction worker with a high school education to the top of the legal profession is a puzzle, to say the least. The law is built around reading—around cases and opinions and scholarly analyses—and Boies is someone for whom reading is a struggle. It seems crazy that he would even have considered the law. But let's not forget that if you are reading this book, then you are a reader—and that means you've probably never had to think of all the shortcuts and strategies and bypasses that exist to get *around* reading.

Boies started college at the University of Redlands, a small private university an hour east of Los Angeles.

Going there was his first break. Redlands was a Small Pond. Boies excelled there. He worked hard and was very well organized—because he knew he had to be. Then he got lucky. Redlands required a number of core courses for graduation, all of which involved heavy reading requirements. In those years, however, one could apply to law school without completing an undergraduate degree. Boies simply skipped the core courses. "I remember when I found out I could go to law school without graduating," he says. "It was so great. I couldn't believe it."

Law school, of course, required even more reading. But Boies discovered that there were summaries of the major cases—guides that would boil down the key point of a long Supreme Court opinion to a page or so. "People might tell you that's an undesirable way to do law school," he says. "But it was functional." Plus, he was a good listener. "Listening," he says, "is something I've been doing essentially all my life. I learned to do it because that was the only way that I could learn. I remember what people say. I remember words they use." So he would sit in class at law school—while everyone else furiously made notes or doodled or lapsed into daydreams or faded in and out—focusing on what was said and committing what he heard to memory. His memory by that point was a formidable instrument. He had been exercising it, after all, ever since his mother read to him as a child and he memorized what she said. His fellow students, as they made notes and doodled and faded in and out, missed things. Their attention was compromised. Boies didn't have that problem. He might not have been a reader, but the things he was forced to do because he could not read well turned out to be even more valuable. He started out at Northwestern Law School, then he transferred to Yale.

When Boies became a lawyer, he did not choose to practice corporate law. That would have been foolish. Corporate lawyers need to work their way through mountains of documents and appreciate the significance of the minor footnote on page 367. He became a litigator, a job that required him to think on his feet. He memorizes what he needs to say. Sometimes in court he stumbles when he has to read something and comes across a word that he cannot process in time. So he stops and spells it out, like a child in a spelling bee. It's awkward. It's more of an eccentricity, though, than an actual problem. In the 1990s, he headed the prosecution team accusing Microsoft of antitrust violations, and during the trial, he kept referring to "login" as "lojin," which is just the kind of mistake a dyslexic makes. But he was devastating in the cross-examination of witnesses, because there was no nuance, no subtle evasion, no peculiar and telling choice of words that he would miss—and no stray comment or revealing admission from testimony an hour or a day or a week before that he would not have heard, registered, and remembered.

"If I could read a lot faster, it would make a lot of things that I do easier," Boies said. "There's no doubt about that. But on the other hand, not being able to read a lot and learning by listening and asking questions means that I need to simplify issues to their basics. And that is very powerful, because in trial cases, judges and jurors—neither of them have the time or the ability to become an expert in the subject. One of my strengths is presenting a case that they can understand." His opponents tend to be scholarly types, who have read every conceivable analysis of the issue at hand. Time and again, they get bogged down in excessive detail. Boies doesn't.

One of his most famous cases—*Hollingsworth v. Schwarzenegger**—involved a California law limiting marriage to a man and woman. Boies was the attorney arguing that the law was unconstitutional, and in the trial's most memorable exchange, Boies destroyed the other side's key expert witness, David Blankenhorn, getting him to concede huge chunks of Boies's case.

"One of the things you tell a witness when you're preparing them is take your time," Boies said. "Even when you don't need to. Because there will be some times when you need to slow down, and you don't want to show the examiner by your change of pace that this is something that you need time on. So—when were you born?" He spoke carefully and deliberately. "'It...was...1941.' You don't say, 'ItwasMarcheleventh1941atsix-thirtyinthemorning,' even though you're not trying to hide it. You want your response to be the same for the easy things as for the harder things so that you don't reveal what's easy and what's hard by the way you answer."

When Blankenhorn paused just a bit too much in certain crucial moments, Boies caught it. "It was tone and pace and the words he used. Some of it comes from

---

* When Blankenhorn took the stand in January of 2010, the case was called *Perry v. Schwarzenegger;* it became *Hollingsworth v. Perry* at the Supreme Court level in 2013.

pauses. He'd slow down when he was trying to think of how to phrase something. He was somebody who as you probed him and listened to him, you could hear areas where he was uncomfortable—where he would use an obscuring word. And by being able to zero in on those areas, I was able to get him to admit the key elements of our case."

4.

Boies has a particular skill that helps to explain why he is so good at what he does. He's a superb listener. But think about how he came to develop that skill. Most of us gravitate naturally toward the areas where we excel. The child who picks up reading easily goes on to read even more and becomes even better at it, and ends up in a field that requires a lot of reading. A young boy named Tiger Woods is unusually coordinated for his age and finds that the game of golf suits his imagination, and so he likes to practice golf. And because he likes to practice so much, he gets even better, and on and on, in a virtuous circle. That's "capitalization learning": we get good at something by building on the strengths that we are naturally given.

But desirable difficulties have the opposite logic. In their CRT experiments, Alter and Oppenheimer made students excel by making their lives harder, by forcing them to compensate for something that had been taken away from them. That's what Boies was doing as well when he learned to listen. He was compensating. He had no choice. He was such a terrible reader that he had to scramble and adapt and come up with some kind of strategy that allowed him to keep pace with everyone around him.

Most of the learning that we do is capitalization learning. It is easy and obvious. If you have a beautiful voice and perfect pitch, it doesn't take much to get you to join a choir. "Compensation learning," on the other hand, is really hard. Memorizing what your mother says while she reads to you and then reproducing the words later in such a way that it sounds convincing to all those around you requires that you confront your limitations. It requires that you overcome your insecurity and humiliation. It requires that you focus hard enough to memorize the words, and then have the panache to put on a successful performance. Most people with a serious disability cannot master all those steps. But those who can are *better* off than they would have been otherwise, because what is learned out of necessity is inevitably more powerful than the learning that comes easily.

It is striking how often successful dyslexics tell versions of this same compensation story. "It was horrible to be in school," a man named Brian Grazer told me. "My body chemistry would always change. I would be anxious, really anxious. It would take forever to do a simple homework assignment. I would spend hours daydreaming because I couldn't really read the words. You'd find yourself sitting in one place for an hour and a half accomplishing nothing. Through seventh, eighth, ninth, and tenth grade, I was getting mostly Fs, with an occasional D and maybe a C. I was only passing because my mom wouldn't let them put me back."

So how did Grazer get through school? Before any test

or exam, he would start to plan and strategize, even in elementary school. "I would get together with someone the night before," he said. "What are you going to do? How do you think you will answer these questions? I'd try and guess the questions, or if there was a way to get the questions or the tests beforehand, I would."

By the time he hit high school, he'd developed a better strategy. "I challenged all my grades," he went on, "which meant that literally every time I got my grade in high school, after the report cards came out, I would go back to each teacher and do a one-on-one. I would argue my D into a C and my C into a B. And almost every time—ninety percent of the time—I got my grade changed. I would just wear them down. I got really good at it. I got confident. In college, I would study, knowing that I was going to have this hour-long meeting afterward with my professor. I learned how to do everything possible to sell my point. It was really good training."

All good parents try to teach their children the art of persuasion, of course. But a normal, well-adjusted child has no need to take those lessons seriously. If you get As in school, you never need to figure out how to negotiate your way to a passing grade, or to look around the room as a nine-year-old and start strategizing about how to make it through the next hour. But when Grazer practiced negotiation, just as when Boies practiced listening, he had a gun to his head. He practiced day in, day out, year after year. When Grazer said that was "really good training," what he meant was learning to talk his way from a position of weakness to a position of strength turned out to be the perfect preparation for the profession he ended up in.

Grazer is now one of the most successful movie producers in Hollywood of the past thirty years.* Would Brian
Grazer be where he is if he weren't a dyslexic?

5.

Let's dig a little deeper into this strange association between what is essentially a neurological malfunction and
career success. In the Big Pond chapter, I talked about
the fact that being on the outside, in a less elite and less
privileged environment, can give you more freedom to
pursue your own ideas and academic interests. Caroline
Sacks would have had a better chance of practicing the
profession she loved if she had gone to her second-choice
school instead of her first choice. Impressionism, simi-
larly, was possible only in the tiny gallery that virtually
no one went to, not in the most prestigious art show on
earth.

Dyslexics are outsiders as well. They are forced to
stand apart from everyone else at school because they can't
do the thing that school requires them to do. Is it possible
for that "outsiderness" to give them some kind of advantage down the line? To answer that question, it is worth
thinking about the kind of personality that characterizes
innovators and entrepreneurs.

Psychologists measure personality through what is
called the Five Factor Model, or "Big Five" inventory,

---

* Among Grazer's many films: *Splash, Apollo 13, A Beautiful Mind,* and *8 Mile.* He
was also mentioned in my book *Blink,* discussing the art of casting actors.

which assesses who we are across the following dimensions.*

Neuroticism
(sensitive/nervous versus secure/confident)
Extraversion
(energetic/gregarious versus solitary/reserved)
Openness
(inventive/curious versus consistent/cautious)
Conscientiousness
(orderly/industrious versus easygoing/careless)
Agreeableness
(cooperative/empathic versus self-interested/antagonistic)

The psychologist Jordan Peterson argues that innovators and revolutionaries tend to have a very particular mix of these traits—particularly the last three: openness, conscientiousness, and agreeableness.

Innovators have to be open. They have to be able to imagine things that others cannot and to be willing to challenge their own preconceptions. They also need to be conscientious. An innovator who has brilliant ideas but lacks the discipline and persistence to carry them out is merely a dreamer. That, too, is obvious.

But crucially, innovators need to be *dis*agreeable. By disagreeable, I don't mean obnoxious or unpleasant. I

---

* The "Big Five" is the standard that social psychologists use to measure personality. Social scientists are not always big fans of personality tests like, say, the Myers-Briggs, because they think those "lay" tests overlook key traits or mischaracterize others.

mean that on that fifth dimension of the Big Five personality inventory, "agreeableness," they tend to be on the far
end of the continuum. They are people willing to take *social* risks—to do things that others might disapprove of.

That is not easy. Society frowns on disagreeableness.
As human beings we are hardwired to seek the approval of
those around us. Yet a radical and transformative thought
goes nowhere without the willingness to challenge conven-
tion. "If you have a new idea, and it's disruptive and you're
agreeable, then what are you going to do with that?" says
Peterson. "If you worry about hurting people's feelings
and disturbing the social structure, you're not going to put
your ideas forward." As the playwright George Bernard
Shaw once put it: "The reasonable man adapts himself to
the world: the unreasonable one persists in trying to adapt
the world to himself. Therefore all progress depends on the
unreasonable man."

A good example of Peterson's argument is the story of
how the Swedish furniture retailer IKEA got its start. The
company was founded by Ingvar Kamprad. His great innovation was to realize that much of the cost of furniture
was tied up in its assembly: putting the legs on the table not
only costs money but also makes shipping the table really
expensive. So he sold furniture that hadn't yet been assembled, shipped it cheaply in flat boxes, and undersold all his
competitors.

In the mid-1950s, however, Kamprad ran into trouble.
Swedish furniture manufacturers launched a boycott of
IKEA. They were angry at his low prices, and they
stopped filling his orders. IKEA faced ruin. Desperate for
a solution, Kamprad looked south and realized just across

the Baltic Sea from Sweden was Poland, a country with much cheaper labor and plenty of wood. That's Kamprad's openness: few companies were outsourcing like that in the early 1960s. Then Kamprad focused his attention on making the Polish connection work. It wasn't easy. Poland in the 1960s was a mess. It was a Communist country. It had none of the infrastructure or machinery or trained workforce or legal protections of a Western country. But Kamprad pulled it off. "He is a micromanager," says Anders Åslund, a fellow at the Peterson Institute for International Economics. "That's why he succeeded where others failed. He went out to these unpleasant places, and made sure things worked. He's this extremely stubborn character." That's conscientiousness.

But what is the most striking fact about Kamprad's decision? It's the year he went to Poland: 1961. The Berlin Wall was going up. The Cold War was at its peak. Within a year, East and West would come to the brink of nuclear war during the Cuban Missile Crisis. The equivalent today would be Walmart setting up shop in North Korea. Most people wouldn't even think of doing business in the land of the enemy for fear of being branded a traitor. Not Kamprad. He didn't care a whit for what others thought of him. That's disagreeableness.

Only a very small number of people have the creativity to think of shipping furniture flat and outsourcing in the face of a boycott. An even smaller number have not only those kinds of insights but also the discipline to build a first-class manufacturing operation in an economic backwater. But to be creative and conscientious *and* have the strength of mind to defy the Cold War? That's rare.

Dyslexia doesn't necessarily make people more open. Nor does it make them more conscientious (although it certainly might). But the most tantalizing possibility raised by the disorder is that it might make it a little bit easier to be disagreeable.

6.

Gary Cohn grew up in a suburb of Cleveland, in northeast Ohio. His family was in the electrical contracting business. This was in the 1970s, at a time before dyslexia was routinely diagnosed. He was held back a year in elementary school because he couldn't read.[*] But, he said, "I didn't do any better the second time than I did the first time." He had a discipline problem. "I sort of got expelled from elementary school," he explained. "I think when you hit the teacher, you get expelled. It was one of those disruptive incidents....I was being abused. The teacher put me under her desk and rolled her chair in and started kicking me. So I pushed the chair back, hit her in the face, and walked out. I was in fourth grade."

He called that period in his life "the ugly years." His parents didn't know what to do. "It was probably the most frustrating part of my life, which is saying a lot." He went on: "Because it wasn't that I wasn't trying. I was working

---

[*] Dyslexia, it should be pointed out, affects only reading. Cohn's facility with numbers was unaffected. The one person who believed in him throughout his childhood, Cohn says, was his grandfather, and it was because his grandfather realized that young Gary had committed the entire inventory of the family's plumbing supplies business to memory.

really, really hard, and no one understood that part of the equation. They literally thought that I was conscientiously making decisions to be a disruptive kid, to not learn, to hold the class back. You know what it's like, you're a six- or seven- or eight-year-old kid, and you're in a public school setting, and everyone thinks you're an idiot, so you try to do funny things to try to create some social esteem. You'd try to get up every morning and say, today is going to be better, but after you do that a couple of years, you realize that today is going to be no different than yesterday. And I'm going to have to struggle to get through and I'm going to struggle to survive another day, and we'll see what happens."

His parents took him from school to school, trying to find something that worked. "All my mother wanted me to do was graduate high school," Cohn said. "I think if you'd asked her, she'd have said, 'The happiest day of my life will be if he graduates high school. Then he can go drive a truck, but at least he'll have a high school degree.'" On the day he finally did graduate, Cohn's mother was a fountain of tears. "I've never seen anyone cry so much in my life," he said.

When Gary Cohn was twenty-two, he got a job selling aluminum siding and window frames for U.S. Steel in Cleveland. He had just graduated from American University after a middling academic career. One day just before Thanksgiving, while visiting the company's sales office on Long Island, he persuaded his manager to give him the day off and ventured down to Wall Street. A few summers earlier, he had been an intern at a local brokerage firm and had become interested in trading. He headed to the commodities exchange, which was part of the old World Trade Center complex.

"I think I'm going to get a job," he said. "But there's nowhere to go. It's all secure. So I go up to the observation deck and watch the guys and think, Can I talk to them? Then I walk down to the floor with the security gate and stand at the security gate, like someone's going to let me in. Of course no one is. And then literally right after the market's closed, I see this pretty well-dressed guy running off the floor, yelling to his clerk, 'I've got to go, I'm running to LaGuardia, I'm late, I'll call you when I get to the airport.' I jump in the elevator, and I say, 'I hear you're going to LaGuardia.' He says, 'Yeah.' I say, 'Can we share a cab?' He says, 'Sure.' I think this is awesome. With Friday afternoon traffic, I can spend the next hour in the taxi getting a job."

The stranger Cohn had jumped into the cab with happened to be high up at one of Wall Street's big brokerage firms. And just that week, the firm had opened a business buying and selling options.

"The guy was running the options business but did not know what an option was," Cohn went on. He was laughing at the sheer audacity of it all. "I lied to him all the way to the airport. When he said, 'Do you know what an option is?' I said, 'Of course I do, I know everything, I can do anything for you.' Basically by the time we got out of the taxi, I had his number. He said, 'Call me Monday.' I called him Monday, flew back to New York Tuesday or Wednesday, had an interview, and started working the next Monday. In that period of time, I read McMillan's *Options as a Strategic Investment* book. It's like the Bible of options trading."

It wasn't easy, of course, since Cohn estimates that on a good day, it takes him six hours to read twenty-two pages.* He buried himself in the book, working his way through one word at a time, repeating sentences until he was sure he understood them. When he started at work, he was ready. "I literally stood behind him and said, 'Buy those, sell those, sell those,'" Cohn said. "I never owned up to him what I did. Or maybe he figured it out, but he didn't care. I made him tons of money."

Cohn isn't ashamed of his beginnings on Wall Street. But it would be a mistake, at the same time, to say that he is proud of them. He is smart enough to know that a story about bluffing your way into your first job isn't altogether flattering. He told it, instead, in the spirit of honesty. It was *This is who I am.*

Cohn was required in that taxi ride to play a role: to pretend to be an experienced options trader when in fact he was not. Most of us would have foundered in that situation. We aren't used to playing someone other than ourselves. But Cohn had been playing someone other than himself since elementary school. *You know what it's like, you're a six- or seven- or eight-year-old kid, and you're in a public school setting, and everyone thinks you're an idiot, so you try to do funny things to try to create some social esteem.* Better to play the clown than to be thought of as

---

*This chapter is about that long. If Gary Cohn wants to read about himself, he will have to sit down and clear a substantial space on his schedule. "To really understand it, read it, comprehend it, look up all the words I didn't know, look up the word and realize, oh, that's not the word, I'm looking it up wrong, that's two hours for three days in a row," he said. He's a busy man. That's unlikely to happen. "Good luck with your book I'm not going to read," he said, laughing, at the end of our interview.

an idiot. And if you've been pretending to be someone else your whole life, how hard is it to bluff your way through a one-hour cab ride to LaGuardia?

More important, most of us wouldn't have jumped in that cab, because we would have worried about the potential social consequences. The Wall Street guy could have seen right through us—and told everyone else on Wall Street that there's a kid out there posing as an options trader. Where would we be then? We could get tossed out of the cab. We could go home and realize that options trading is over our heads. We could show up on Monday morning and make fools of ourselves. We could get found out, a week or a month later, and get fired. Jumping in the cab was a *dis*agreeable act, and most of us are inclined to be agreeable. But Colm? He was selling aluminum siding. His mother thought that he would be lucky to end up a truck driver. He had been kicked out of schools and dismissed as an idiot, and, even as an adult, it took him six hours to read twenty-two pages because he had to work his way word by word to make sure he understood what he was reading. He had nothing to lose.

"My upbringing allowed me to be comfortable with failure," he said. "The one trait in a lot of dyslexic people I know is that by the time we got out of college, our ability to deal with failure was very highly developed. And so we look at most situations and see much more of the upside than the downside. Because we're so accustomed to the downside. It doesn't faze us. I've thought about it many times, I really have, because it defined who I am. I wouldn't be where I am today without my dyslexia. I never would have taken that first chance."

Dyslexia—in the best of cases—forces you to develop skills that might otherwise have lain dormant. It also forces you to do things that you might otherwise never have considered, like doing your own version of Kamprad's disagreeable trip to Poland or hopping in the cab of someone you've never met and pretending to be someone you aren't. Kamprad, in case you are wondering, is dyslexic. And Gary Cohn? It turns out he was a really good trader, and it turns out that learning how to deal with the possibility of failure is really good preparation for a career in the business world. Today he is the president of Goldman Sachs.

CHAPTER FIVE

Emil "Jay" Freireich

1.

When Jay Freireich was very young, his father died suddenly. The Freireichs were Hungarian immigrants who were running a restaurant in Chicago. It was just after the stock market crash in 1929. They lost everything. "They found him in the bathroom," Freireich said. "I think it was suicide, because he felt all alone. He had come to Chicago because he had a brother there. When the crash occurred, the brother left town. He had a wife, two small children, no money, a restaurant gone. He must have been pretty desperate."

Freireich's mother went to work in a sweatshop, sewing brims on hats. She made two cents a hat. She didn't speak much English. "She had to work eighteen hours a day, seven days a week, to make enough money to have an apartment for us to rent," Freireich went on. "We never saw her. We had a little apartment on the west side of Humboldt Park, bordering the ghetto. She couldn't leave a two-year-old and a five-year-old all alone, so she found an immigrant Irish lady who worked for room and board. My parent, from the age of two, was this Irish maid. We loved her. She was my mother. Then, when I was nine, my mother met a Hungarian man who had lost his wife and had one son, and she married him. It was a marriage of convenience. He couldn't take care of his son by himself, and she didn't have anybody. He was a really bitter, shriveled guy. So they got married and my mother left the sweatshop and appeared back on the scene, and they couldn't afford the maid anymore. So they fired her. They fired my *mother.* I never forgave my mother for that."

The family moved from one apartment to another. They had protein one day a week. Freireich remembers being sent from store to store looking for a bottle of milk for four cents, because the normal price of five cents was more than the family could afford. He spent his days on the street. He stole. He wasn't close to his sister. She was more disciplinarian than friend. He didn't like his stepfather. In any case, the marriage didn't last. He didn't like his mother either. "Whatever mind she had was destroyed in the sweatshops," he said. "She was an angry person. And when she married this ugly guy, who brought this person in—my half brother—who got half of everything I used to get, and then she fired *my* mother…" His voice trailed off.

Freireich was sitting at his desk. He was wearing a white coat. Everything he was talking about was both long ago and—in another, more important sense—not long ago at all. "I can't remember her ever hugging or kissing me or anything like that," he said. "She never talked about my father. I have no idea whether he was nice to her or mean. I never heard a word. Do I ever think about what he might have been like? All the time. I have one picture." Freireich turned in his chair and clicked on a file of pictures on his computer. Up came a grainy early-twentieth-century photograph of a man who, not surprisingly, looked a lot like Freireich himself. "That's the only picture of him my mother ever had," he said. The edges of the photo were uneven. It had been cropped from a much larger family photograph.

I asked about the Irish maid who raised him. What was her name? He stopped short—a rare pause for him. "I don't know," he said. "It will pop into my head, I'm sure." He sat still for a moment and concentrated. "My sister would remember, my mother would remember. But they are no longer alive. I have no living relatives—just two cousins." He paused again. "I want to call her Mary. And that may actually be her name. But my mother's name was Mary. So I may be confusing it…"

Freireich was eighty-four years old when we talked. But it would be a mistake to call this an age-related memory lapse. Jay Freireich does not have memory lapses. I interviewed him for the first time one spring and then again six months later, and again after that, and every time, he would recall dates and names and facts with clocklike precision, and if he went over the same ground as he had on some previous occasion, he would stop himself and say, "I know I said this to you before." He could not retrieve the name of the woman who raised him because everything from those years was so painful that it had been pushed to the furthest recesses of his mind.

2.

In the years leading up to the Second World War, the British government was worried. If, in the event of war, the German Air Force launched a major air offensive against London, the British military command believed that there was nothing they could do to stop it. Basil Liddell Hart, one of the foremost military theorists of the day, estimated that in the first week of any German attack, London could see a quarter of a million civilian deaths and injuries. Winston Churchill described London as "the greatest target in the world, a kind of tremendous, fat, valuable cow, tied up to attract the beast of prey." He predicted that the city would be so helpless in the face of attack that between three and four million Londoners would flee to the countryside. In 1937, on the eve of the war, the British military command issued a report with the direst prediction of all: a sustained German bombing attack would leave six hundred thousand dead and 1.2 million wounded and create mass panic in the streets. People would refuse to go to work. Industrial production would grind to a halt. The army would be useless against the Germans because it would be preoccupied with keeping order among the millions of panicked civilians. The country's planners briefly considered building a massive network of underground bomb shelters across London, but they abandoned the plan out of a fear that if they did, the people who took refuge there would never come out. They set up several psychiatric hospitals just outside the city limits to handle what they expected would be a flood of psychological casualties. "There is every chance," the report stated, "that this could cost us the war."

In the fall of 1940, the long-anticipated attack began. Over a period of eight months—beginning with fifty-seven consecutive nights of devastating bombardment—German bombers thundered across the skies above London, dropping tens of thousands of high-explosive bombs and more than a million incendiary devices. Forty thousand people were killed, and another forty-six thousand were injured. A million buildings were damaged or destroyed. In the city's East End, entire neighborhoods were laid waste. It was everything the British government officials had feared—except that every one of their predictions about how Londoners would react turned out to be wrong.

The panic never came. The psychiatric hospitals built on the outskirts of London were switched over to military use because no one showed up. Many women and children were evacuated to the countryside as the bombing started. But people who needed to stay in the city by and large stayed. As the Blitz continued, as the German assaults grew heavier and heavier, the British authorities began to observe—to their astonishment—not just courage in the face of the bombing but something closer to indifference. "In October 1940 I had occasion to drive through South-East London just after a series of attacks on that district," one English psychiatrist wrote just after the war ended:

> Every hundred yards or so, it seemed, there was a bomb crater or wreckage of what had once been a house or shop. The siren blew its warning and I looked to see what would happen. A nun seized the hand of a child she was escorting and hurried on. She and I seemed to be the only

ones who had heard the warning. Small boys continued to play all over the pavements, shoppers went on haggling, a policeman directed traffic in majestic boredom and the bicyclists defied death and the traffic laws. No one, so far as I could see, even looked into the sky.

I think you'll agree this is hard to believe. The Blitz was *war.* The exploding bombs sent deadly shrapnel flying in every direction. The incendiaries left a different neighborhood in flames every night. More than a million people lost their homes. Thousands crammed into makeshift shelters in subway stations every night. Outside, between the thunder of planes overhead, the thud of explosions, the rattle of anti-aircraft guns, and the endless wails of ambulances, fire engines, and warning sirens, the noise was unrelenting. In one survey of Londoners, on the night of September 12, 1940, a third said that they had gotten no sleep the night before, and another third said they got fewer than four hours. Can you imagine how New Yorkers would have reacted if one of their office towers had been reduced to rubble not just once but every night *for two and a half months?*

The typical explanation for the reaction of Londoners is the British "stiff upper lip"—the stoicism said to be inherent in the English character. (Not surprisingly, this is the explanation most favored by the British themselves.) But one of the things that soon became clear was that it wasn't just the British who behaved this way. Civilians from other countries also turned out to be unexpectedly resilient in the face of bombing. Bombing, it became clear, didn't have the effect that everyone had thought it would have. It wasn't until the end of the war that the puzzle was solved by the Canadian psychiatrist J. T. MacCurdy, in a book called *The Structure of Morale*.

MacCurdy argued that when a bomb falls, it divides the affected population into three groups. The first group is the people killed. They are the ones for whom the experience of the bombing is—obviously—the most devastating. But as MacCurdy pointed out (perhaps a bit callously), "the morale of the community depends on the reaction of the survivors, so from that point of view, the killed do not matter. Put this way the fact is obvious, corpses do not run about spreading panic."

The next group he called the *near misses*:

They feel the blast, they see the destruction, are horrified by the carnage, perhaps they are wounded, but they survive deeply impressed. "Impression" means, here, a powerful reinforcement of the fear reaction in association with bombing. It may result in "shock," a loose term that covers anything from a dazed state or actual stupor to jumpiness and preoccupation with the horrors that have been witnessed.

Third, he said, are the *remote misses*. These are the people who listen to the sirens, watch the enemy bombers overhead, and hear the thunder of the exploding bombs. But the bomb hits down the street or the next block over. And for them, the consequences of a bombing attack are exactly the opposite of the near-miss group. They survived, and the second or third time that happens, the emotion associated with the attack, MacCurdy wrote, "is a feeling of excitement with a flavour of invulnerability." A near miss leaves you traumatized. A remote miss makes you think you are invincible.

In diaries and recollections of Londoners who lived through the Blitz, there are countless examples of this phenomenon. Here is one:

> When the first siren sounded I took my children to our dug-out in the garden and I was quite certain we were all going to be killed. Then the all-clear went without anything having happened. Ever since we came out of the dug-out I have felt sure nothing would ever hurt us.

Or consider this, from the diary of a young woman whose house was shaken by a nearby explosion:

> I lay there feeling indescribably happy and triumphant. "I've been *bombed!*" I kept on saying to myself, over and over again—trying the phrase on, like a new dress, to see how it fitted. "I've been bombed!...I've been bombed—*me!*"
>
> It seems a terrible thing to say, when many people were killed and injured last night; but never in my whole life have I ever experienced such *pure and flawless happiness.*

So why were Londoners so unfazed by the Blitz? Because forty thousand deaths and forty-six thousand injuries—spread across a metropolitan area of more than eight million people—means that there were many more remote misses who were emboldened by the experience of being

bombed than there were near misses who were traumatized by it.

"We are all of us not merely liable to fear," MacCurdy
went on.

> We are also prone to be afraid of being afraid, and the con-
> quering of fear produces exhilaration....When we have
> been afraid that we may panic in an air-raid, and, when it
> has happened, we have exhibited to others nothing but a
> calm exterior and we are now safe, the contrast between
> the previous apprehension and the present relief and feel-
> ing of security promotes a self-confidence that is the very
> father and mother of courage.

In the midst of the Blitz, a middle aged laborer in a button-
factory was asked if he wanted to be evacuated to the
countryside. He had been bombed out of his house twice.
But each time he and his wife had been fine. He refused.

"What, and miss all this?" he exclaimed. "Not for all
the gold in China! There's never been nothing like it!
Never! And never will be again."

3.

The idea of desirable difficulty suggests that not all difficulties are negative. Being a poor reader is a real obstacle,
unless you are David Boies and that obstacle turns you
into an extraordinary listener, or unless you are Gary
Cohn and that obstacle gives you the courage to take
chances you would never otherwise have taken.

MacCurdy's theory of morale is a second, broader perspective on this same idea. The reason Winston Churchill and the English military brass were so apprehensive about the German attacks on London was that they assumed that a traumatic experience like being bombed would have the same effect on everyone: that the only difference between near misses and remote misses would be the degree of trauma they suffered.

But to MacCurdy, the Blitz proved that traumatic experiences can have two completely different effects on people: the same event can be profoundly damaging to one group while leaving another *better off*. That man who worked in a button factory and that young woman whose house was shaken by the bomb were better off for their experience, weren't they? They were in the middle of a war. They couldn't change that fact. But they were freed of the kinds of fears that can make life during wartime unendurable.

Dyslexia is a classic example of this same phenomenon. Many people with dyslexia don't manage to compensate for their disability. There are a remarkable number of dyslexics in prison, for example: these are people who have been overwhelmed by their failure at mastering the most basic of academic tasks. Yet this same neurological disorder in people like Gary Cohn and David Boies can also have the opposite effect. Dyslexia blew a hole in Cohn's life—leaving a trail of misery and anxiety. But he was very bright, and he had a supportive family and more than a little luck and enough other resources that he was able to weather the worst effects of the blast and emerge stronger. Too often, we make the same mistake as the British did and jump to the conclusion that there is only one kind of response to something terrible and traumatic. There isn't. There are two—which brings us back to Jay Freireich and the childhood he could not allow himself to remember.

4.

When Jay Freireich was nine years old, he contracted tonsillitis. He was very sick. The local physician—Dr. Rosenbloom—came to his family's apartment to remove his inflamed tonsils. "I never saw a man in those years," Freireich said. "Everyone I knew was a woman. If you saw a man, he was dirty and in overalls. But Rosenbloom—he had a suit and tie and he was dignified and kind. So from the age of ten I used to dream about becoming a famous doctor. I never thought of any other career."

In high school, his physics teacher took a shine to him and told him he should go to college. "I said, 'What do I need?' He said, 'Well, probably if you get twenty-five dollars, I think you can make it.' It was 1942. Things were better. But people still weren't very well off. Twenty-five dollars wasn't small stuff. I don't think my mother had ever seen twenty-five dollars. She said, 'Well, let me see what I can do.' A couple of days later, she appeared. She had found a Hungarian lady whose husband died and left her money, and believe it or not, she gave my mother twenty-five dollars. Instead of keeping it, my mother gave it to me. So here I am. I'm sixteen years old. And I'm very optimistic."

Freireich took the train from Chicago to Champaign-Urbana, where the University of Illinois was located. He rented a bedroom in a rooming house. He got a job waiting tables in a sorority house to pay his tuition, with the added bonus that he could feed himself from the leftovers. He did well and was accepted to medical school, after which he began his internship at Cook County Hospital, the major public hospital in Chicago.

Medicine in those years was a genteel profession. Doctors held a privileged social position and typically came from upper-middle-class backgrounds. Freireich was not like that. Even today, in his eighties, Freireich is an intimidating man, six foot four and thick through the chest and shoulders. His head is oversize—even for a body as large as his—making him seem bigger still. He is a talker, fluent and relentless and loud, his voice inflected with the hard vowels of his native Chicago. In moments of special emphasis, he has the habit of shouting and pounding the table with his fist—which, memorably, once resulted in his shattering a glass conference table. (The immediate aftermath was later described as the only time anyone had ever seen Freireich silenced.)

At one point, he dated a woman from a much more affluent family than his. She was refined and sophisticated. Freireich was a bruiser from Humboldt Park who looked and sounded like the muscle for some Depression-era gangster. "She took me to the symphony. It was the first time I'd ever heard classical music," he remembered. "I'd never seen a ballet. I'd never seen a play. Outside of our little TV that my mother purchased, I had no education to speak of. There was no literature, no art, no music, no dance, no nothing. It was just food. And not getting killed or beaten up. I was pretty raw."*

Freireich was a research associate in hematology in Boston. From there, he was drafted into the army and chose to complete his military service at the National Cancer Institute, just outside Washington, DC. He was, by all accounts, a brilliant and dedicated physician, the first at the hospital in the morning and the last to leave. But he remained never more than a step away from his tumultuous beginnings. He had a volcanic temper. He had no patience, no gentleness. One colleague remembers his unforgettable first impression of Freireich: "a giant, in the back of the room, yelling and screaming on the phone." Another remembers him as "completely irrepressible. He would say whatever came into his mind." Over the course of his career, he would end up being fired seven times, the first time during his residency when he angrily defied the head nurse at Presbyterian Hospital in Chicago. One of his former co-workers remembers Freireich coming across a routine error made by one of his medical residents. A minor laboratory finding had been overlooked. "The patient died," the doctor said. "It wasn't because of the error. Jay screamed at him right there in the ward, in front of five or six doctors and nurses. He called him a murderer, and the guy broke down and cried." Almost everything said about Freireich by his

---

* When Freireich was completing his medical training, a distant relative died and left him six hundred dollars. "I had a patient, a used-car dealer who said he'd sell me a used car," Freireich said. "It was a 1948 Pontiac. One night I was drunk and out partying with some girls, and I drove into the side of a brand-new Lincoln. I should have gone to jail for it, but the police came over and recognized me immediately as a county intern, so they said, 'We'll take care of it.'" This was what it was like being a doctor in those days. It is safe to say this doesn't happen anymore.

friends contains a "but." I love him, *but* we nearly came to blows. I invited him to my house, *but* he insulted my wife. "Freireich remains to this day one of my closest friends," said Evan Hersh, an oncologist who worked with Freireich at the beginning of his career. "We take him to our weddings and bar mitzvahs. I love him like he is a father. But he was a tiger in those days. We had several terrible run-ins. There were times I wouldn't speak to him for weeks."

Is it at all surprising that Freireich would be this way? The reason most of us do not scream "Murderer!" at our coworkers is that we can put ourselves in their shoes; we can imagine what someone else is feeling and create that feeling in ourselves. We can take that route because we have been supported and comforted and understood in our suffering. That support gives us a model of how to feel for others: it is the basis for empathy. But in Freireich's formative years, every human connection ended in death and abandonment—and a childhood as bleak as that leaves only pain and anger in its wake.

Once, in the middle of reminiscing about his career, Freireich burst into an attack on the idea that terminally ill cancer patients be given hospice care at the end of their lives. "You have all these doctors who want to do hospice care. I mean, how can you treat a person like that?" When Freireich gets worked up about something, he raises his voice, and his jaw sets. "Do you say, 'You've got cancer, you're certainly going to die. You've got pain and it's horrible. I'm gonna send you to a place where you can die pleasantly'? *I would never say that to a person.* I would say, 'You're suffering. You've got pain. I'm going to relieve your suffering. Are you gonna die? Maybe not. I see miracles every day.' There's no possibility of being pessimistic when people are dependent on you for their only optimism. On Tuesday morning, I make teaching rounds, and sometimes the medical fellows say, 'This patient is eighty years old. It's hopeless.' Absolutely not! It's challenging, it's not hopeless. You have to come up with something. You have to figure out a way to help them, because people *must have hope* to live." He was nearly shouting now. "I was *never* depressed. I never sat with a parent and cried about a child dying. That's nothing I would ever do in my role as a doctor. As a parent I might do it. My kids died, I'd probably go crazy. But as a doctor, you swear to give people hope. That's your job."

Freireich continued on in this vein for several more minutes until the full force of his personality became nearly overwhelming. We all want a physician who doesn't give up and who doesn't lose hope. But we also want a physician who can stand in our shoes and understand what we are feeling. We want to be treated with dignity, and treating people with dignity requires empathy. Could Freireich do that? *I was* never *depressed. I never sat with a parent and cried about a child dying.* If we were asked if we would wish a childhood like Freireich's on anyone, we would almost certainly say no because we could not imagine that any good could come of it. You can't have a remote miss from that kind of upbringing.

Or can you?

5.

In the early 1960s, a psychologist named Marvin Eisenstadt started a project interviewing "creatives"—innovators and artists and entrepreneurs—looking for patterns and trends. As he was analyzing the responses, he noticed an odd fact. A surprising number had lost a parent in childhood. The group he was studying was so small that Eisenstadt knew there was a possibility that what he was seeing was just chance. But the fact nagged at him. What if it wasn't chance? What if it meant something? There had been hints in the psychological literature. In the 1950s, while studying a sample of famous biologists, the science historian Anne Roe had remarked in passing on how many had at least one parent who died while they were young. The same observation was made a few years later in an informal survey of famous poets and writers like Keats, Wordsworth, Coleridge, Swift, Edward Gibbon, and Thackeray. More than half, it turned out, had lost a father or mother before the age of fifteen. The link between career achievement and childhood bereavement was one of those stray facts that no one knew what to do with. So Eisenstadt decided to embark on a more ambitious project.

"It was 1963, 1964," Eisenstadt remembers. "I started with the *Encyclopedia Britannica* and then it turned into both *Britannica* and the *Encyclopedia Americana*." Eisenstadt made a list of every person, from Homer to John F. Kennedy, whose life merited more than one column in either encyclopedia. That, he felt, was a rough proxy for achievement. He now had a list of 699 people. He then began systematically tracking down biographical information for everyone on the list. "It took me ten years," Eisenstadt says. "I was reading all kinds of foreign-language books, I went to California and to the Library of Congress, and to the genealogical library in New York City. I tracked down as many parental-loss profiles as I could, until I felt I had good statistical results."

Of the 573 eminent people for whom Eisenstadt could find reliable biographical information, a quarter had lost at least one parent before the age of ten. By age fifteen, 34.5 percent had had at least one parent die, and by the age of twenty, 45 percent. Even for the years before the twentieth century, when life expectancy due to illness and accidents and warfare was much lower than it is today, those are astonishing numbers.

At the same time as Eisenstadt was pursuing his research, the historian Lucille Iremonger set out to write a history of England's prime ministers. Her focus was on the period from the beginning of the nineteenth century to the start of the Second World War. What sort of backgrounds and qualities, she wondered, predicted the kind of person capable of rising to the top of British politics at a time when it was the most powerful country in the world? Like Eisenstadt, however, she got sidetracked by a fact that, as she wrote, "occurred so frequently that I began to wonder whether it was not of more than passing significance." Sixty-seven percent of the prime ministers in her sample lost a parent before the age of sixteen. That's roughly twice the rate of parental loss during the same period for members of the British upper class—the socioeconomic segment from which most prime ministers came. The same pattern can be found among American presidents. Twelve of the first forty-four U.S. presidents—beginning with George Washington and going all the way up to Barack Obama—lost their fathers while they were young.*

Since then, the topic of difficult childhoods and parental loss has cropped up again and again in the scholarly literature. There is a fascinating passage in an essay by the psychologist Dean Simonton, for example, in which he tries to understand why so many gifted children fail to live up to their early promise. One of the reasons, he concludes, is that they have "inherited an excessive amount of psychological health." Those who fall short, he says, are children "too conventional, too obedient, too unimaginative, to make the big time with some revolutionary idea." He goes on: "Gifted children and child prodigies seem most likely to emerge in highly supportive family conditions. In contrast, geniuses have a perverse tendency of growing up in more adverse conditions."

I realize these studies make it sound as if losing a parent is a good thing. "People always kid me and say, 'Oh, you mean I'd be better off if I don't have parents, or if I murder my father?'" Eisenstadt says. "The idea that some people could be successful without parents is a very threatening concept because the common idea is that parents help you. Parents are essential to your life." And that, Eisenstadt stresses, is absolutely true. Parents *are* essential. Losing a father or a mother is the most devastating thing that can happen to a child. The psychiatrist Felix Brown has found

---

* The twelve are George Washington, Thomas Jefferson, James Monroe, Andrew Jackson, Andrew Johnson, Rutherford Hayes, James Garfield, Grover Cleveland, Herbert Hoover, Gerald Ford, Bill Clinton, and Barack Obama.

that prisoners are somewhere between two and three times more likely to have lost a parent in childhood than is the population as a whole. That's too great a difference to be a coincidence. There are, clearly, an enormous number of direct hits from the absence of a parent.[*]

The evidence produced by Eisenstadt, Iremonger, and the others, however, suggests that there is also such a thing as a remote miss from the death of a parent. Your father can commit suicide and you can suffer from a childhood so unspeakable that you push it to the furthest corners of your memory—and still some good can end up coming from that. "This is not an argument in favour of orphanhood and deprivation," Brown writes, "but the existence of these eminent orphans does suggest that in certain circumstances a virtue can be made of necessity."[†]

6.

When Jay Freireich arrived at the National Cancer Institute in 1955, he reported to Gordon Zubrod, the head of

---

[*] Brown begins with these haunting lines from Wordsworth, whose mother died when he was eight:

> *She who was the heart*
> *And hinge of all our learnings and our loves:*
> *She left us destitute and, as we might,*
> *Trooping together.*

[†] Or, as the English essayist Thomas De Quincey famously put it: "It is, or it is not, according to the nature of men, an advantage to be orphaned at an early age."

cancer treatment. Zubrod assigned him to the children's leukemia ward, on the second floor of the main hospital building in the center of campus.*

Childhood leukemia was then one of the most terrifying of all cancers. It struck without warning. A child as young as one or two would come down with a fever. The fever would persist. Then came a violent headache that would not let up, followed by infections, one after another, as the child's body lost its ability to defend itself. Then came the bleeding.

"Dr. Zubrod came around once a week to see how we were doing," Freireich remembered, "and he said to me, 'Freireich, this place is like an abattoir! There's blood all over the goddamn place. We have to clean it up!' It was true. The kids bled from everywhere—through their stool, urine—that's the worst part. They paint the ceiling. They bleed from out of their ears, from their skin. There was blood on everything. The nurses would come to work in the morning in their white uniforms and go home covered in blood."

The children would bleed internally, into their livers and spleens, putting them in extraordinary pain. They would turn over in their beds and get terrible bruises. Even a nosebleed was a potentially fatal event. You'd squeeze the child's nose and put ice on it. That wouldn't work. You'd pack gauze into the child's nostrils. That wouldn't work. You'd call in an ear, nose, and throat spe-

---

* If you want to understand the full scientific context of the fight against leukemia, there is no better source than Siddhartha Mukherjee's Pulitzer Prize–winning *The Emperor of All Maladies: A Biography of Cancer*. Mukherjee has a full chapter on the war on leukemia. It is well worth reading.

cialist who would go in through the mouth and pack the nasal passage from behind with gauze—which then had to be pulled forward into the nose. The idea was to apply pressure on the blood vessels from inside the nasal cavity. You can imagine how painful that was for the child. Plus, it rarely worked, so you'd take out the gauze—and the bleeding would start all over again. The goal of the second floor was to find a cure for leukemia. But the problem was that controlling the bleeding was so difficult that most of the children were dead before anyone could figure out how to help them.

"When they came to the hospital, ninety percent of the kids would be dead in six weeks," Freireich said. "They would bleed to death. If you're bleeding in your mouth and nose, then you can't eat. You stop eating. You try to drink. You gag. You vomit. You get diarrhea from the blood in the stools. So you starve to death. Or you get an infection and then you get pneumonia, then you get fever, and then you get convulsions, and then..." He let his voice trail off.

Doctors did not last long on the leukemia floor. It was too much. "You got there at seven in the morning," one physician who worked on the second floor in those years remembers. "You left at nine at night. You had to do everything. I would come home every day, completely destroyed psychologically. I became a stamp collector. I would sit down at ten o'clock at night with my stamps, because it was the only way to take my mind off work. The parents were afraid. Nobody would even go into the children's room. They would stand at the door. Nobody wanted to work there. I had seventy kids who died on me that year. It was a nightmare."*

Not for Freireich. *I was* never *depressed. I never sat with a parent and cried about a child dying.* Freireich teamed up with another researcher at NCI named Tom Frei. Together, they became convinced that the problem was a lack of platelets—the irregularly shaped cell fragments that float around in human blood. The leukemia was destroying the children's ability to make them, and without platelets their blood couldn't clot. This was a radical idea. One of Freireich's bosses at NCI—a world expert in the field of hematology named George Brecher—was skeptical. But Freireich thought Brecher wasn't counting the platelets correctly when he did his analysis. Freireich was meticulous. He used a more sophisticated method-

---

* In the 1960s, the daughter of the novelist Peter de Vries died of leukemia. He wrote a heartbreaking novel based on the experience called *The Blood of the Lamb*. De Vries writes:

> So we were back in the Children's Pavilion, and there was again the familiar scene: the mothers with their nearly dead, the false face of mercy, the Slaughter of the Innocents. A girl with one leg came unsteadily down the hall between crutches, skillfully encouraged by nurses. Through the pane in a closed door a boy could be seen sitting up in bed, bleeding from everything in his head; a priest lounged alertly against the wall, ready to move in closer. In the next room a boy of five was having Methotrexate pumped into his skull, or, more accurately, was watching a group of mechanics gathered solemnly around the stalled machine. In the next a baby was sitting up watching a television set on which a panel show was in progress...Among the parents and children, flung together in a hell of prolonged farewell, wandered forever the ministering vampires from Laboratory, sucking samples from bones and veins to see how went with each the enemy that had marked them all. And the doctors in their butchers' coats, who severed the limbs and gouged the brains and knifed the vitals where the demon variously dwelt, what did they think of these best fruits of ten million hours of dedicated toil? They hounded the culprit from organ to organ and joint to joint till nothing remained over which to practice their art: the art of prolonging sickness.

ology and zeroed in on subtle changes in the platelets at really low levels, and to him the connection was clear: the lower the platelet count, the worse the bleeding. The children needed fresh platelets—over and over again, in massive doses.

The NCI blood bank wouldn't give Freireich fresh blood for his transfusions. It was against regulations. Freireich pounded on the table with his fists, shouting out, *"You're gonna kill people!"* "You have to be careful who you say that kind of thing to," Dick Silver, who worked at NCI with Freireich, says. "Jay didn't care."

Freireich went out and recruited blood donors. The father of one of his patients was a minister, and he brought in twenty members of his congregation. Standard procedure in blood transfusions in the mid-1950s was steel needles, rubber tubes, and glass bottles. But it turned out that platelets stuck to those surfaces. So Freireich had the idea of switching to the brand-new technology of silicon needles and plastic bags. The bags were called sausages. They were enormous. "They were *this* big," said Vince DeVita, who was one of Freireich's medical fellows in those years. He held his hands far apart. "And you have this kid, who is only *this* big." He held his hands much closer together. "It was like watering a flowerpot with a fire hose. If you don't do it right, you put the kids into heart failure. The clinical director of NCI at the time was a guy named Berlin. He saw the [sausage] and said to Jay, 'You're insane.' He told Jay he was going to fire him if he kept doing platelet transfusions." Freireich ignored him. "Jay being Jay," DeVita went on, "he decided if he couldn't do it, he didn't want to work there anyway." The bleeding stopped.

7.

Where did Freireich's courage come from? He's such an imposing and intimidating presence that it is easy to imagine him emerging from his mother's womb, fists already clenched. But MacCurdy's idea about near and remote misses suggests something quite different—that courage is in some sense acquired.

Take a look again at what MacCurdy wrote about the experience of being in the London Blitz:

> We are all of us not merely liable to fear, we are also prone to be afraid of being afraid, and the conquering of fear produces exhilaration....When we have been afraid that we may panic in an air-raid, and, when it has happened, we have exhibited to others nothing but a calm exterior and we are now safe, the contrast between the previous apprehension and the present relief and feeling of security promotes a self-confidence that is the very father and mother of courage.

Let us start with the first line: *We are all of us not merely liable to fear, we are also prone to be afraid of being afraid.* Because no one in England had been bombed before, Londoners assumed the experience would be terrifying. What frightened them was their prediction about how they would feel once the bombing started.* Then German bombs dropped like hail for months and months, and millions of

---

*The prediction we make about how we are going to feel in some future situation is called "affective forecasting," and all of the evidence suggests that we are terrible affective forecasters. The psychologist Stanley J. Rachman, for example, has done things like

remote misses who had predicted that they would be terrified of bombing came to understand that their fears were overblown. They were fine. And what happened then? *The conquering of fear produces exhilaration.* And: *The contrast between the previous apprehension and the present relief and feeling of security promotes a self-confidence that is the very father and mother of courage.*

Courage is not something that you already have that makes you brave when the tough times start. Courage is what you earn when you've been through the tough times and you discover they aren't so tough after all. Do you see the catastrophic error that the Germans made? They bombed London because they thought that the trauma associated with the Blitz would destroy the courage of the British people. In fact, it did the opposite. It created a city of remote misses, who were more courageous than they had ever been before. The Germans would have been better off not bombing London at all.

The next chapter of *David and Goliath* is about the American civil rights movement, when Martin Luther King Jr. brought his campaign to Birmingham, Alabama. There is one part of the Birmingham story that is worth touching on now, though, because it is a perfect example of this idea of acquired courage.

One of King's most important allies in Birmingham was a black Baptist preacher named Fred Shuttlesworth, who had been leading the fight against racial segregation in

---

take a group of people terrified of snakes and then show them a snake. Or take a group of claustrophobics and have them stand in a small metal closet. What he finds is that the actual experience of the thing that was feared is a lot less scary than the person imagined.

the city for years. On Christmas morning in 1956, Shuttlesworth announced that he was going to ride the city's
segregated buses in defiance of the city's laws forbidding
blacks from traveling with whites. The day before the
protest, on Christmas night, his house was bombed by
members of the Ku Klux Klan. The Klan was trying to do
to Shuttlesworth what the Nazis had been trying to do to
the English during the Blitz. But they, too, misunderstood
the difference between a near and a remote miss.

In Diane McWhorter's magnificent history of the civil
rights campaign in Birmingham, *Carry Me Home,* she describes what happened as the police and neighbors came
running toward the smoking ruins of Shuttlesworth's
house. It was late at night. Shuttlesworth had been lying in
bed. They feared he was dead:

> A voice rose from the wreckage: "I'm not coming out
> naked." And, after a few moments, Shuttlesworth
> emerged in the raincoat someone threw into the parson-
> age's rubble. He was not crippled, not bloodied or blind;
> he was not even deaf, though the blast had blown win-
> dows out of houses a mile away.... Shuttlesworth raised a
> biblical hand to the concerned neighbors, and said, "The
> Lord has protected me. I am not injured."...
>
> A big cop was crying. "Reverend, I know these people,"
> he said of the bombers. "I didn't think they would go this far.
> If I were you, I'd get out of town. These people are vicious."
>
> "Well, Officer, you're not me," Shuttlesworth said.
> "Go back and tell your Klan brothers that if the Lord
> saved me from this, I'm here for the duration. The fight is
> just beginning."

That's a classic remote miss. Shuttlesworth wasn't killed. (A direct hit.) He wasn't maimed or badly injured. (A near miss.) He was unscathed. Whatever the Klan had hoped to accomplish had gone badly awry. Shuttlesworth was now less afraid than he had been before.

The next morning, members of his congregation pleaded with him to call off the protest. He refused. McWhorter continues:

> "Hell, yeah, we're going to ride," the cussing preacher said and addressed his board. "Find you any kind of crack you can to hide in if you're scared, but I'm walking downtown after this meeting and getting on the bus. I'm not going to look back to see who's following me." His voice deepened into the preacher register. "Boys step back," he ordered, "and men step forward."

A few months later, Shuttlesworth decided to personally take his daughter to enroll at the all-white John Herbert Phillips High School. As he drove up, a crowd of angry white men gathered around his car. Here is McWhorter again:

> To the child's disbelief, her father stepped out of the car. The men lunged at Shuttlesworth, baring brass knuckles, wooden clubs, and chains. Scampering west across the sidewalk, he was repeatedly knocked down. Someone had pulled his coat up over his head so that he couldn't lower his arms.... "We've got this son of a bitch now," a man yelled. "Let's kill him," the crowd screamed. From a white female cheering section came advice to "kill the motherfucking nigger and it will be all over." Men began smashing the windows of the car.

So, what happened to Shuttlesworth? Not much. He managed to crawl back into the car. He went to the hospital and was found to have minor kidney damage and some scratches and bruises. He checked himself out that afternoon, and that evening from the pulpit of his church, he told his congregation that he had only forgiveness for his attackers.

Shuttlesworth must have been someone of great resolve and strength. But when he climbed unscathed out of the wreckage of his house, he added an extra layer of psychological armor. *We are all of us not merely liable to fear, we are also prone to be afraid of being afraid, and the conquering of fear produces exhilaration....The contrast between the previous apprehension and the present relief and feeling of security promotes a self-confidence that is the very father and mother of courage.*

And then what happened at Phillips High School? Another remote miss! Upon leaving the hospital, Shuttlesworth told reporters, "Today is the second time within a year that a miracle has spared my life." If one remote miss brings exhilaration, we can only imagine what two bring.

Not long afterward, Shuttlesworth brought a colleague, Jim Farmer, to meet with Martin Luther King at a church in Montgomery, Alabama. Outside, an angry mob had gathered, waving Confederate flags. They began to rock the car. The driver reversed and tried an alternate route, only to be blocked once more. What did Shuttlesworth do? Just like at Phillips High School, he got *out of* the car. Here again is McWhorter:

Coke bottles shattered car windows around him as he paused to register a strange smell, his first whiff of tear gas. Then he beckoned Farmer out of the car and strode into the mob. Farmer followed, "scared as hell," trying to shrink his bon vivant's ample body into Shuttlesworth's thin shadow. The goons parted, their clubs went slack, and Shuttlesworth walked up to the doors of First Baptist without a thread on his jacket disturbed. "Out of the way" was all he had said. "Go on. Out of the way."

That's *three* remote misses.

Losing a parent is not like having your house bombed or being set upon by a crazed mob. It's worse. It's not over in one terrible moment, and the injuries do not heal as quickly as a bruise or a wound. But what happens to children whose worst fear is realized—and then they discover that they are still standing? Couldn't they also gain what Shuttlesworth and the Blitz remote misses gained—a self-confidence that is the very father and mother of courage?*

---

* "I had a patient like this many years ago," the New York psychiatrist Peter Mezan told me. "He'd built an empire. But talk about a catastrophic childhood. His mother died in front of him when he was six, with his father standing over her, screaming at her in rage. She was having a convulsion. The father was then murdered because he was a gangster, and he and his sibling were sent to an orphanage. He grew up where there was nothing except to overcome. So he was willing to take chances that other people wouldn't take. I think he felt that there was nothing to lose." To Mezan, there was no mystery—in his experience over the years—between this kind of outsize pathology in childhood and the larger-than-life successes that some of those bereaved children would have later in adulthood. The fact of having endured and survived such trauma had a liberating effect. "These are people who are able to break the frame of the known world—what's believed, what's assumed, what's common sense, what's familiar, what everyone takes for granted, whether it's about cancer or the laws of physics," he said. "They are not confined to the frame. They have the ability to step outside it, because I think the usual frame of childhood didn't exist for them. It was shattered."

"The officer who took Shuttlesworth to jail," McWhorter writes of another of Shuttlesworth's many run-ins with white authority, "struck him, kicked him in the shin, called him a monkey, and then goaded him, 'Why don't you hit me?' Shuttlesworth replied, 'Because I love you.' He folded his arms and smiled the rest of the way to jail, where, forbidden to sing or pray, he took a nap."

8.

The work that Freireich had done in stopping the bleeding was a breakthrough. It meant that children could now be kept alive long enough that the underlying cause of their illness could be treated. But leukemia was an even harder problem. Only a handful of drugs were known to be of any use at all against the disease. There were the cell-killing drugs 6-MP and methotrexate, and there was the steroid prednisone. But each was potentially severely toxic and could be given in limited doses only, and because it could be given in limited doses only, it could wipe out only some of a child's cancer cells. The patient would get better for a week or so. Then the cells that had survived would start to multiply, and the cancer would come roaring back.

"One of the consultants at the clinical center was a man named Max Wintrobe," Freireich said. "He was world-famous because he wrote the first textbook of hematology, and he had written a review of the current state of the treatment of leukemia in children. I have a quotation from him that I show my students to this day. It says, 'These drugs cause more harm than good because they just prolong the agony. The patients all die anyway. The drugs make them worse, so you shouldn't use them.' This was the world's authority."

But Frei and Freireich and a companion group at the Roswell Park Memorial Institute in Buffalo led by James Holland became convinced that the medical orthodoxy had it backwards. If the drugs weren't killing enough cancer cells, didn't that mean that the children needed more aggressive treatment, not less? Why not *combine* 6-MP and methotrexate? They each attacked cancer cells in different ways. They were like the army and the navy. Maybe the cells that survived 6-MP would be killed by methotrexate. And what if they added prednisone into the mix? It could be the air force, bombing from the air while the other drugs attacked from the land and sea.

Then Freireich stumbled across a fourth drug, one derived from the periwinkle plant. It was called vincristine. Someone from the drug company Eli Lilly brought it by the National Cancer Institute for researchers to study. No one knew much about it, but Freireich had a hunch that it might work against leukemia. "I had twenty-five kids dying," he said. "I had nothing to offer them. My feeling was, I'll try it. Why not? They're going to die anyway." Vincristine showed promise. Freireich and Frei tried it out on children who no longer responded to the other drugs, and several went into temporary remission. So Frei and Freireich went to the NCI's research oversight board to ask for permission to test all four drugs together: army, navy, air force, marines.

Cancer is now routinely treated with drug "cocktails," complicated combinations of two or three or even four or five medications simultaneously. But in the early 1960s, it was unheard of. The drugs available to treat cancer in those years were considered just too dangerous. Even vincristine, Freireich's prized new discovery, was utterly terrifying. Freireich learned that the hard way. "Did it have side effects? You bet," he said. "It caused serious depression, neuropathies. The kids got paralyzed. When you get a toxic dose, you end up in coma. Of the first fourteen children we treated, one or two actually died. Their brains were totally fried." Max Wintrobe thought the humane approach was not to use any drugs at all. Freireich and Frei wanted to use *four,* all at once. Frei went before the NCI advisory board to ask for approval. He got nowhere.

"There was a senior hematologist on the board by the name of Dr. Carl Moore, who happened to be a friend of my father's from St. Louis," Frei remembered years later. "I had always considered him a friend, too. But my presentation struck him as being outrageous. He didn't deal in pediatric diseases like childhood leukemia, so he talked about Hodgkin's disease in adults. He said that if you have a patient who has widespread Hodgkin's disease, then it's best to tell that patient to go to Florida and enjoy life. If patients are having too many symptoms from their Hodgkin's disease, you treat them with a little X-ray or possibly a little nitrogen mustard, but give the smallest dose possible. Anything more aggressive than that is unethical, and giving four drugs at a time is unconscionable."

Frei and Freireich were desperate. They went to their boss, Gordon Zubrod. Zubrod had been through the wars with Freireich over the platelets controversy. He had only reluctantly approved the vincristine experiment. He was responsible for what happened on the second floor. If somehow things didn't go well, he would be the one hauled before a congressional committee. Can you imagine? Two renegade researchers are giving experimental and highly toxic cocktails of drugs to four- and five-year-olds at a government laboratory. He had grave reservations. But Frei and Freireich persisted. Actually, Frei persisted; Freireich isn't the kind of person who can be trusted with a delicate negotiation. "I couldn't have done anything without Tom," Freireich admitted. "Frei is the inverse of me. He is deliberate and very humane." Yes, the drugs were all poisons, Frei argued. But they were poisonous in different ways, which meant that if you were careful with the dosages—and if you were aggressive enough in the way you treated the side effects—the children could be kept alive. Zubrod gave in. "It was crazy," Freireich said. "But smart and correct. I thought about it and I knew it would work. It was like the platelets. It had to work!"

The trial was called the VAMP regimen. Some of the clinical associates—the junior doctors assisting on the ward—refused to take part. They thought Freireich was insane. "I had to do it all myself," Freireich said. "I had to order the drugs. I had to mix them. I had to inject them. I had to do the blood counts. I had to measure the bleeding. I had to do the bone marrows. I had to count the slides." There were thirteen children in the initial round of the trial. The first was a young girl. Freireich started her off with a dose that turned out to be too high, and she almost died. He sat with her for hours. He kept her going with antibiotics and respirators. She pulled through, only to die later when her cancer returned. But Frei and

Freireich were learning. They tinkered with the protocol and moved on to patient number two. Her name was Janice. She recovered, as did the next child and the next child. It was a start.

The only problem was that the cancer wasn't gone. A handful of malignant cells was still lurking. One bout of chemotherapy wouldn't be enough, they realized. So they started up another round. Would the disease return? It did. They needed to try again. "We gave them three treatments," Freireich said. "Twelve of the thirteen relapsed. So I decided, there's only one way to do this. We are going to continue treating them every month—for a year."*

"If people thought I was crazy before, now they thought I was completely crazy," Freireich went on. "These were children who seemed completely normal, in complete remission, walking around, playing football, and I was going to put them in the hospital again and make them sick again. No platelets. No white cells. Hemorrhage. Infection." VAMP wiped out the children's immune system. They were defenseless. For their parents, it was

---

* The idea of administering repeated bouts of chemotherapy—even after the patient appeared cancer free—came from M. C. Li and Roy Hertz at the National Cancer Institute in the late 1950s. Li hit choriocarcinoma—a rare cancer of the uterus—with round after round of methotrexate until he finally drove it from his patients' bodies. It was the first time a solid tumor had ever been cured by chemotherapy. When Li first proposed the idea, he was told to stop. People thought it was barbaric. He persisted. He was fired—*even though he cured his patients.* "That was what the atmosphere was like," DeVita says. "I remember there was a grand rounds around that time, to discuss choriocarcinoma. And the subject of conversation was whether this was a case of spontaneous remission. No one could even get their heads around the idea that the methotrexate had actually cured the patient." Needless to say, Freireich speaks of Li, even today, with awe. Once at a scientific meeting, a speaker slighted Li's accomplishments, and Freireich leapt up and roared, in the middle of the proceeding, *"M. C. Li cured choriocarcinoma!"*

agony. In order to have a chance at life—they were told—their child had to be brought savagely and repeatedly to the brink of death.

Freireich threw himself into the task, using every ounce of his energy and audacity to keep his patients alive. In those days, when a patient developed a fever, the physician took a blood culture, and when the results came back, the doctor matched the infection with the most appropriate antibiotic. Antibiotics were never given in combination. You gave a second antibiotic only when the first one stopped working. "One of the first things Jay said to us was, no deal," DeVita remembered. "These kids spike a fever, you treat them immediately, and you treat them with combinations of antibiotics, because they're going to be dead in three hours if you don't." DeVita had an antibiotic that he had been told should never be administered in the spinal fluid. Freireich told him to give it to a patient—in the spinal fluid. "Freireich told us to do things," DeVita said, "that we had been taught were heretical.

"He was subject to so much criticism," DeVita continued. "The clinical associates thought that what he was doing was completely nuts. He carried the weight of it. They would insult him—especially the guys from Harvard. They used to stand in the back of the room and heckle. He would say something, and they would say, 'Sure, Jay, and I'm going to fly to the moon.' It was awful, and Jay was there, all the time, hovering over you, looking at every lab test, going over every chart. God help you if you didn't do something for one of his patients. He was ferocious. He would do things and say things that got him into trouble, or go to some meeting and insult someone and Frei would have to come in and smooth things over. Did he care what people thought of him? Maybe. But not enough to stop doing what he thought was right.*

"How Jay did it," he said finally, "I don't know."

But we do know, don't we? He had been through worse.

In 1965, Freireich and Frei published "Progress and Perspectives in the Chemotherapy of Acute Leukemia" in *Advances in Chemotherapy,* announcing that they had developed a successful treatment for childhood leukemia.†

Today, the cure rate for this form of cancer is more than 90 percent. The number of children whose lives have been saved by the efforts of Freireich and Frei and the re-

---

* Freireich stories are legion. At one point he ventured up to the twelfth floor of the NCI's clinical center, which housed the ward for adults who had chronic myeloid leukemia. CML is a form of leukemia that overproduces white blood cells. The patients' cell-making machinery goes into overdrive. The children Freireich was treating, by contrast, had acute lymphocytic leukemia. It's a cancer that results in the overproduction of defective white blood cells—which is why they are helpless in the face of infection. So Freireich began taking blood from adults with cancer of the blood on the twelfth floor and giving it to children with cancer of the blood on the second floor. Was it considered unusual to take white cells from CML patients? *"Insane,"* Freireich said, looking back on that experiment. "Everyone said it was insane. What if the children ended up somehow getting CML as well? What if it made them even sicker?" Freireich shrugged. "This was an environment where the kids had one hundred percent mortality in months. We had nothing to lose."

† I have simplified the leukemia story. See Mukherjee's *The Emperor of All Maladies* for a more complete version. After Freireich and Frei demonstrated that they could make progress against leukemia with previously unheard-of doses of chemotherapy drugs, the oncologist Donald Pinkel took over and pushed that logic even further. It was Pinkel's group, at St. Jude's Children's Research Hospital in Memphis, that pioneered "total therapy," which is best described as VAMP squared. Today's overwhelmingly successful leukemia treatments are essentially Pinkel's supercharged version of the VAMP regimen.

searchers who followed in their footsteps is in the many, many thousands.

9.

Does this mean that Freireich should be glad he had the childhood he had? The answer is plainly no. What he went through as a child no child should ever have to endure. Along the same lines, I asked every dyslexic I interviewed the question posed at the beginning of the previous chapter: Would they wish dyslexia on their own children? Every one of them said no. Grazer shuddered at the thought. Gary Cohn was horrified. David Boies has two boys who are both dyslexic, and watching them grow up in an environment where reading early and well counted for everything nearly broke his heart. Here were one of the top producers in Hollywood, one of the most powerful bankers on Wall Street, and one of the best trial lawyers in the country—all of whom recognized how central their dyslexia was to their success. Yet they also knew firsthand what the price of that success was—and they could not bring themselves to wish that same experience on their own children.

But the question of what any of us would wish on our children is the wrong question, isn't it? The right question is whether we as a society *need* people who have emerged from some kind of trauma—and the answer is that we plainly do. This is not a pleasant fact to contemplate. For every remote miss who becomes stronger, there are countless near misses who are crushed by what they have been through. There are times and places, however, when all of us depend on people who have been hardened by their experiences.* Freireich had the courage to think the unthinkable. He experimented on children. He took them through pain no human being should ever have to go through. And he did it in no small part because he understood from his own childhood experience that it is possible to emerge from even the darkest hell healed and restored. Leukemia was a direct hit. He turned it into a remote miss.

At one point, in the midst of his battle, Freireich realized that the standard method of monitoring the children's cancer—taking a blood sample and counting the number of cancer cells under a microscope—wasn't good enough. Blood was misleading. A child's blood could look cancer free. But the disease could still be lurking in her bone marrow—which meant that you had to go through the painful process of gathering bone marrow samples, over and over again, month after month, until you were sure the cancer was gone. Max Wintrobe heard what Freireich was up to and tried to stop him. Freireich was torturing the patients, Wintrobe said. He was not wrong. His was the empathetic response. But it is also the response that would never have led to a cure.

---

* In his memoir *The Theory and Practice of Hell,* Eugen Kogon writes of what happened at the German concentration camp Buchenwald whenever the Nazis came to the leaders of the camp and demanded that they select for the gas chambers those from among their own ranks who were "socially unfit." Not to comply meant disaster; the Nazis would then turn the prisoner leadership over to the "greens"—the sadistic criminal element also interned at Buchenwald alongside Jews and political prisoners. On "no account," Kogon writes, could the "pure of heart" be asked to make that decision. Sometimes human survival demands that we commit harm in the cause of some greater good—and, Kogon writes, "the more tender one's conscience, the more difficult it was to make such decisions."

"We used to do bone marrows by grabbing their legs like this," Freireich told me. He held one of his giant hands out, as if wrapped around a child's tiny femur. "We'd stick the needle in without anesthesia. Why no anesthesia? Because they'd scream just as much when you gave them an anesthesia shot. It's an eighteen- or nineteen-gauge needle straight into the shinbone, right below the knee. The kids are hysterical. The parents and nurses hold the kid down. We did that for every cycle. We needed to know if their bone marrow had recovered."

When he said the words "grabbing their legs like this," an involuntary grimace passed across Freireich's face, as if for a moment he could feel what an eighteen-gauge needle straight into the shinbone of a small child felt like, and as if the feeling of that pain would give him pause. But then, as quickly as it appeared, it was gone.

10.

When Jay Freireich was doing his medical training, he met a nurse named Haroldine Cunningham. He asked her out on a date. She said no. "All the young doctors were pretty aggressive," she remembers. "He had a reputation for being very outspoken. He called a couple of times, and I didn't go." But one weekend, Cunningham went to visit her aunt in a suburb outside of Chicago—and the phone rang. It was Freireich. He had taken the train out from Chicago and was calling from the train station. "He said, 'I'm here,'" she remembers. "He was very persistent." This was the early 1950s. They have been married ever since.

Freireich's wife is as small as Freireich is enormous, a tiny woman with a deep and obvious reservoir of strength. "I see the man. I see his needs," she said. He would come home from the hospital late at night, from the blood and the suffering, and she would be there. "She is the first person who ever loved me," Freireich said simply. "She is my angel from heaven. She found me. I think she detected something in me that could be nourished. I defer to her in all things. She keeps me going every day."

Haroldine grew up poor as well. Her family lived in a tiny apartment outside Chicago. When she was twelve, she tried the bathroom door—and couldn't get in. "My mother had locked the door," she said. "I got the neighbor from downstairs, who was the landlord. He opened the window and got in. We called the hospital. She died there. You don't really know when you're twelve or thirteen years old what is going on, but I knew she was unhappy. My father was away, of course. He was not a terrific father."

She sat in the chair in her husband's office, this woman who carved an island of calm out of the turbulence of her husband's life. "You have to realize, of course, that love doesn't always save people you want to save. Somebody asked me once, weren't you angry? And I said, no, I wasn't, I understood her misery.

"There are things that either build you up or put you down. Jay and I have that in common."

CHAPTER SIX

Wyatt Walker

"DE RABBIT IS DE SLICKEST O'
ALL DE ANIMALS DE LAWD EVER
MADE."

1.

The most famous photograph in the history of the American civil rights movement was taken on May 3, 1963, by Bill Hudson, a photographer for the Associated Press. Hudson was in Birmingham, Alabama, where Martin Luther King Jr.'s activists had taken on the city's racist public safety commissioner Eugene "Bull" Connor. The photo was of a teenage boy being attacked by a police dog. Even to this day, it has not lost its power to shock.

Hudson gave his roll of film from that day to his editor, Jim Laxon. Laxon looked through Hudson's photos until he came to the boy leaning into the dog. He was, he said later, riveted by the "saintly calm of the young [man] in the snarling jaws of the German shepherd." He hadn't felt that way about a photograph since he published a Pulitzer Prize–winning photo seventeen years before of a woman jumping from an upper-story window in a hotel fire in Atlanta.

Laxon took the picture and sent it out over the wires. The next day, the *New York Times* published it above the fold across three columns on the front page of its Saturday paper, as did virtually every major paper in the country. President Kennedy saw the photograph and was appalled. The secretary of state, Dean Rusk, worried that it would "embarrass our friends abroad and make our enemies joyful." The photo was discussed on the floor of Congress and in countless living rooms and classrooms. For a time, it seemed like Americans could talk of little else. It was an image, as one journalist put it, that would "burn forever...the thin, well-dressed boy seeming to be leaning into the dog, his arms limp at his side, calmly staring straight ahead as though to say—'Take me, here I am.'" For years, Martin Luther King and his army of civil rights activists had been fighting the thicket of racist laws and policies that blanketed the American South—the rules that made it hard or impossible for blacks to get jobs, vote, get a proper education, or even to use the same water fountain as a white person. Suddenly, the tide turned. A year later, the U.S. Congress passed the landmark Civil Rights Act of 1964, one of the most important pieces of legislation in the history of the United States. The Civil Rights Act, it has often been said, was "written in Birmingham."

2.

In 1963, when Martin Luther King came to Birmingham, his movement was in crisis. He had just spent nine months directing protests against segregation in Albany, Georgia, two hundred miles to the south, and he had limped away from Albany without winning any significant concessions. The biggest victory the civil rights movement had won to that point had been the Supreme Court's decision in the famous *Brown v. Board of Education* case in 1954, declaring segregation of public schools to be unconstitutional. But almost a decade had passed and the public schools of the Deep South were still as racially divided as ever. In the 1940s and early 1950s, most Southern states had been governed by relatively moderate politicians who were at least willing to acknowledge the dignity of black people. Alabama had a governor in those years named "Big Jim" Folsom, who was fond of saying "all men are just alike." By the early sixties, all the moderates were gone. The state-houses were in the control of hard-line segregationists. The South seemed to be moving backwards.

And Birmingham? Birmingham was the most racially divided city in America. It was known as "the Johannes-burg of the South." When a busload of civil rights ac-tivists were on their way to Birmingham, the local police stood by while Klansmen forced their bus to the side of the road and set it afire. Black people who tried to move into white neighborhoods had their homes dynamited by the city's local Ku Klux Klansmen so often that Birm-ingham's other nickname was Bombingham. "In Birming-ham," Diane McWhorter writes in *Carry Me Home,* "it was held a fact of criminal science that the surest way to stop a crime wave—burglaries, rapes, whatever—was to go out and shoot a few suspects. ('This thing's getting out of hand,' a [police] lieutenant might say. 'You know what we've got to do.')"

Eugene "Bull" Connor, the city's public safety com-missioner, was a short, squat man with enormous ears and a "bullfrog voice." He came to prominence in 1938 when a political conference was held in downtown Birmingham with both black and white delegates. Connor tied a long rope to a stake in the lawn outside the auditorium, and ran the rope down the center of the aisle and insisted—in accordance with the city's segregation ordinances—that black people stay to one side of the line, and whites to the other. One of the attendees at the meeting was the president's wife, Eleanor Roosevelt. She was sitting on the "wrong" side and Connor's people had to force her to move to the white side. (Imagine someone trying that on Michelle Obama.)* Connor liked to spend his mornings at the Molton Hotel downtown, doing shots of 100 proof Old Grand-Dad Bourbon, and sayings things like, A Jew is just a "nigger turned inside out." People used to tell jokes about Birmingham, of the sort that weren't really jokes: A black man in Chicago wakes up one morning and tells his wife that Jesus had come to him in a dream and told him to go to Birmingham. She is horrified: "Did Jesus say He'd go with you?" The husband replies: "He said He'd go as far as Memphis."

Upon arriving in Birmingham, King called a meeting of his planning team. "I have to tell you," he said, "that in my judgment, some of the people sitting here today will not come back alive from this campaign." Then he went around the room and gave everyone a mock eulogy. One of King's aides would later admit that he never wanted to go to Birmingham at all: "When I kissed my wife and children good-bye down on Carol Road in Atlanta, I didn't think I would ever see them again."

King was outgunned and overmatched. He was the overwhelming underdog. He had, however, an advan-

---

* In William Nunnelley's biography of Connor, titled *Bull Connor,* Nunnelley identifies the relevant section of the Birmingham city code as section 369, which prohibited serving "white and colored people" in the same room unless they were separated by a partition seven feet high with separate entrances.

tage—of the same paradoxical variety as David Boies's dyslexia or Jay Freireich's painful childhood. He was from a community that had *always* been the underdog. By the time the civil rights crusade came to Birmingham, African-Americans had spent a few hundred years learning how to cope with being outgunned and overmatched. Along the way they had learned a few things about battling giants.

3.

At the center of many of the world's oppressed cultures stands the figure of the "trickster hero." In legend and song, he appears in the form of a seemingly innocuous animal that triumphs over others much larger than himself through cunning and guile. In the West Indies, slaves brought with them from Africa tales of a devious spider named Anansi.[*] Among American slaves, the trickster was often the short-tailed Brer Rabbit.[†] "De rabbit is de slickest o' all de animals de Lawd ever made," one ex-slave recounted in an interview with folklorists a hundred years ago:

---

[*] My mother, who is West Indian, was taught Anansi stories as a child and told them to my brothers and me when we were young. Anansi is a rascal, who is not above cheating and sacrificing his own children (of which he invariably has many) for his own ends. My mother is a proper Jamaican lady, but on the subject of Anansi she becomes the picture of mischief.

[†] In *Black Culture and Black Consciousness: Afro-American Folk Thought from Slavery to Freedom,* Lawrence Levine writes: "The rabbit, like the slaves who wove tales about him, was forced to make do with what he had. His small tail, his natural portion of intellect—these would have to suffice, and to make them do he resorted to any means at his disposal—means which may have made him morally tainted but which allowed him to survive and even to conquer."

He ain't de biggest, an he ain't de loudest but he sho' am de slickest. If he gits in trouble he gits out by gittin' somebody else in. Once he fell down a deep well an' did he holler and cry? No siree. He set up a mighty mighty whistling and a singin', an' when de wolf passes by he heard him an' he stuck his head over an' de rabbit say, "Git 'long 'way f'om here. Dere ain't room fur two. Hit's mighty hot up dere and nice an' cool down here. Don' you git in dat bucket an' come down here." Dat made de wolf all de mo' onrestless and he jumped into the bucket an' as he went down de rabbit come up, an' as dey passed de rabbit he laughed an' he say, "Dis am life; some go up and some go down."

In the most famous Brer Rabbit story, Brer Fox traps Rabbit by building a baby doll out of tar. Brer Rabbit tries to engage the tar baby and instead gets stuck, and the more he tries to free himself from the tar, the more hopelessly entangled he becomes. "I don't care what you do wid' me, Brer Fox," Rabbit pleads to the gloating Fox, "but don't fling me in dat briar-patch." Brer Fox, of course, does just that—and Rabbit, who was born and bred in the briar patch, uses the thorns to separate himself from the doll and escapes. Fox is defeated. Rabbit sits cross-legged on a nearby log, triumphantly "koamin' de pitch outen his har wid a chip."

Trickster tales were wish fulfillments in which slaves dreamed of one day rising above their white masters. But as the historian Lawrence Levine writes, they were also "painfully realistic stories which taught the art of surviving and even triumphing in the face of a hostile environment."

African-Americans were outnumbered and overpowered, and the idea embedded in the Brer Rabbit stories was that the weak could compete in even the most lopsided of contests if they were willing to use their wits. Brer Rabbit *understood* Brer Fox in a way that Brer Fox did not understand himself. He realized his opponent Fox was so malicious that he couldn't resist giving Rabbit the punishment Rabbit said he desperately wanted to avoid. So Rabbit *tricked* Fox, gambling that he could not bear the thought that a smaller and lesser animal was enjoying himself so much. Levine argues that over the course of their long persecution, African-Americans took the lessons of the trickster to heart:

> The records left by nineteenth-century observers of slavery and by the masters themselves indicate that a significant number of slaves lied, cheated, stole, feigned illness, loafed, pretended to misunderstand the orders they were given, put rocks in the bottom of their cotton baskets in order to meet their quota, broke their tools, burned their masters' property, mutilated themselves in order to escape work, took indifferent care of the crops they were cultivating, and mistreated the livestock placed in their care to the extent that masters often felt it necessary to use the less efficient mules rather than horses since the former could better withstand the brutal treatment of the slaves.

Dyslexics compensate for their disability by developing other skills that—at times—can prove highly advantageous. Being bombed or orphaned can be a near-miss experience and leave you devastated. Or it can be a remote miss and leave you stronger. These are David's opportunities: the occasions in which difficulties, paradoxically, turn out to be desirable. The lesson of the trickster tales is the third desirable difficulty: the unexpected freedom that comes from having nothing to lose. The trickster gets to break the rules.

The executive director of the Southern Christian Leadership Conference, the organization led by King, was Wyatt Walker. Walker was on the ground in Birmingham from the beginning, marshaling King's meager army against the forces of racism and reaction. King and Walker were under no illusions that they could fight racism the conventional way. They could not defeat Bull Connor at the polls, or in the streets, or in the court of law. They could not match him strength for strength. What they could do, though, was play Brer Rabbit and try to get Connor to throw them in the briar patch.

"Wyatt," King said, "you've got to find the means to create a crisis, to make Bull Connor tip his hand." That is exactly what Walker did. And the crisis created by Wyatt Walker was the photograph of a teenage boy being attacked by a police dog—leaning in, his arms limp, as if to say, "Take me, here I am."

4.

Wyatt Walker was a Baptist minister from Massachusetts. He joined up with Martin Luther King in 1960. He was King's "nuts and bolts" man, his organizer and fixer. He was a mischief maker—slender, elegant, and intellectual, with a pencil-thin mustache and a droll sense of humor. Every Wednesday afternoon he reserved for a round of golf. To him, women were always "dahlin'," as in "I'm not hard to get along with, dahlin's. I just have to have perfection." As a young man he joined the Young Communist League because—as he would always say, tongue planted firmly in cheek—it was one of the only ways a black person in those years could meet white women. "In college," the historian Taylor Branch writes, "he acquired dark-rimmed glasses that gave his face the look of a brooding Trotskyite."* Once, when he was preaching in Petersburg, a small town in Virginia, he showed up at the local whites-only public library with his family and a small entourage in tow, with the intention of getting arrested for breaking the town's segregation laws. What book did he check out that he could wave in front of the assembled photographers and reporters? A biography of the great hero of the white South, Robert E. Lee, the Civil War general who led the Confederate Army in its battle to defend slavery. That was vintage Wyatt Walker. He was perfectly happy to be carted off to jail for breaking Petersburg's segregation laws. But he made sure to rub the town's nose in its own contradictions at the same time.

In Birmingham, King, Walker, and Fred Shuttlesworth formed a triumvirate. Shuttlesworth was the longtime face

---

* The historian Taylor Branch writes of Walker: "Walker was a hotspur. As a New Jersey high school student in the 1940s, he had heard Paul Robeson say that if being for freedom and equality meant being a Red, then he was a Red. Walker promptly joined the Young Communist League. One of his high school papers was a five-year plan for a Soviet-type economy in the United States, and he dreamed of carrying out technically ingenious assassinations against leading segregationists."

of the Birmingham civil rights struggle, the local preacher whom the Klan could not kill. King was the prophet, gracious and charismatic. Walker stayed in the shadows. He did not allow himself to be photographed with King. Even in Birmingham, many of Bull Connor's people had no idea what Walker looked like. King and Shuttlesworth were equipped with a certain serenity. Walker was not. "If you get in my way, I'll run smack dab over you" is how Walker described his management style. "I don't have time for 'good morning, good afternoon; how do you feel.' We've got a revolution on our hands."

Once, in Birmingham, when King was giving a speech, a two-hundred-pound white man charged the stage and began pummeling King with his fists. As King's aides rushed to defend him, McWhorter writes:

> They were astounded to watch King become his assailant's protector. He held him solicitously and, as the audience began singing Movement songs, told him that their cause was just, that violence was self-demeaning, that "we're going to win." Then King introduced him to the crowd, as though he were a surprise guest. Roy James, a twenty-four-year-old native New Yorker who lived in an American Nazi Party dormitory in Arlington, Virginia, began to weep in King's embrace.

King was a moral absolutist who did not stray from his principles even when under attack. Walker liked to call himself a pragmatist. He was once attacked by a "mountain of a man"—six foot six, 260 pounds—when he was standing in front of a courthouse in North Carolina.

Walker didn't embrace his assailant. He got up and came back at him, and each time the man's blows sent Walker tumbling down the courthouse steps, he picked himself up and came back for more. The third time, Walker recalled later, "he caught me good, knocked me almost senseless. And I went back up a fourth time. By this time, you know, if I'd had my razor I'd have cut him."

One famous night, the three of them—Walker, King, and Shuttlesworth—were about to preach to fifteen hundred people at the First Baptist Church in Montgomery, when the church was surrounded by an angry white mob threatening to burn the building down. King, predictably enough, took the high road. "The only way we are going to save the people upstairs," he told the others, "is we who are the leadership have to give ourselves up to the mob." Shuttlesworth, imperturbable as always, agreed: "Yeah, well if that what we have to do, let's do it." Walker? He looked over at King and said to himself: "This man must be out of his goddam mind."* (At the last moment, federal troops came and dispersed the crowd.) Later, Walker would embrace nonviolence. But he always gave the sense that turning the other cheek wasn't something that came naturally.

"At times I would accommodate or alter my morality for the sake of getting a job done because I was the guy having to deal with the results," he said once. "I did it consciously; I had no choice. I wasn't dealing with a moral situation when I dealt with a Bull Connor." Walker loved

---

* Walker continued: "We were just going to give ourselves up to the mob and felt that would appease them. Let them beat us to death, I guess."

to play tricks on Connor. "I have come to Birmingham to ride the Bull," he announced, eyes twinkling, upon his arrival. He might put on a Southern drawl, and call in some imaginary complaint to the local police about "niggers" headed somewhere in a protest, sending them off on a wild goose chase. Or he might lead a march that wasn't a march, one that went around and around, through office lobbies and down alleyways, until the police were tearing out their hair. "Oh, man, it was a great time to be alive," he said, recalling the antics he got up to in Birmingham. Walker knew better than to tell King all that he was doing. King would disapprove. Walker kept his mischief to himself.

"I think Negroes like myself have developed almost a mental catalog of the tone of voices of how a white face speaks to them," Walker told the poet Robert Penn Warren in a long interview just after the Birmingham campaign ended. "But everything that a white person says is interpreted by the nuance of the tone of voice, or maybe the hang of the head, or the depth of tone, or the sharpness of the tongue, you know—things that in the ordinary, normal ethnic frame of reference would have no meaning, take on tremendous and deep and sharp meaning."

Warren then brought up the trickster folktales of the African-American tradition. You can almost see a sly smile cross Walker's face: "Yes," he replied, he found "pure joy" in poking fun at the "master," telling him "one thing that you knew he wanted to hear and really meaning something else."

People called Martin Luther King "Mr. Leader" or, in lighter moments, "De Lawd." Walker was Brer Rabbit.

5.

The plan Walker devised for Birmingham was called Project C—for confrontation. The staging ground was the city's venerable 16th Street Baptist Church, next to Kelly Ingram Park, and a few short blocks from downtown Birmingham. Project C had three acts, each designed to be bigger and more provocative than the last. It began with a series of sit-ins at local businesses. That was to draw media attention to the problem of segregation in Birmingham. At night, Shuttlesworth and King would lead mass meetings for the local black community to keep morale high. The second stage was a boycott of downtown businesses, to put financial pressure on the white business community to reconsider their practices toward their black customers. (In department stores, for example, blacks could not use the washrooms or the changing rooms, for fear that a surface or an item of clothing once touched by a black person would then touch a white person.) Act three was a series of mass marches to back up the boycott and fill up the jails—because once Connor ran out of cells he could no longer make the civil rights problem go away simply by arresting the protesters. He would have to deal with them directly.

Project C was a high-stakes operation. For it to work, Connor had to fight back. As King put it, Connor had to be induced to "tip his hand"—thereby revealing his ugly side to the world. But there was no guarantee that he would do that. King and Walker had just come from running their long campaign in Albany, Georgia, and they had failed there because the Albany police chief, Laurie Pritchett, had refused to take the bait. He told his police officers not to use violence or excessive force. He was friendly and polite. His views on civil rights may have been unevolved, but he treated King with respect. The Northern press came to Albany to cover the confrontation between white and black, and found—to their surprise—they quite liked Pritchett. When King was finally thrown in jail, a mysterious well-dressed man—sent, legend had it, by Pritchett himself—came the next day and bailed him out. How can you be a martyr if you get bailed out of jail the instant you get there?

At one point, Pritchett moved into a downtown motel so that he could be on call should any violence erupt. In the midst of a long negotiating session with King, Pritchett was handed a telegram by his secretary. As Pritchett recalled, years later:

> I...must have shown some concern over [it] because Dr. King asked me if it was bad news. I said, "No, it's not bad news, Dr. King. It just so happens this is my twelfth weddin' anniversary, and my wife has sent me a telegram." And he says—I never will forget this and this shows the understandin' which we had—he said, "You mean this is your anniversary?" And I said, "That's right," and I said, "I haven't been home in at least three weeks." And he said, "Well, Chief Pritchett, you go home tonight, no, right now. You celebrate your anniversary. I give you my word that nothing will happen in Albany, Georgia, till tomorrow, and you can go, take your wife out to dinner, do anything you want to, and tomorrow at ten o'clock, we'll resume our efforts."

Pritchett would not throw King in the briar patch. It was

hopeless. Not long afterward, King packed his bags and left town.*

Walker realized that a setback in Birmingham so soon after the Albany debacle would be disastrous. In those years, the evening news on television was watched in an overwhelming number of American households, and Walker wanted desperately to have Project C front and center on American television screens every night. But he knew that if the campaign was perceived to be faltering, the news media could lose interest and go elsewhere.

"As a general principle, Walker asserted that everything must build," Taylor Branch writes. "If they showed strength, then outside support would grow more than proportionately. Once started, however, they could not fall back....In no case, said Walker, could the Birmingham campaign be smaller than Albany. That meant they must be prepared to put upwards of a thousand people in jail at one time, maybe more."

Several weeks in, Walker saw his campaign begin to lose that precious momentum. Many blacks in Birmingham were worried—justifiably—that if they were seen with King, they would be fired by their white bosses. In April, one of King's aides spoke before seven hundred people at a church service and could persuade only nine of them to

---

* Pritchett actually came to Birmingham and warned Bull Connor about King and Walker. He wanted to teach Connor how to handle the civil rights tricksters. But Connor wasn't inclined to listen. "I never will forget, when we entered his office," Pritchett remembers, "his back was to us...some big executive chair, you know, and when he turned around, there was this little man—you know, in stature. But he had this boomin' voice, and he was tellin' me that they closed the course that day...said, 'They can play golf, but we put concrete in the holes. They can't get the ball in the holes.' And this gave me some indication as to what type of man he was."

march with him. The next day, Andrew Young—another of King's men—tried again, and this time found only seven volunteers. The local conservative black paper called Project C "wasteful and worthless." The reporters and photographers assembled there to record the spectacle of black-on-white confrontation were getting restless. Connor made the occasional arrest but mostly just sat and watched. Walker was in constant contact with King as King commuted back and forth between Birmingham and his home base in Atlanta. "Wyatt," King told him for the hundredth time, "you've got to find some way to make Bull Connor tip his hand." Walker shook his head. "Mr. Leader, I haven't found the key yet, but I'm going to find it."

The breakthrough came on Palm Sunday. Walker had twenty-two protesters ready to go. The march would be led by King's brother, Alfred Daniel, known as A.D. "Our mass meeting was slow getting together," Walker recalled. "We were supposed to march at something like two-thirty, and we didn't march until about four. In that time, people, being aware of the demonstration, collected out on the streets. By the time they got ready to march, there were a thousand people up and down this three-block area, lining up all along the sides as spectators, watching."

The next day, Walker opened the newspapers to read the media's account of what had happened, and to his surprise he discovered the reporters had gotten it all wrong. The papers said eleven hundred demonstrators had marched in Birmingham. "I called Dr. King and said, 'Dr. King, I've got it!'" Walker recalled. "'I can't tell you on the phone, but I've got it!' So what we did each day was we dragged out our meetings until people got home from work late in the afternoon. They would form out on the side and it would look like a thousand folks. We weren't marching but twelve, fourteen, sixteen, eighteen. But the papers were reporting fourteen hundred."

It was a situation straight out of one of the most famous of all trickster tales—the story of Terrapin, a lowly turtle who finds himself in a race with Deer. He hides just by the finish line and places his relatives up and down the course, at strategic intervals, to make it seem like he is running the whole race. Then at the finish line, he emerges just ahead of Deer to claim victory. Deer is completely fooled, since, as Terrapin knows, to Deer, all turtles "am so much like annurrer you can't tell one from turrer."

Underdogs have to be students of the nuances of white expression—the hang of the head, the depth of tone, or the sharpness of the tongue. Their survival depends on it. But those in positions of power have no need to *look* at the weak. Deer had disdain for the lowly Terrapin. To him, a turtle was a turtle. The comfortable elite of Birmingham were just like Deer. "They can only see...through white eyes," Walker explained, gleefully. "They cannot distinguish even between Negro demonstrators and Negro spectators. All they know is Negroes."*

Connor was an arrogant man who liked to swagger around Birmingham saying, "Down here we make our

---

* This was a running theme with Walker. One time in Birmingham, the city filed an injunction against the Southern Christian Leadership Conference, which meant that Walker had to appear in court. The question was: If Walker was tied up in court, how would he run the campaign? Walker's answer was to register with the court and then have someone else show up in his place every day thereafter. Why not? He said, "You know, all niggers look alike anyway."

own law." He sat drinking his bourbon every morning at the Molton Hotel, loudly predicting that King would "run out of niggers." Now he looked out the window and saw Terrapin ahead of him at every turn. He was in shock. Those imaginary one thousand protesters were a *provocation*. "Bull Connor had something in his mind about not letting these niggers get to city hall," Walker said. "I prayed that he'd keep trying to stop us....Birmingham would have been lost if Bull had let us go down to the city hall and pray. If he had let us do that and stepped aside, what else would be new? There would be no movement, no publicity." *Please, Brer Connor, please. Whatever you do, don't throw me in the briar patch.* And of course that's just what Connor did.

A month into the protest, Walker and King stepped up the pressure. One of the Birmingham team, James Bevel, had been working with local schoolchildren, instructing them in the principles of nonviolent resistance. Bevel was a Pied Piper: a tall, bald, hypnotic speaker who wore a yarmulke and bib overalls and claimed to hear voices. (McWhorter calls him a "militant out of Dr. Seuss.") On the last Monday in April, he dropped off leaflets at all of the black high schools around the county: "Come to 16th Street Baptist Church at noon on Thursday. Don't ask permission." The city's most popular black disc jockey—Shelley "the Playboy" Stewart—sent out the same message to his young listeners: "Kids, there's gonna be a party at the park."* The FBI

---

* Stewart was a huge figure in Birmingham. Every African-American teenager listened to his show. The second part of his message to his listeners was "Bring your toothbrushes, because lunch will be served." "Toothbrushes" was code for "be dressed and prepared to spend a few nights in jail."

got wind of the plan and told Bull Connor, who announced that any child who skipped school would be expelled. It made no difference. The kids came in droves. Walker called the day the children arrived "D Day."

At one o'clock, the doors to the church opened, and King's lieutenants began sending the children out. They held signs saying "Freedom" or "I'll Die to Make This Land My Home." They sang "We Shall Overcome" and "Ain't Gonna Let Nobody Turn Me Around." Outside the church, Connor's police officers waited. The children dropped to their knees and prayed, then filed into the open doors of the paddy wagons. Then another dozen came out. Then another dozen, and another, and another—until Connor's men had begun to get an inkling that the stakes had been raised again.

A police officer spotted Fred Shuttlesworth. "Hey, Fred, how many more have you got?"

"At least a thousand more," he replied.

"God A'mighty," the officer said.

By the end of the day, more than six hundred children were in jail.

The next day—Friday—was "Double-D Day." This time fifteen hundred schoolchildren skipped school to come down to 16th Street Baptist. At one o'clock, they began filing out of the church. The streets surrounding Kelly Ingram Park were barricaded by police and firefighters. There was no mystery about why the firefighters had been called in. They had high-pressure hoses on their fire trucks, and "water cannons," as they were also known, had been a staple of crowd control since the 1930s in the early days of Nazi Germany. Walker knew that if the demonstrations grew so large that they overwhelmed the Birmingham police, Connor would be sorely tempted to turn on the hoses. He *wanted* Connor to turn on the hoses. "It was hot in Birmingham," he explained. "I told [Bevel] to let the pep rally go on a while and let these firemen sit out there and bake in the sun until their tempers were like hair triggers."

And the dogs? Connor had been itching to use the city's K-9 Corps. Earlier that spring, in a speech, Connor had vowed to combat the civil right protesters with one hundred German shepherd police dogs. "I want 'em to see the dogs work," Connor growled, as things began to get out of control in Kelly Ingram Park—and nothing made Walker happier than that. He had children marching in the streets, and now Connor wanted to let German shepherds loose on them? Everyone in King's camp knew what it would look like if someone published a photograph of a police dog lunging at a child.

Connor stood watch as the children came closer. "Do not cross," he said. "If you come any further, we will turn the fire hoses on you." Connor's jails were full. He couldn't arrest anyone else, because he had nowhere to put them. The children kept coming. The firemen were hesitant. They were not used to controlling crowds. Connor turned to the fire chief: "Turn 'em on, or go home." The firemen turned on their "monitor guns," valves that turned the spray of their hoses into a high-pressure torrent. The children clung to one another and were sent sprawling backwards. The force of the water ripped some of the marchers' shirts from their bodies and flung others against walls and doorways.

Back at the church, Walker began deploying waves of

children to the other end of the park to open another front. Connor had no more fire trucks. But he was determined that none of the marchers cross over into "white" Birmingham. "Bring the dogs," Connor ordered, calling in eight K-9 units. "Why did you bring old Tiger out?" Connor shouted at one of his police officers. "Why didn't you bring a meaner dog—this one is not the vicious one!" The children came closer. A German shepherd lunged at a boy. He leaned in, arms limp, as if to say, "Take me, here I am." On Saturday, the picture ran on the front page of every newspaper around the country.

6.

Does Wyatt Walker's behavior make you uncomfortable? James Forman, who was a key figure in the civil rights movement in those years, was with Walker when Connor first deployed the K-9 units. Forman says that Walker started jumping with joy. "We've got a movement. We've got a movement. We had some police brutality." Forman was stunned. Walker was as aware as any of them just how dangerous Birmingham could be. He had been in the room when King gave everyone a mock eulogy. How could he be jumping up and down at the sight of protesters being attacked by police dogs?[*]

After D Day, King and Walker heard it from all sides. The judge processing the arrested marchers said that the

---

[*] Forman writes: "It seemed very cold, cruel, and calculating to be happy about police brutality coming down on innocent people...no matter what purpose it served."

people who "misled those kids" into marching "ought to be put under the jail." On the floor of Congress, one of Alabama's congressmen called the use of children "shameful." The mayor of Birmingham denounced the "irresponsible and unthinking agitators" who were using children as "tools." Malcolm X—the black activist who was in every way more radical than King—said "real men don't put their children on the firing line." The *New York Times* editorialized that King was engaged in "perilous ventures in brinkmanship" and *Time* scolded him for using children as "shock troops." The U.S. attorney general, Robert F. Kennedy, warned that "schoolchildren participating in street demonstrations is a dangerous business," and said, "An injured, maimed or dead child is a price that none of us can afford to pay."*

On the Friday night, after the second day of children's protests, King spoke at 16th Street Baptist Church to the parents of those who had been arrested that day and the day before. They knew full well the dangers and humiliations of being a black person in Birmingham. *Jesus said He'd go as far as Memphis.* Can you imagine how they felt with their children at that moment languishing in Bull Connor's jails? King stood up and tried to make light of the situation: "Not only did they stand up in the water, they went *under* the water!" he said. "And dogs? Well, I'll

---

* King thought long and hard before agreeing to use the children. He had to be talked into it by James Bevel. Their eventual conclusion was that if someone was old enough to belong to a church—to have made a decision of that importance to their life and soul—then they were old enough to fight for a cause of great importance to their life and soul. In the Baptist tradition, you could join a church once you were of school age. That meant that King approved of using children as young as six or seven against Bull Connor.

tell you. When I was growing up, I was dog bitten...for *nothing*. So I don't mind being bitten by a dog for standing up for freedom!"

Whether or not any of the parents were buying this is unclear. King plunged on: "Your daughters and sons are in jail....Don't worry about them....They are suffering for what they believe, and they are suffering to make this nation a better nation." *Don't worry about them?* Taylor Branch writes that there were rumors—"true and false"—about "rats, beatings, concrete beds, overflowing latrines, jailhouse assaults, and crude examinations for venereal disease." Seventy-five and eighty children were packed into cells intended for eight. Some had been bused out to the state fairground and held without food and water in stockades in the pouring rain. King's response? "Jail helps you to rise above the miasma of everyday life," he said blithely. "If they want some books, we will get them. I catch up on my reading every time I go to jail."

Walker and King were trying to set up that picture—the German shepherd lunging at the boy. But to get it, they had to play a complex and duplicitous game. To Bull Connor, they pretended that they had a hundred times more supporters than they did. To the press, they pretended that they were shocked at the way Connor let his dogs loose on their protesters—while at the same time, they were jumping for joy behind closed doors. And to the parents whose children they were using as cannon fodder, they pretended that Bull Connor's prisons were a good place for their children to catch up on their reading.

But we *shouldn't* be shocked by this. What other options did Walker and King have? In the traditional fable of the Tortoise and the Hare, told to every Western school-child, the Tortoise beats the Hare through sheer persistence and effort. Slow and steady wins the race. That's an appropriate and powerful lesson—but only in a world where the Tortoise and the Hare are playing by the same rules, and where everyone's effort is rewarded. In a world that isn't fair—and no one would have called Birmingham in 1963 fair—the Terrapin has to place his relatives at strategic points along the racecourse. The trickster is not a trickster by nature. He is a trickster by necessity. In the next great civil rights showdown in Selma, Alabama, two years later, a photographer from *Life* magazine put down his camera in order to come to the aid of children being roughed up by police officers. Afterward, King reprimanded him: "The world doesn't know this happened, because you didn't photograph it. I'm not being cold-blooded about it, but it is so much more important for you to take a picture of us getting beaten up than for you to be another person joining in the fray." He *needed* the picture. In response to the complaints over the use of children, Fred Shuttlesworth said it best: "We got to use what we got."

A dyslexic, if she or he is to succeed, is in exactly the same position, of course. That's part of what it means to be "disagreeable." Gary Cohn leapt into the taxi, pretending he knew about options trading, and it is remarkable how many successful dyslexics have had a similar moment in their careers. Brian Grazer, the Hollywood producer, got a three-month internship after college as a clerk in the business affairs department at the Warner Bros. studio. He pushed a cart around. "I was in a big office with two union secretaries," he remembers. "My boss had worked for Jack Warner. He was putting in his last hours. He was a great guy. There was this great office there, and I said to him, 'Can I have it?' The office was bigger than my office today. He said, 'Sure. Use it.' It became the Brian Grazer business. I could do my eight-hour workdays in one hour. I would use my office and my position to get access to all the legal contracts, business contracts, the treatments being submitted to Warner Brothers—why they passed, what they considered. I used that year to gain knowledge and information about the movie business. I would call someone every single day. And I would say, 'I'm Brian Grazer. I work at Warner Brothers business affairs. I want to meet you.'"

He was eventually fired, but only after he had stretched his three-month term to a year and sold two ideas to NBC for five thousand dollars each.

Grazer and Cohn—two outsiders with learning disabilities—played a trick. They bluffed their way into professions that would have been closed to them. The man in the cab assumed that no one would be so audacious as to say he knew how to trade options if he didn't. And it never occurred to the people Brian Grazer called that when he said he was Brian Grazer from Warner Brothers, what he meant was that he was Brian Grazer who pushed the mail cart around at Warner Brothers. What they did is not "right," just as it is not "right" to send children up against police dogs. But we need to remember that our definition of what is right is, as often as not, simply the way that people in positions of privilege close the door on those on the outside. David has nothing to lose, and because he has nothing to lose, he has the freedom to thumb his nose at the rules set by others. That's how people with brains a little bit different from the rest of ours get jobs as options traders and Hollywood producers—and a small band of protesters armed with nothing but their wits have a chance against the likes of Bull Connor.

"I still t'ink Ise de fas'est runner in de worl'," the bewildered Deer complains after a race in which Terrapin has done something that would get him banished from every competition in the world. "Maybe you air," Terrapin responds, "but I kin head ou off wid sense."

7.

The boy in Bill Hudson's famous photograph is Walter Gadsden. He was a sophomore at Parker High in Birmingham, six foot tall and fifteen years old. He wasn't a marcher. He was a spectator. He came from a conservative black family that owned two newspapers in Birmingham and Atlanta that had been sharply critical of King. Gadsden had taken off school that afternoon to watch the spectacle unfolding around Kelly Ingram Park.

The officer in the picture is Dick Middleton. He was a modest and reserved man. "The K-9 Corps," McWhorter writes, "was known for attracting straight arrows who wanted none of the scams and payoffs that often came with a regular beat. Nor were the dog handlers known for being race ideologues." The dog's name is Leo.

Now look at the faces of the black bystanders in the background. Shouldn't they be surprised or horrified? They're not. Next, look at the leash in Middleton's hand. It's taut, as if he's trying to restrain Leo. And look at Gadsden's left hand. He's gripping Middleton on the forearm. Look at Gadsden's left leg. He's kicking Leo, isn't he? Gadsden would say later that he had been raised around dogs and had been taught how to protect himself. "I automatically threw my knee up in front of the dog's head," he said. Gadsden wasn't the martyr, passively leaning forward as if to say, "Take me, here I am." He's steadying himself, with a hand on Middleton, so he can deliver a sharper blow. The word around the movement, afterward, was that he'd broken Leo's jaw. Hudson's photograph is not at all what the world thought it was. It was a little bit of Brer Rabbit trickery.

You got to use what you got.

"Sure, people got bit by the dogs," Walker said, looking back twenty years later. "I'd say at least two or three. But a picture is worth a thousand words, dahlin'."*

---

* Walker makes a similar claim about the famous photographs of protesters being hit by Connor's water cannons. The people in the photographs, he says, were spectators like Gadsden, not demonstrators. And they had been standing outside 16th Street Baptist Church all afternoon—on a typically humid Birmingham spring day. They were hot. "They had gathered in the park, which is a shaded area. And the firemen had set up their hoses at two corners of the park, one on Fifth Street and one on Sixth Street. And the mood was like a Roman holiday; it was festive. There wasn't anybody among the spectators who were angry, and they had waited so long, and it was beginning to get dark now. So, somebody heaved a brick because they knew that in fact, they had been saying, 'Turn the water hose on. Turn the water hose on.' And Bull Connor, then somebody threw a brick, and he started turning them on, see. So they just danced and played in the hose spray. This famous picture of them holding hands, it was just a frolic of them trying to stand up [unintelligible] and some of them were getting knocked down by the hose. They'd get up and run back and it would slide them along the pavement. Then they began bringing the hose up from the other corner, and instead of Negroes [unintelligible] they ran to the hose. It was a, it was a holiday for them. And this went on for a couple of hours. It was a joke, really. All in good humor and good spirit. Not any vitriolic response on the part of even the Negro spectators, which to me, again, was an example of the changing spirit, you know. When Negroes once had been cowed in the presence of policemen and maybe water hoses, here they had complete disdain for them. Made a joke out of it."

Part Three

The Limits of Power

I returned, and saw under the sun, that the race is not to the swift, nor the battle to the strong, neither yet bread to the wise, nor yet riches to men of understanding, nor yet favor to men of skill; but time and chance happeneth to them all.

Ecclesiastes 9:11

CHAPTER SEVEN

Rosemary Lawlor

"I WASN'T BORN THAT WAY. THIS
WAS FORCED UPON ME."

1.

When the Troubles began in Northern Ireland, Rosemary Lawlor was a newlywed. She and her husband had just bought a house in Belfast. They had a baby. It was the summer of 1969, and Catholics and Protestants—the two religious communities that have lived uneasily alongside each other throughout the country's history—were at each other's throats. There were bombings and riots. Gangs of Protestant militants—Loyalists, as they were called—roamed the streets, burning down houses. The Lawlors were Catholic, and Catholics have always been a minority in Northern Ireland. Every day, they grew more frightened.

"I'd come home at night," Lawlor said, "and there would be writing on the door: 'Taigs out.' 'Taigs' is a derogatory word for an Irish Catholic. Or 'No Pope here.'

197

Another night we were there, we were very lucky. A bomb came into the backyard and didn't explode. One day I went to knock on my neighbor's door, and I realized that she was gone. I found out that day that a lot of people had gone. So when my husband, Terry, came home from work, I said, 'Terry, what's going on here?' And he said, 'We're in danger.'

"We left the home that night. We had no phone. You remember, this is in the days before mobiles. We walked out. The fear was in me. I put my son in his pram. I gathered up best we could pieces of clothes for him and ourselves. There was a tray at the bottom of the pram, and we stuffed them all in the tray. And Terry says to me, 'Right, Rosie, we're just going to walk straight out of here and we're gonna smile at everybody.' I was trembling. I was a teenage mum, a teenage girl who got married, nineteen, married, new baby, new world, new life. Taken away from me like that. D'you know? And I have no power to stop it. Fear is an awful thing, and I remember being really, really scared."

The safest place they knew was the all-Catholic neighborhood of Ballymurphy, in West Belfast, where Lawlor's parents lived. But they had no car, and with Belfast in turmoil, no taxi wanted to venture into a Catholic neighborhood. Finally they tricked a cab into stopping by saying their baby was sick and needed to get to a hospital. They shut the car door and Terry told the driver, "I want you to take us to Ballymurphy." The driver said, "Oh, no, I'm not doing that." But Terry had a poker, and he took it out, and he placed the point against the back of the driver's neck and said, "You're going to take us." The cabdriver drove them to the edge of Ballymurphy and stopped. "I don't care if you stick that in me," he said. "I'm not going any further." The Lawlors gathered up their baby and their worldly possessions and ran for their lives.

At the beginning of 1970, things got worse. That Easter, there was a riot in Ballymurphy. The British Army was called in: a fleet of armored cars with barbed wire on their bumpers patrolled the streets. Lawlor would push her pram past soldiers with automatic rifles and tear-gas grenades. One weekend in June, there was a gun battle in the bordering neighborhood: a group of Catholic gunmen stepped into the middle of the road and opened fire on a group of Protestant bystanders. In response, Protestant Loyalists tried to burn down a Catholic church near the docks. For five hours, the two sides fought, locked in deadly gun battle. Hundreds of fires burned across the city. By the end of the weekend, six people were dead and more than two hundred injured. The British home secretary responsible for Northern Ireland flew up from London, surveyed the chaos, and ran back to his plane. "For God's sake, bring me a large Scotch," he said, burying his head in his hands. "What a bloody awful country."

A week later, a woman came through Ballymurphy. Her name was Harriet Carson. "She was famous for hitting Maggie Thatcher over the head with a handbag at City Hall," Lawlor said. "I knew her growing up. Harriet was coming around with two lids of pots, and she was banging them together and she was shouting, 'Come on, come out, come out. The people in the Lower Falls are getting murdered.' She was shouting it up. And I went out to the door. My family was all there. And she was shouting, 'They're locked in their houses. Their children can't get

milk, and they haven't got anything for a cup of tea, and
there's no bread, and come out, come out, we need to do
something!'"

The Lower Falls is an all-Catholic neighborhood just
down the hill from Ballymurphy. Lawlor had gone to
school in the Lower Falls. Her uncle lived there, as did
countless cousins. She knew as many people in the Lower
Falls as she did in Ballymurphy. The British Army had put
the entire neighborhood under curfew while they searched
for illegal weapons.

"I didn't know what 'curfew' meant," Lawlor said.
"Hadn't a clue. I had to say to somebody, 'What does
that mean?' She said, 'They're not allowed out of their
houses.' I said, 'How can they do that?' I was totally
stunned. Stunned. 'What do you mean?' 'The people are
locked in their houses. They can't get out for bread or
milk.' While the Brits, the British Army, were kicking
in doors and wracking and ruinin' and searchin', I was,
'What?' The biggest thought in everybody's mind was,
there are people locked in their houses, and there's children. You have to remember, some houses then had
twelve, fifteen kids in them. D'you know? That's the way
it was. 'What do you mean they can't get out of their
houses?'" They were *angry*.

Rosemary Lawlor is now in her sixties, a sturdily built
woman with ruddy cheeks and short, white-blond hair
swept to the side. She was a seamstress by trade, and she
was dressed with flair: a bright floral blouse and white
cropped pants. She was talking about things that had happened half a lifetime ago. But she remembered every moment.

"My father said, 'The Brits, they'll turn on us. They say they're in here to protect us. They'll turn on us — you wait and see.' And he was one hundred percent right. They turned on us. And the curfew was the start of it."

2.

The same year that Northern Ireland descended into chaos, two economists — Nathan Leites and Charles Wolf Jr. — wrote a report about how to deal with insurgencies. Leites and Wolf worked for the RAND Corporation, the prestigious think tank started after the Second World War by the Pentagon. Their report was called *Rebellion and Authority*. In those years, when the world was exploding in violence, everyone read Leites and Wolf. *Rebellion and Authority* became the blueprint for the war in Vietnam, and for how police departments dealt with civil unrest, and for how governments coped with terrorism. Its conclusion was simple:

> Fundamental to our analysis is the assumption that the population, as individuals or groups, behaves "rationally," that it calculates costs and benefits to the extent that they can be related to different courses of action, and makes choices accordingly....Consequently, influencing popular behavior requires neither sympathy nor mysticism, but rather a better understanding of what costs and benefits the individual or the group is concerned with, and how they are calculated.

In other words, getting insurgents to behave is fundamentally a math problem. If there are riots in the streets of Belfast, it's because the costs to rioters of burning houses and smashing windows aren't high enough. And when Leites and Wolf said that "influencing popular behavior requires neither sympathy nor mysticism," what they meant was that nothing mattered but that calculation. If you were in a position of power, you didn't have to worry about how lawbreakers *felt* about what you were doing. You just had to be tough enough to make them think twice.

The general in charge of the British forces in Northern Ireland was a man straight out of the pages of *Rebellion and Authority*. His name was Ian Freeland. He had served with distinction in Normandy during the Second World War and later fought insurgencies in Cyprus and Zanzibar. He was trim and forthright, with a straight back and a square jaw and a firm hand: he "conveyed the correct impression of a man who knew what needed to be done and would do it." When he arrived in Northern Ireland, he made it plain that his patience was limited. He was not afraid to use force. He had his orders from the prime minister: the British Army "should deal toughly, and be seen to deal toughly, with thugs and gunmen."

On June 30, 1970, the British Army received a tip. There were explosives and weapons hidden in a house at 24 Balkan Street in the Lower Falls, they were told. Freeland immediately dispatched five armored cars filled with soldiers and police officers. A search of the house turned up a cache of guns and ammunition. Outside, a crowd gathered. Someone started throwing stones. Stones turned into petrol bombs. A riot started. By ten p.m. the British had

had enough. An army helicopter armed with a loudspeaker circled the Lower Falls, demanding that all residents stay inside their homes or face arrest. As the streets cleared, the army launched a massive house-to-house search. Disobedience was met with firm and immediate punishment. The next morning, a triumphant Freeland took two Protestant government officials and a pack of journalists on a tour of the neighborhood in the back of an open flatbed truck, surveying the deserted streets like—as one soldier later put it—"the British Raj on a tiger hunt."

The British Army went to Northern Ireland with the best of intentions. The local police force was overwhelmed, and they were there simply to help—to serve as a peacekeeper between Northern Ireland's two warring populations. This was not some distant and foreign land: they were dealing with their own country, their own language, and their own culture. They had resources and weapons and soldiers and experience that dwarfed those of the insurgent elements that they were trying to contain. When Freeland toured the empty streets of the Lower Falls that morning, he believed that he and his men would be back home in England by the end of the summer. But that's not what happened. Instead, what should have been a difficult few months turned into thirty years of bloodshed and mayhem.

In Northern Ireland, the British made a simple mistake. They fell into the trap of believing that because they had resources, weapons, soldiers, and experience that dwarfed those of the insurgent elements that they were trying to contain, it did not matter what the people of Northern Ireland thought of them. General Freeland believed Leites and Wolf when they said that "influencing popular behavior requires neither sympathy nor mysticism." And Leites and Wolf were wrong.

"It has been said that most revolutions are not caused by revolutionaries in the first place, but by the stupidity and brutality of governments," Seán MacStiofáin, the provisional IRA's first chief of staff, said once, looking back on those early years. "Well, you had that to start with in [Northern Ireland], all right."

3.

The simplest way to understand the British mistake in Northern Ireland is to picture a classroom. It's a kindergarten class, a room with brightly colored walls covered in children's drawings. Let's call the teacher Stella.

The classroom was videotaped as part of a project at the Curry School of Education at the University of Virginia, and there is more than enough footage to provide a good sense of the kind of teacher Stella is and the kind of classroom she has. Even after a few minutes, it is abundantly clear that things aren't going well.

Stella is sitting in a chair at the front of the room. She's reading out loud from a book that she is holding up to one side: "...seven slices of tomatoes," "eight juicy olives," "nine chunks of cheese...." A girl is standing in front of her, reading along, and all around her, the class is in chaos, a mini-version of Belfast in the summer of 1970. A little girl is doing cartwheels across the room. A little boy is making faces. Much of the class seems to be paying no attention at all. Some of the students have actually turned themselves entirely around, so that they have their backs to Stella.

If you were to walk in on Stella's class, what would you think? I'm guessing your first reaction would be that she has a group of unruly children. Maybe she teaches in a school in a poor neighborhood and her students come from troubled families. Maybe her students come to school without any real respect for authority or learning. Leites and Wolf would say that she really needs to use some discipline. Children like that need a firm hand. They need rules. If there is no order in the classroom, how can any learning take place?

The truth is, though, that Stella's school isn't in some terrible neighborhood. Her students aren't particularly or unusually unruly. When the class begins, they are perfectly well behaved and attentive, eager and ready to learn. They don't seem like bad apples at all. They only start to misbehave well into the lesson, and only in response to the way Stella is behaving. *Stella* causes the crisis. How so? By doing an appalling job of teaching the lesson.

Stella had the girl from the class reading alongside her as a way of engaging the rest of the students. But the pacing of the back-and-forth between the two of them was excruciatingly slow and wooden. "Look at her body language," one of the Virginia researchers, Bridget Hamre, said as we watched Stella. "Right now she is just talking to this one kid, and no one else is getting in." Her colleague Robert Pianta added: "There's no rhythm. No pace. This is going nowhere. There is no value in what she's doing."

Only then did the class begin to deteriorate. The little

boy started making faces. When the child started doing cartwheels, Stella missed it entirely. Three or four students to the immediate right of the teacher were still gamely trying to follow along, but Stella was so locked onto the book that she wasn't giving them any encouragement. Meanwhile, to Stella's left, five or six children had turned themselves around. But that was because they were bewildered, not because they were disobedient. Their view of the book was completely blocked by the little girl standing in front of Stella. They had no way of following along. We often think of authority as a response to disobedience: a child acts up, so a teacher cracks down. Stella's classroom, however, suggests something quite different: disobedience can also be a response to authority. If the teacher doesn't do her job properly, then the child will *become* disobedient.

"With classrooms like this one, people will call what is happening a behavioral issue," Hamre said. We were watching one of Stella's kids wiggling and squirming and contorting her face and altogether doing whatever she could to avoid her teacher. "But one of the things we find is that this sort of thing is more often an engagement problem than a behavioral problem. If the teacher is actually doing something interesting, these kids are quite capable of being engaged. Instead of responding in a 'let me control your behavior' way, the teacher needs to think, 'How can I do something interesting that will prevent you from misbehaving in the first place?'"

The next video Pianta and Hamre played was of a third-grade teacher giving homework to her students. Each student was given a copy of the assignment, and the teacher and the class read the instructions aloud together. Pianta was aghast. "Just the idea that you would be choral reading a set of instructions to a bunch of eight-year-olds is almost disrespectful," he said. "I mean, why? Is there any instructional purpose?" They know how to read. It is like a waiter in a restaurant giving you the menu and then proceeding to read every item to you just as it appears on the page.

A boy sitting next to the teacher raises his hand midway through the reading, and without looking at him, the teacher reaches out, grabs his wrist, and pushes his hand back down. Another child starts to actually do the assignment—an entirely logical action, given the pointlessness of what the teacher is doing. The teacher addresses him, sharply. "Sweetie. This is *home*work." It was a moment of discipline. The child had broken the rules. The teacher had responded, firmly and immediately. If you were to watch that moment with the sound turned off, you would think of it as Leites and Wolf perfectly applied. But if you were to listen to what the teacher was saying and think about the incident from the child's perspective, it would become clear that it is having anything but its intended effect. The little boy isn't going to come away with a renewed appreciation of the importance of following the rules. He is going to come away angry and disillusioned. Why? Because the punishment is completely arbitrary. He can't speak up and give his own side of the story. *And wants to learn.* If that little boy became defiant, it was because his teacher made him that way, just as Stella turned an eager and attentive student into someone who did cartwheels across the floor. When people in authority want the rest of us to behave, it matters—first and foremost—how *they* behave.

This is called the "principle of legitimacy," and legitimacy is based on three things. First of all, the people who are asked to obey authority have to feel like they have a voice—that if they speak up, they will be heard. Second, the law has to be predictable. There has to be a reasonable expectation that the rules tomorrow are going to be roughly the same as the rules today. And third, the authority has to be fair. It can't treat one group differently from another.

All good parents understand these three principles implicitly. If you want to stop little Johnnie from hitting his sister, you can't look away one time and scream at him another. You can't treat his sister differently when she hits him. And if he says he really didn't hit his sister, you have to give him a chance to explain himself. *How* you punish is as important as the act of punishing itself. That's why the story of Stella is not all that surprising. Anyone who has ever sat in a classroom knows that it is important for teachers to earn the respect of their students.

What is harder to understand, however, is the importance of these same principles when it comes to law and order. We know our parents and our teachers, so it makes sense that legitimacy should matter a lot inside the home or the school. But the decision about whether to rob a bank or shoot someone seems like it belongs to a very different category, doesn't it? That's what Leites and Wolf meant when they said that fighting criminals and insurgents "requires neither sympathy nor mysticism." They were saying that at that level, the decision to obey the law is a function of a rational calculation of risks and benefits. It *isn't* personal. But that's precisely where they went wrong, because getting criminals and insurgents to behave turns out to be as dependent on legitimacy as getting children to behave in the classroom.

4.

Let me give you an example. It involves an experiment that has been going on for the past few years in the New York City neighborhood of Brownsville. Brownsville is home to just over a hundred thousand people, and it lies in the eastern part of Brooklyn, past the elegant brownstones of Park Slope and the synagogues of Crown Heights.[*] For more than a century, it has been among the most destitute corners of New York City. There are eighteen public housing projects in Brownsville, more than in any other part of the city, and they dominate the skyline: block upon block of bleak, featureless brick-and-concrete developments. As the crime rate in New York City fell dramatically over the past twenty years, Brownsville always remained a step behind, plagued by groups of teenagers who roamed the streets, mugging passersby. From time to time, the police would flood the streets with extra officers. But the effect was never more than temporary.

In 2003, a police officer named Joanne Jaffe took over as head of the city's Housing Bureau, the group with pri-

---

[*] An impressive number of famous people have come from Brownsville over the years: two heavyweight boxing champions (Mike Tyson and Riddick Bowe); the composer Aaron Copland; the Three Stooges (played by Moe and Shemp Howard [later replaced by his brother Curly] and Larry Fine); the television host Larry King—not to mention a long list of professional basketball, football, and baseball stars. The operative words, though, are *"come from* Brownsville." Nobody who can help it stays in Brownsville.

mary responsibility for the Brownsville projects. She decided to try something new. Jaffe began by making a list of all of the juveniles in Brownsville who had been arrested at least once in the previous twelve months. That search yielded 106 names, corresponding to 180 arrests. Jaffe's assumption was that anyone arrested for a mugging had probably committed somewhere between twenty and fifty other crimes that never came to the attention of the police, so by her rule of thumb, her 106 juveniles were responsible for as many as five thousand crimes in the previous year.

She then put together a task force of police officers and had them contact every name on the list. "We said to them, 'You're in the program,'" Jaffe explained. "'And the program is that we're going to give you a choice. We want to do everything we can to get you back in school, to help you get a high school diploma, to bring services to your family, find out what's needed in the household. We will provide job opportunities, educational opportunities, medical—everything we can. We want to work with you. But the criminal conduct has to stop. And if it doesn't stop and you get arrested for anything, we're going to do everything to keep you in jail. I don't care how minor it is. We are going to be all over you.'"

The program was called J-RIP, for Juvenile Robbery Intervention Program. There was nothing complicated about it—at least on the surface. J-RIP was standard-issue, high-intensity modern policing. Jaffe put her J-RIP task force in a trailer in the parking lot of a housing project, not off in a station house somewhere. She made every surveillance tool available to her J-RIP team. They made lists of each J-RIPper's associates—the people they had been arrested with. They went on Facebook and down-loaded photos of their friends and looked for gang affili-ations. They talked to brothers and sisters and mothers, and they put together giant, poster-size maps showing the networks of friendships and associations that surrounded each person—the same way an intelligence organization might track the movements of suspected terrorists.

"I have people out there 24/7," Jaffe said. "So when a J-RIPper is arrested, I'm willing to send in a team if I have to. I don't care if it's the Bronx, or the middle of the night. There have got to be dire consequences. They've got to know what's going to happen. It's got to be swift. If you get arrested, you're going to see my face."

She went on, "I tell them, 'You can slam the door when I come to your house. But I'll see you on the street. I'll say hello to you. I'll learn everything about you. You go from Brooklyn to the Bronx, I'll know what trains you take.' We say to someone, 'Johnnie, come into the J-RIP office tomorrow,' and Johnnie comes in, and we say, 'You were stopped in the Bronx last night. You got a summons.' He says, 'What?' 'You were with Raymond Rivera and Mary Jones.' 'How do you know that?' They started thinking we were all over the place. Since we had developed a folder on each kid, we'd show them what we had on them. We'd say, 'These are all your buddies. Here's all your information. Here are your pictures. We know you're part of this devel-opment. We know you might be a part of a crew. We know your world.' We started learning about where they're sup-posed to go to school, who they're hanging out with at school. When they're not in school, we get a call. So my J-RIP team goes out and wakes them up and says, 'Get up!'"

But this was only part of Jaffe's strategy. She also did things that don't sound like typical policing strategy. She spent a lot of time, for example, finding the *right* kind of officer to serve on the task force. "I couldn't put just any cop in there," she said, sounding more like a social worker than a police chief. "I had to have a cop that loves kids. I had to have a cop that didn't have an ounce of negativity about them, and who had the ability to help sway kids and push them in the right direction." To head the group, she finally settled on David Glassberg, a gregarious former narcotics officer with children of his own.

She was also obsessed, from the very beginning, with meeting the families of her J-RIPpers. She wanted to know them. It turned out to be surprisingly difficult. In her first attempt, she sent letters to every home, inviting the families to come to a local church for a group session. No one showed up. Then Jaffe and her team went door-to-door. Once again, they got nowhere. "We ended up going to each family, one hundred and six kids," she said. "They would say, 'Fuck you. Don't come into my house.'"

The breakthrough finally came months into the program. "There's this one kid," Jaffe said. She made up a name for him: Johnnie Jones. "He was a *bad* kid. He was fourteen, fifteen then. He lived with a seventeen- or eighteen-year-old sister. His mother lived in Queens. Even the mother hated us. There was no one for us to reach out to. So now, November of the first year, 2007, Dave Glassberg comes to my office, Wednesday before Thanksgiving.

"He says, 'All the guys, all the people on the team, chipped in and we bought Johnnie Jones and his family Thanksgiving dinner tonight.'

"And I said, 'You're kidding.' This was a *bad* kid.

"And he goes, 'You know why we did it? This is a kid that we're gonna lose but there are seven other kids in that family. We had to do something for them.'

"I had tears in my eyes. Then he said, 'Well, we have all these other families. What are we going to do?' It's ten a.m., day before Thanksgiving, and I said, 'Dave, what if I go to the police commissioner and see if I can get two thousand bucks and see if we can buy a turkey for every family? Could we do it?'"

She went upstairs to the executive level of police head-quarters, and begged for two minutes with the police commissioner. "I said, 'This is what Dave Glassberg did with the team. I want to buy a hundred and twenty-five turkeys. Can I get money somewhere?' He said yes. Glassberg put his men on overtime. They found frozen turkeys and refrigerated trucks, and that night went door-to-door in the Brownsville projects. We put them in a bag, and we did a flyer: 'From our family to your family, Happy Thanksgiving.'"

Jaffe was sitting in her office at New York police head-quarters in downtown Manhattan. She was in full uni-form—tall and formidable, with a head of thick black hair and more than a hint of Brooklyn in her voice.

"We'd knock," she continued. "Momma or Grandma would open the door and say, 'Johnnie, the police are here'—just like that. I'd say, 'Hi, Mrs. Smith, I'm Chief Jaffe. We have something for you for Thanksgiving. We just want to wish you a happy Thanksgiving.' And they'd be, 'What is this?' And they'd say, 'Come in, come in,' and they would drag you in, and the apartments were so hot, I mean, and then, 'Johnnie, come here, the police are here!' And there's all these people running around, hugging and crying. Every family—I did five—there was hugging and crying. And I always said the same thing: 'I know sometimes you can hate the police. I understand all that. But I just want you to know, as much as it seems that we're harassing you by knocking on your door, we really do care, and we really do want you to have a happy Thanksgiving.'"

Now, why was Jaffe so obsessed with meeting her J-RIPpers' families? *Because she didn't think the police in Brownsville were perceived as legitimate.* Across the United States, an astonishing number of black men have spent some time in prison. (To give you just one statistic, 69 percent of black male high school dropouts born in the late seventies have done time behind bars.) Brownsville is a neighborhood full of black male high school dropouts, which means that virtually every one of those juvenile delinquents on Jaffe's list would have had a brother or a father or a cousin who had served time in jail.[*] If that many

---

* Here are the U.S. imprisonment rates by race and education level.

WHITE MEN	1945–49	1960–64	1975–79
High school dropouts	4.2	8.0	15.3
High school only	0.7	2.5	4.1
Some college	0.7	0.8	1.2
BLACK MEN	1945–49	1960–64	1975–79
High school dropouts	14.7	41.6	69.0
High school only	10.2	12.4	18.0
Some college	4.9	5.5	7.6

The key statistics are the ones in boldface. *Sixty-nine percent* of all black male high school dropouts born between 1975 and 1979 have spent time behind bars. That's Brownsville in a nutshell.

214

people in your life have served time behind bars, does the law seem fair anymore? Does it seem predictable? Does it seem like you can speak up and be heard? What Jaffe realized when she came to Brownsville was that the police were seen as the enemy. And if the police were seen as the enemy, how on earth would she be able to get fifteen- and sixteen-year-olds—already embarked on a course of mugging and stealing—to change their ways? She could threaten them and warn them of the dire consequences of committing more crimes. But these were *teenagers,* stubborn and defiant by nature, who had already drifted into a life of crime. Why should they listen to her? She represented the institution that had put their fathers and brothers and cousins in prison. She needed to win back the respect of the community, and to do that, she needed the support of the families of her J-RIPpers. Her little speech on that first Thanksgiving—*I know sometimes you can hate the police. I understand all that. But I just want you to know, as much as it seems that we're harassing you by knocking on your door, we really do care, and we really do want you to have a happy Thanksgiving*—was a plea for legitimacy. She was trying to get families who had been on the wrong side of the law—sometimes for generations—to see that the law could be on their side.

After the success with the turkeys, Jaffe started Christmas-toy giveaways. The J-RIP task force started playing basketball with their young charges. They took them out for sushi dinners. They tried to get them summer jobs. They drove them to doctor appointments. Then Jaffe started a Christmas dinner, where every J-RIPper was invited along with his entire family. "You know what I do at the Christmas dinner with my J-RIP kids?" Jaffe said. "They act all tough in front of their friends. So I hug each one of them. It's always 'Come on. Let's hug.'" Jaffe is not a small woman. She is strong and imposing. Imagine her approaching some skinny teenager with her arms wide open. A hug from her would swallow him up.

This sounds like something out of a bad Hollywood movie, doesn't it? Turkeys on Thanksgiving! Hugging and crying! The reason most police departments around the world haven't followed Jaffe's lead is that what she did doesn't *seem* right. Johnnie Jones was a bad kid. Buying food and toys for people like him seems like the worst form of liberal indulgence. If the police chief in your town announced, in the face of a major crime wave, that she was going to start hugging and feeding the families of the criminals roaming the streets, you'd be speechless—right? Well, take a look at what happened in Brownsville.

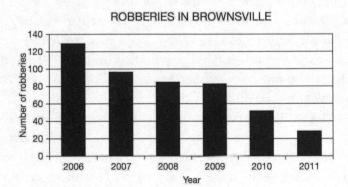

ROBBERIES IN BROWNSVILLE

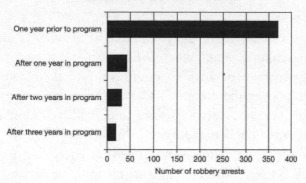

ROBBERY ARRESTS J-RIPPERS

When Leites and Wolf wrote that "influencing popular behavior requires neither sympathy nor mysticism," they meant that the power of the state was without limits. If you wanted to impose order, you didn't have to worry about what those whom you were ordering about thought of you. You were above that. But Leites and Wolf had it backwards. What Jaffe proved was that the powerful *have to* worry about how others think of them—that those who give orders are acutely vulnerable to the opinions of those whom they are ordering about.

That was the mistake General Freeland made in the Lower Falls. He didn't look at what was happening through the eyes of people like Rosemary Lawlor. He thought he'd ended the insurgency when he rode around the hushed streets of the Lower Falls like a British Raj on a tiger hunt. Had he bothered to drive up the street to Ballymurphy, where Harriet Carson was banging the lids of pots and saying, "Come on, come out, come out. The people in the Lower Falls are getting murdered," he would have realized the insurgency was just beginning.

5.

July in Northern Ireland is the height of what is known as "marching season," when the country's Protestant Loyalists organize parades to commemorate their long-ago victories over the country's Catholic minority. There are church parades, "arch, banner and hall" parades, commemorative band parades, and "blood and thunder" and "kick-the-Pope" flute band parades. There are parades with full silver bands, parades with bagpipes, parades with accordions, and parades with marchers wearing sashes and dark suits and bowler hats. There are hundreds of parades in all, involving tens of thousands of people, culminating every year in a massive march on the twelfth of July that marks the anniversary of the victory by William of Orange in the Battle of the Boyne in 1690, when Protestant control over Northern Ireland was established once and for all.

The night before the Twelfth, as it is known, marchers around the country hold street parties and build enormous bonfires.* When the fire is at its height, the group chooses a symbol to burn. In past years, it has often been

---

* In Belfast, the Twelfth march wends its way through the city and ends up in the "Field," a large staging area where the crowd gathers for public speeches. Here is a sample of one speech given in 1995. Keep in mind that this is after the Downing Street Declaration that officially began the peace process in Northern Ireland:

> We have read the history books, from 200 years ago. The Roman Catholics forming into groups known as the Defenders, to get rid of the so called heretic dogs, better known by you and I as Protestant people. Well today is no different from 1795. There is a Pope on the throne, a Polish Pope who was around in the days of Hitler and the concentration camps of Auschwitz when they stood back and watched thousands go out to death without one word of condemnation.

an effigy of the Pope or some hated local Catholic official. Here's how one Twelfth ditty goes, sung to the tune of "Clementine":

> *Build a bonfire, build a bonfire,*
> *Stick a Catholic on the top,*
> *Put the Pope right in the middle,*
> *And burn the fucking lot.** *

Northern Ireland is not a large country. Its cities are dense and compact, and as the Loyalists march by each summer in their bowler hats and sashes with flutes, they inevitably pass by the neighborhoods of the people whose defeat they are celebrating. The central artery of Catholic West Belfast is, in places, no more than a few minutes' walk from the street that runs through the heart of Protestant West Belfast. There are places in Belfast where the houses of Catholics back directly onto the backyards of Protestants, in such close proximity that each house has a giant metal grate over its backyard to protect the inhabitants against debris or petrol bombs thrown by their neighbors. On

---

* There are many versions of this children's rhyme, of course. A slightly less offensive version is sung by fans of Manchester United about their archrival Liverpool. (A "scouser," incidentally, refers to someone from Liverpool or who speaks with the Liverpudlian accent. The Beatles were scousers.)

> *Build a bonfire, build a bonfire,*
> *Put the scousers on the top,*
> *Put the city in the middle,*
> *And we'll burn the fuckin' lot.*

As you might expect, numerous highly enthusiastic renditions of this rhyme are available on YouTube.

the night before the Twelfth, when Loyalists lit bonfires around the city, people in Catholic neighborhoods would smell the smoke and hear the chants and see their flag going up in flames.

In marching season, violence *always* erupts in Northern Ireland. One of the incidents that began the Troubles was in 1969 after two days of riots broke out when a parade passed through a Catholic neighborhood. When the marchers went home, they went on a rampage through the streets of West Belfast, burning down scores of homes.* The gun battles the following summer that so tried Freeland's patience also happened during Protestant marches. Imagine that every summer U.S. Army veterans from the Northern states paraded through the streets of Atlanta and Richmond to commemorate their long-ago victory in the American Civil War. In the dark years of Northern Ireland, when Catholic and Protestant were at each other's throats, that's what marching season felt like.

When the residents of the Lower Falls looked up that afternoon and saw the British Army descend on their neighborhood, they were then as desperate as anyone to see law and order enforced in Belfast. But they were equally anxious about *how* law and order would be enforced. Their world did not seem fair. The Twelfth, when

---

* The next day, a Loyalist mob burned the Catholic neighborhood along Bombay Street to the ground. The Loyalists, who are fond of their verse, had a ditty for that attack as well:

> On the 15th of August, we took a little trip
> Up along Bombay Street and burned out all the shit.
> We took a little petrol, and we took a little gun
> And we fought the bloody Fenians till we had them on the run.

either their flag or their Pope would be burned in giant bonfires, was only days away. The institution charged with keeping both sides apart during marching season was the police force, the Royal Ulster Constabulary. But the RUC was almost entirely Protestant. It belonged to the other side. The RUC had done almost nothing to try to stop the riots the previous summer; a tribunal convened by the British government concluded, after the Protestant Loyalists had torched houses, that the RUC officers had "failed to take effective action." Journalists at the scene reported Loyalists going up to police officers and asking them if they could borrow their weapons. One of the reasons the British Army had been brought into Northern Ireland was to serve as an impartial referee between Protestant and Catholic. But England was an overwhelmingly Protestant country, so it seemed only natural to Northern Ireland's beleaguered Catholics that the sympathies of the soldiers would ultimately lie with the Protestants. When a big Loyalist march had run through Ballymurphy in the Easter before the curfew, British soldiers had stood between the marchers and the residents, ostensibly to act as a buffer. But the troops faced the Catholics on the sidewalk and stood with their backs to the Loyalists—as if they saw their job as to protect the Loyalists from the Catholics but not the Catholics from the Loyalists.

General Freeland was trying to enforce the law in Belfast, but he needed to first ask himself if he had the legitimacy to enforce the law—and the truth is, he didn't. He was in charge of an institution that the Catholics of Northern Ireland believed, with good reason, was thoroughly sympathetic to the very people who had burned down the houses of their friends and relatives the previous summer. And when the law is applied in the absence of legitimacy, it does not produce obedience. It produces the opposite. It leads to backlash.*

The great puzzle of Northern Ireland is why it took the British so long to understand this. In 1969, the Troubles resulted in thirteen deaths, seventy-three shootings, and eight bombings. In 1970, Freeland decided to get tough with thugs and gunmen, warning that anyone caught throwing gasoline bombs was "liable to be shot." What happened? The historian Desmond Hamill writes:

> The [IRA] retaliated by saying that they would shoot soldiers, if Irishmen were shot. The Protestant Ulster Volunteer Force—an extreme and illegal paramilitary unit—quickly joined in, offering to shoot a Catholic in return for every soldier shot by the IRA. The *Times* quoted a Belfast citizen saying: "Anyone who isn't confused here doesn't really understand what is going on."

That year, there were 25 deaths, 213 shootings, and 155 bombings. The British stood firm. They cracked down even harder—and in 1971, there were 184 deaths, 1,020 bombings, and 1,756 shootings. Then the British drew a line in the sand. The army instituted a policy known as "internment." Civil rights in Northern Ireland were suspended. The country was flooded with troops, and the

---

* As Sinn Féin leader Gerry Adams would say years later, the curfew's result was that "thousands of people…who had never had any time for physical force now accepted it as a practical necessity."

army declared that anyone suspected of terrorist activities could be arrested and held in prison, indefinitely, without charges or trial. So many young Catholic men were rounded up during internment that in a neighborhood like Ballymurphy, everyone had a brother or a father or a cousin in prison. If that many people in your life have served time behind bars, does the law seem fair anymore? Does it seem predictable? Does it seem like you can speak up and be heard? Things got even worse. In 1972, there were 1,495 shootings, 531 armed robberies, 1,931 bombings, and 497 people killed. One of those 497 was a seventeen-year-old boy named Eamon. Eamon was Rosemary Lawlor's little brother.*

"Eamon appeared at my door," Lawlor said. "He said to me, 'I'd love to stay here for a day or two.' And I said, 'Why don't you?' He said, 'Ma would have a fit. She would go ballistic.' Then he confided in myself and my husband that he was getting harassed by the British Army. Every time he was out, every corner he turned, everywhere he went, they were stopping him and they threatened him."

Was he actually working with the IRA? She didn't know, and she said it didn't matter. "We were all suspects in their eyes," she went on. "That's the way it was. And Eamon was shot, shot by a British soldier. Him and another fellow were having a smoke, and one shot rang out, and Eamon got it. He lived for eleven weeks. He died on the sixteenth of January, at seventeen and a half years of

---

* By the way, things didn't get much better in 1973. The British cracked down even harder that year, and there were 171 civilians killed, 5,018 shootings, 1,007 explosions, 1,317 armed robberies, and 17.2 tons of explosives seized by the army.

age." She began to tear up. "My father never worked again at the dock. My mother was destroyed, heartbroken. It's forty years ago this year. It's still rough."

Lawlor was a young wife and mother, living what she had expected would be a normal life in modern Belfast. But then she lost her home. She was threatened and harassed. Her relatives down the hill were imprisoned in their homes. Her brother was shot and killed. She never wanted any of it, nor asked for any of it, nor could even make sense of what happened. "That was my life, my whole new life," she said. "And then this was forced upon me. And I go, This is not right. D'you know? Here are my people I grew up with in school, being burnt out of their houses. The British Army that came in to protect us has now turned on us and is wracking and ruining. I became hooked. I don't mean that flippantly. I became that way because I can't sit in the house while this is going on. I can't be a nine-to-five mother.

"People call it the Troubles," she continued. "It was war! The British Army was out there with armored cars and weapons and you name it. That's a war zone we lived in. The British Army came in here with every means that they had available to put us down. And we were like rubber dolls—we'd just bounce back up again. Don't get me wrong. We got hurt on the way down. A lot of people had heartache. I suffered from anger for a long, long time, and I've apologized to my children for that. But the circumstances dictated that. It wasn't how I was. I wasn't born that way. This was forced upon me."

6.

When General Freeland's men descended on the Lower Falls, the first thing the neighbors did was run to St. Peter's Cathedral, the local Catholic church just a few blocks away. The defining feature of the Lower Falls, like so many of the other Catholic neighborhoods of West Belfast, was its religiosity. St. Peter's was the heart of the neighborhood. Four hundred people would attend mass at St. Peter's on a typical *weekday.* The most important man in the community was the local priest. He came running. He went up to the soldiers. The raid must be done quickly, he warned them, or there would be trouble.

Forty-five minutes passed, and the soldiers emerged with their haul: fifteen pistols, a rifle, a Schmeisser submachine gun, and a cache of explosives and ammunition. The patrol packed up and left, turning onto a side street that would take them out of the Lower Falls. In the interim, however, a small crowd had gathered, and as the armored cars turned the corner, a number of young men ran forward and started throwing stones at the soldiers. The patrol stopped. The crowd grew angry. The soldiers responded with tear gas. The crowd grew angrier. Stones turned to petrol bombs and petrol bombs to bullets. A taxi driver said he had seen someone carrying a submachine gun heading for Balkan Street. The rioters set up roadblocks to slow the army's advance: a truck was set ablaze, blocking the end of the street. The soldiers fired even more tear gas, until the wind had carried it clear across the Lower Falls. The crowd grew angrier still.

Why did the patrol stop? Why didn't they just keep

going? Lingering in the neighborhood is exactly what the priest told them *not* to do. The priest went back to the soldiers and pleaded with them again. If they stopped the tear gas, he said, he would get the crowd to stop throwing stones. The soldiers didn't listen. Their instructions were to get tough and be seen to get tough with thugs and gunmen. The priest turned back toward the crowd. As he did, the soldiers fired off another round of tear gas. The canisters fell at the feet of the priest, and he staggered across the street, leaning on a windowsill as he gasped for air. In a neighborhood so devout that four hundred people would show up for mass on a typical weekday, *the British Army gassed the priest.*

That was when the riot started. Freeland called in reinforcements. To subdue a community of eight thousand people—packed into tiny houses along narrow streets—the British brought in three thousand troops. And not just any troops. To a fiercely Catholic neighborhood, Freeland bought in soldiers from the Royal Scots—one of the most obviously and self-consciously Protestant regiments in the entire army. Army helicopters circled overhead, ordering the residents by megaphone to stay inside their homes. Roadblocks were placed at every exit. A curfew was declared, and a systematic house-by-house search began. Twenty- and twenty-one-year-old soldiers, still smarting from the indignity of being pelted with stones and petrol bombs, forced their way into home after home, punching holes in walls and ceilings, ransacking bedrooms. Listen to one of those British soldiers, looking back on what happened that night:

A guy still in his pajamas came out cursing, wielding a lamp, and whacked Stan across the head. Stan dodged the next one and decked the bloke with his rifle butt. I knew full well that a lot of the lads were taking this opportunity to vent their anger over things already done. Heads were being cracked and houses trashed from top to bottom. Everything in the houses became a mass of rubble, but, out of the blur, little sharp details still cut through: school photos; smiley family pictures (cracked); trinkets and crucifixes (snapped); kids crying; crunching on the glass of the Pope's picture; unfinished meals and bad wallpaper; coloured toys and TV noise and radio crackle; painted plates; shoes; a body in the hall, flattened against the wall....This is when I did feel like we'd invaded.

Three hundred and thirty-seven people were arrested that night. Sixty were injured. Charles O'Neill, a disabled air force veteran, was run over and killed by a British armored car. As his body lay on the ground, one of the soldiers poked a bystander with a baton and said, "Move on, you Irish bastard—there are not enough of you dead." A man named Thomas Burns was shot by a soldier on the Falls Road at eight p.m. as he stood with a friend who was boarding up the windows of his store. When his sister came to pick up his body, she was told he had no business being on the street at that time. At eleven p.m., an elderly man named Patrick Elliman, thinking the worst was over, went out in his bedroom slippers and shirtsleeves for a pre-bedtime stroll. He died in a burst of army gunfire. One of the neighborhood accounts of the curfew says of Elliman's death:

That very night British troops actually entered and quartered themselves in the shot man's home, the distraught sister having been moved to the other brother's up the street. This tasteless intrusion into the abandoned home was discovered the next afternoon during the interval in the "curfew" when the brother, with his daughter and son-in-law, went down to the house and found the door broken down, a window broken, kit lying on the floor, shaving tackle on the settee, and used cups in the scullery. Neighbors informed them that the soldiers had dossed down in the upstairs rooms as well.

A door broken down. A window broken. Dirty dishes left in the sink. Leites and Wolf believed that all that counts are rules and rational principles. But what actually matters are the hundreds of small things that the powerful do—or don't do—to establish their legitimacy, like sleeping in the bed of an innocent man you just shot accidentally and scattering your belongings around his house.

By Sunday morning, the situation inside the Lower Falls was growing desperate. The Lower Falls was not a wealthy neighborhood. Many of the adults were unemployed or, if they were not, relied on piecework. The streets were crowded, and the homes were narrow—cheaply built nineteenth-century terraced redbrick row houses, with one room to a floor, and bathrooms in the backyard. Very few houses had a refrigerator. They were dark and damp. People bought bread daily because it grew moldy otherwise. But the curfew was now thirty-six hours old—and there was no bread left. The Catholic neighborhoods of West Belfast are packed so tightly together, and linked by so many ties of marriage and blood, that word spread quickly from one to the next about the plight of the Lower Falls. Harriet Carson walked through Ballymurphy, banging together the lids of pots. Next came a woman named Máire Drumm.* She had a bullhorn. She marched through the streets, shouting to the women: "Come out! Fill your prams with bread and milk! The children haven't gotten any food."

The women started to gather in groups of two and four and ten and twenty, until they numbered in the thousands. "Some people still had their rollers in their hair, and their scarves over their head," Lawlor remembered. "We linked arms and sang, 'We shall overcome. We shall overcome someday.'

"We got down to the bottom of the hill," she went on. "The atmosphere was electric. The Brits were standing with their helmets and their guns—all ready. Their batons were out. We turned and went down the Grosvenor Road, singing and shouting. I think the Brits were in awe. They couldn't believe that these women with prams were coming down to take them on. I remember seeing one Brit standing there scratching his head, going, 'What do we do with all these women? Do we go into riot situation here?' Then we turned onto Slate Street, where the school was—*my school.* And the Brits were there. They come flying out [of the school], and there was hand-to-hand fighting. We got the hair pulled out of us. The Brits just grabbed us, threw us up against the walls. Oh, aye. They beat us,

---

* Six years later, Drumm was shot to death in her bed by Protestant extremists while she was being treated at Mater Hospital in Belfast.

like. And if you fell, you had to get up very quickly, because you didn't want to get trampled. They came out with brutality. I remember standing up on top of a car and having a look at what was going on in the front. Then I saw a man with shaving cream on his face, and putting his braces on—and all of a sudden the soldiers stopped beating us."

The man putting his braces on was the commanding officer of the Slate Street checkpoint. He might have been the only voice of sanity on the British side that day, the only one who understood the full dimensions of the catastrophe unfolding. A heavily armed group of soldiers was beating up a group of pram-pushing women, coming to feed the children of the Lower Falls.* He told his men to stop.

"You have to understand, the march was still coming down the road, and the people at the back hadn't a clue what was going on at the front," Lawlor went on. "They kept coming. Women were crying. People started coming out of their houses—pulling people in because there were so many injured. Once all the people started coming out of their houses, the Brits lost control. Everyone came out on the streets—hundreds and hundreds of people. It was like a domino effect. One street they'd come out, next thing you know, doors are opening on another street, another street, and another street. The Brits gave up. They had their hands up. The women forced—and we forced and we forced—until we got in, and we got in and we

---

* One of the many legends of the Lower Falls curfew is that the prams pushed by marchers had two purposes. The first was to bring milk and bread into the Lower Falls. The second was to take guns and explosives out—past the unsuspecting eyes of the British Army.

broke the curfew. I've often thought about it. God, it was like—Everybody was jubilant. It was like—*We did it.*

"I remember coming home and suddenly felt very shaky and upset and nervous about the whole episode, do you know? I remember speaking to my father about it afterward. I said, 'Daddy, your words came true. They turned on us.' And he said, 'True. British Army—that's what they do.' He was right. They turned on us. And that was the start of it."

CHAPTER EIGHT

Wilma Derksen

"WE HAVE ALL DONE SOMETHING
DREADFUL IN OUR LIVES, OR
HAVE FELT THE URGE TO."

1.

One weekend in June of 1992, Mike Reynolds's daughter came home from college to go to a wedding. She was eighteen, with long honey-blond hair. Her name was Kimber. She was a student at the Fashion Institute of Design and Merchandising in Los Angeles. Home was Fresno, several hours to the north, in California's Central Valley. After the wedding, she stayed on to have dinner with an old friend, Greg Calderon. She was wearing shorts and boots and her father's red-and-black-checked sports coat.

Reynolds and Calderon ate at the Daily Planet restaurant, in Fresno's Tower District. They had coffee and then wandered back to her Isuzu. It was 10:41 p.m. Reynolds opened the passenger door for Calderon, then walked around the car to the driver's side. As she did, two young men on a stolen Kawasaki motorcycle moved slowly out of a parking lot just down the street. They were wearing helmets with shaded visors. The driver, Joe Davis, had a long list of drug and gun convictions. He had just been paroled from Wasco State Prison after serving time for auto theft. On the back of the motorcycle was Douglas Walker. Walker had been in and out of jail seven times. Both men were crystal-meth addicts. Earlier in the evening, they had attempted a carjacking on Shaw Avenue, Fresno's main thoroughfare. "I wasn't really thinking much a nothing, you know," Walker would say months later when asked about his state of mind that night. "When it happens, it happens, you know. It just happened suddenly. We were just out doing what we do. I mean, that's all I can tell you."

Walker and Davis pulled up alongside the Isuzu, using the weight of the motorcycle to pin Reynolds against her car. Calderon jumped out of the passenger's seat, running around the back of the car. Walker blocked his way. Davis grabbed at Reynolds's purse. He pulled out a .357 magnum handgun and placed it against her right ear. She resisted. He fired. Davis and Walker jumped back on the motorcycle and sped through a red light. People came running out of the Daily Planet. Someone tried to stanch the bleeding. Calderon drove back to Reynolds's parents' house but couldn't wake them. He called and got their answering machine. Finally, at two-thirty in the morning, he got through. Mike Reynolds heard his wife cry out, "In the head! She's been shot in the head!" Kimber died a day later.

"Father-daughter relationships are kind of a real special thing," Mike Reynolds said not long ago, looking back on that awful night. He is an older man now. He limps and has lost most of his hair. He sat at a table in his study, in his rambling Mission-style home in Fresno not more than a five-minute drive from the street where his daughter was shot. On the wall behind him was a photograph of Kimber. In the kitchen, next door, was a painting of Kimber with angel's wings, ascending to heaven. "You may fight with your wife," he went on, his voice filled with the emotion of the memory. "But your daughter is kind of like the princess—she can do no wrong. And for that matter, her dad is the guy who can fix anything, from a broken tricycle to a broken heart. Daddy can fix everything, and when this happened to our daughter, it was something I couldn't fix. I literally held her hand while she was dying. It's a very helpless feeling." At that moment, he made a vow.

"Everything I've done ever since is about a promise I made to Kimber on her deathbed," Reynolds said. "I can't save your life. But I'm going to do everything in my power to try and prevent this from happening to anybody else."

2.

When Reynolds came home from the hospital, he got a call from Ray Appleton, the host of a popular Fresno talk-radio show. "The town was going berserk," Appleton remembers. "At the time, Fresno was number one in the country in per capita murders—or close to it. But this was just so blatant—in front of a million people, in front of a popular restaurant. I got the word late that night that Kimber had died, and I got hold of Mike. I said, 'Whenever you are ready to come on, let me know.' And he said, 'How about today?' That's where this whole thing began, fourteen hours after his daughter's death."

Reynolds describes the two hours he spent on the Appleton show as the most difficult of his life. He was in tears. "I've never seen devastation like that before," Appleton remembers. In the beginning, the two took calls from people who knew the Reynolds family, or who just wanted to express their sympathy. But then he and Reynolds began to talk about what the murder said about California's justice system, and calls started coming in from clear across the state.

Reynolds went back home and called a meeting. He invited everyone he thought could make a difference, and they sat in his backyard around a long wooden table next to his outdoor barbecue. "We had three judges, people from the police department, lawyers, the sheriff, people from the district attorney's office, people from the community, the school system," he said. "And we were asking, 'Why is this happening? What's causing it?'"

Their conclusion was that in California the penalties associated with breaking the law were too low. Parole was being granted too easily and too quickly. Chronic offenders were being treated no differently than people who were committing crimes for the first time. Douglas Walker, the man on the back of the motorcycle, had his first run-in with the law when he was thirteen years old for trafficking heroin. He had recently been given a temporary release so he could visit his pregnant wife, and he had never returned. Did that make sense?

The group put together a proposal. At Reynolds's insistence, it was short and simple, written in laymen's language. It became known as the Three Strikes Law. Anyone convicted of a second serious or criminal offense in California, it stated, would have to serve double the sentence currently on the books. And anyone convicted of a third offense—and the definition of a third offense included every crime imaginable—would run out of chances entirely and serve a mandatory sentence of twenty-five years to life.* There were no exceptions or loopholes.

Reynolds and his group collected thousands of signatures to qualify for a statewide referendum. There are countless referendum ideas in every California election season, and most never see the light of day. But Three Strikes struck a nerve. It passed with the support of an astonishing 72 percent of the state's voters, and in the spring of 1994, Three Strikes was signed into law, almost word for word the way it was written up in Mike Reynolds's backyard. The criminologist Franklin Zimring called it "the largest penal experiment in American history." There were eighty thousand people behind bars in California's prisons in 1989. Within ten years, that number would double—and along the way, the crime rate in California came tumbling down. Between 1994 and 1998, the homicide rate in California dropped 41.4 percent, rape dropped 10.9 percent, robbery dropped by 38.7 percent, assault dropped by 22.1 percent, burglary dropped by 29.9 percent, and auto theft

---

* In practical terms, Three Strikes meant something like this: First offense (burglary). Before: 2 years. Now: 2 years. Second offense (burglary). Before: 4.5 years. Now: 9 years. Third offense (receiving stolen property). Before: 2 years. Now: 25 years to life. Other states and governments around the world would go on to pass a Three Strikes law of their own. But none went as far as California's version.

dropped by 36.6 percent. Mike Reynolds pledged, on his daughter's deathbed, to ensure that what happened to Kimber would never happen to anyone else—and out of his grief came a revolution.

"Back then, we were seeing twelve murders a day in the state of California. Today it's about six," Reynolds said. "So every day that goes by, I like to think that there's six people alive that wouldn't have been prior to this." He was sitting in the office of his house in Fresno, surrounded by pictures of himself with dignitaries of one sort or another and plaques and signed certificates and framed letters—all testifying to the extraordinary role he has played in the politics of America's largest state. "Every once in a while during the course of your life, you might have an opportunity to save somebody else's life," he went on. "You know, pull 'em out of a burning building, rescue 'em from drowning or some other crazy thing. But how many people get a chance to save six people's lives each and every day? I mean, I think, I'm so lucky."

He paused, as if he were going back over all that had happened in the nearly twenty years since he made that promise to Kimber. He was remarkably articulate and persuasive. It was obvious how, even in the midst of overwhelming grief, he would have been so compelling all those years ago on the Ray Appleton show. He started up again: "Think about the guy that invented safety belts. Do you know his name? I don't. I've got no clue. But think about how many guys that are safe, or people that are safe, as a result of safety belts or air bags or tamper-proof medicine containers. I could sit here and go right through it. Simple devices that are made by Joe Average, just like mc, that have gone on to save numerous lives. Yet we're not looking for any kudos, we're not looking for any pats on the back. All we're looking for is results, and the results are my greatest reward."

The British came to Northern Ireland with the best of intentions and ended up in the middle of thirty years of bloodshed and mayhem. They did not get what they wanted, because they did not understand that power has an important limitation. It has to be seen as legitimate, or else its use has the opposite of its intended effect. Mike Reynolds came to wield extraordinary influence in his home state. There are few other Californians of his generation whose actions and ideas have touched as many people as his have. But in his case, power seemed to have achieved its purpose. Just look at the California crime statistics. He got what he wanted, didn't he?

Nothing could be further from the truth.

3.

Let us go back to the theory of the inverted-U curve that we discussed in the chapter on class size. Inverted-U curves are all about *limits*. They illustrate the fact that "more" is not always better; there comes a point, in fact, when the extra resources that the powerful think of as their greatest advantage only serve to make things worse. The inverted-U shape clearly describes the effects of class size, and it clearly applies as well to the connection between parenting and wealth. But a few years ago, a number of scholars began to make a more ambitious argument, an argument that would end up pulling Mike Reynolds and his claims for Three Strikes into the center of two decades of controversy. What if the relationship between punishment and crime was also an inverted U? In other words, what if—past a certain point—cracking down on crime stopped having any effect on criminals and maybe even started to make crime worse?

At the time Three Strikes was passed, no one considered this possibility. Mike Reynolds and his supporters assumed that every extra criminal they locked up, and every extra year they added to the average sentence, would bring about a corresponding decrease in crime.

"Back then, even first-degree murder was just sixteen years, and you'd do eight," Mike Reynolds explained. He was describing California before his Three Strikes revolution. "It became a very viable option to go into the crime business. The human psyche follows the course of least resistance. The course of least resistance is what's easy, and it's a hell of a lot easier to go out and rob and steal and suck drugs than it is to go out and bust your ass forty hours a week and punch in on a job and take a lot of shit off customers. Who needs that? I can go out there and wave a gun around and make as much as I want as fast as I want, and if I get caught, ninety-five percent of all cases get plea-bargained down. They charge me with this, I'll admit to that, and so let's make a deal. And then third, I'm going to only serve half the time. Weigh all three, the odds are you're going to do one hell of a lot of crime before you ever in fact get caught and prosecuted."

Reynolds was making a version of the argument that Leites and Wolf made in their classic work on deterrence:

Fundamental to our analysis is the assumption that the population, as individuals or groups, behaves "rationally," that it calculates costs and benefits to the extent that they can be related to different courses of action, and makes choices accordingly. In Reynolds's view, criminals found the benefits of committing a crime in California much greater than the risks. The answer, he felt, was to raise the costs of committing a crime so high that it was no longer easier to rob and steal than to work an honest job. And for those who continued to break the law—even in the face of those altered odds—Three Strikes said, Lock them up for the rest of their lives, so they never have a chance to commit another crime again. When it came to law and order, Reynolds and the voters of California believed, "more" was always better.

But is it? Here's where the inverted-U theorist steps in. Let's start with the first assumption—that criminals respond to increases in the cost of crime by committing fewer crimes. This is clearly true when the penalties for breaking the law are really low. One of the best known case studies in criminology is about what happened in the fall of 1969 when the Montreal police went on strike for sixteen hours. Montreal was—and still is—a world-class city in a country that is considered one of the most law-abiding and stable in the world. So, what happened? Chaos. There were so many bank robberies that day—in broad daylight—that virtually every bank in the city had to close. Looters descended on downtown Montreal, smashing windows. Most shocking of all, a long-standing dispute between the city's taxi drivers and a local car service called Murray Hill Limousine Service over the right to pick up passengers from the airport exploded into violence, as if the two sides were warring principalities in medieval Europe. The taxi drivers descended on Murray Hill with gasoline bombs. Murray Hill's security guards opened fire. The taxi drivers then set a bus on fire and sent it crashing through the locked doors of the Murray Hill garage. This is *Canada* we're talking about. As soon as the police returned to work, however, order was restored. The threat of arrest and punishment *worked*.

Clearly, then, there's a big difference between having no penalties for breaking the law and having some penalties—just as there's a big difference between a class of forty students and a class of twenty-five. On the left side of the inverted U curve, interventions make a difference.

But remember, the logic of the inverted-U curve is that the same strategies that work really well at first stop working past a certain point, and that's exactly what many criminologists argue happens with punishment.

Some years ago, for example, the criminologists Richard Wright and Scott Decker interviewed eighty-six convicted armed robbers. Most of what they heard were comments like this:

> I put forth an effort to try not to think about [getting caught....It's] too much of a distraction. You can't concentrate on doing anything if you are thinking, "What's gonna happen if it doesn't go right?" As time went on, if I had made up my mind to do a robbery, [I decided] to be totally focused on that and nothing else.

Or this:

> That's why [my partners and I] get high so much. [We] get
> high and get stupid, then we don't trip off of [the threat
> of getting caught]. Whatever happens, happens....You just
> don't care at the time.

Even when pressed, the criminals interviewed by Decker
and Wright "remained indifferent to threatened sanctions." They just weren't thinking that far ahead.

The murder of his daughter made Reynolds want to
put the fear of God into California's would-be criminals—to make them think twice before crossing the line.
But that strategy doesn't work if criminals think like this.
Joe Davis and Douglas Walker—the two thugs who cor-
nered Kimber Reynolds outside the Daily Planet—were
crystal-meth addicts. Earlier that day, they had attempted a
carjacking in broad daylight. And remember what Walker
said? *I wasn't really thinking much a nothing, you know.
When it happens, it happens, you know. It just happened
suddenly. We were just out doing what we do. I mean,
that's all I can tell you.* Is this the sort of person to think
twice?

"I've talked to family friends who knew Joe and his
brother, and they asked him why he shot Kimber,"
Reynolds once said, looking back on that tragic evening.
"And he said that he already had the purse, so that wasn't
an issue. But that he'd shot her, instead, because of the
way she was looking at him. He shot her because he didn't
think she was taking him seriously, and wasn't giving him
any respect." Reynolds's own words contradict the logic

of Three Strikes. Joe Davis killed Kimber Reynolds because she would not give him the respect he thought he deserved *as he held a gun to her head and grabbed at her purse.* How on earth does changing the severity of punishment deter someone whose brain works like that? You and I are sensitive to increased punishment, because you and I are people with a stake in society. But criminals aren't. As the criminologist David Kennedy writes: "It may simply be that those who stand ready today to take a chance, often on impulse, often while impaired, on what they view as a very small likelihood of an already very serious sanction will stand ready tomorrow to take the same chance on what they still view as a very small likelihood of a somewhat more serious sanction."*

The second argument for Three Strikes—that every extra year a criminal is behind bars is another year he can't commit a crime—is just as problematic. The math doesn't add up. The average age of a California criminal in 2011 at the moment he was convicted of his Third Strike offense, for example, was forty-three. Before Three Strikes came along,

---

* Kennedy goes on to argue that if you examine actual criminal motivations, what you discover is that the calculation of risk and benefits is a "radically subjective" process. Kennedy writes: "What matters in deterrence is *what matters to offenders and potential offenders.* It is benefits and costs as they understand them and define them." As the criminologists Anthony Doob and Cheryl Marie Webster recently concluded in a massive analysis of every major punishment study. "A reasonable assessment of the research to date—with a particular focus on studies conducted in the past decade—is that sentence severity has no effect on the level of crime in society....No consistent body of literature has developed over the last twenty-five to thirty years indicating that harsh sanctions deter." What they were saying is that most countries in the developed world are in the middle part of the curve. Locking up criminals past their criminal peak and threatening younger offenders with something that younger offenders simply don't care about doesn't buy you all that much.

that man might have served something like five years for a typical felony and been released at the age of forty-eight. With Three Strikes, he would serve, at minimum, twenty-five years—and get out at sixty-eight. Logically, the question to ask is: How many crimes do criminals commit between the ages of forty-eight and sixty-eight? Not that many. Take a look at the following graphs, which show the relationship between age and crime both for aggravated assault and murder and for robbery and burglary.

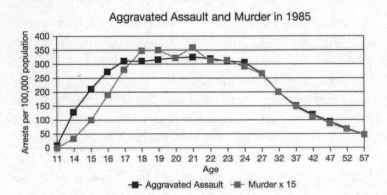

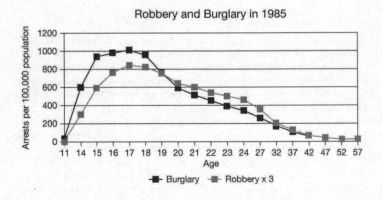

Longer sentences work on young men. But once someone passes that crucial midtwenties mark, all longer sentences do is protect us from dangerous criminals at the point that they become less dangerous. Once again, what starts out as a promising strategy stops working.

Now for the crucial question: Is there a right side to the crime-and-punishment curve—a point where cracking down starts to actually make things *worse*? The criminologist who has made this argument most persuasively is Todd Clear, and his reasoning goes something like this:

Prison has a direct effect on crime: it puts a bad person behind bars, where he can't victimize anyone else. But it also has an indirect effect on crime, in that it affects all the people with whom that criminal comes into contact. A very high number of the men who get sent to prison, for example, are fathers. (One-fourth of *juveniles* convicted of crimes have children.) And the effect on a child of having a father sent away to prison is devastating. Some criminals are lousy fathers: abusive, volatile, absent. But many are not. Their earnings—both from crime and legal jobs—help support their families. For a child, losing a father to prison is an undesirable difficulty. Having a parent incarcerated increases a child's chances of juvenile delinquency between 300 and 400 percent; it increases the odds of a serious psychiatric disorder by 250 percent.

Once the criminal has served his time, he returns to his old neighborhood. There's a good chance he's been psychologically damaged by his time behind bars. His employment prospects have plummeted. While in prison, he's lost many of his noncriminal friends and replaced them with fellow-criminal friends. And now he's back, placing even more strain emotionally and financially on the home that he shattered by leaving in the first place. Incarceration creates collateral damage. In most cases, the harm done by imprisonment is smaller than the benefits; we're still better off for putting people behind bars. But Clear's point is that if you lock up *too* many people for *too* long, the collateral damage starts to outweigh the benefit.[*]

Clear and a colleague—Dina Rose—tested his hypothesis in Tallahassee, Florida.[†] They went across the city and compared the number of people sent to prison in a given neighborhood in one year with the crime rate in that same neighborhood the following year—and tried to estimate, mathematically, if there was a point where the inverted-U curve starts to turn. They found it. "If more than two percent of the neighborhood goes to prison," Clear concluded, "the effect on crime starts to reverse."

This is what Jaffe was talking about in Brownsville.

---

[*] Clear first described his ideas some years ago in a research paper entitled "Backfire: When Incarceration Increases Crime." It presented ten arguments for why putting a very large number of people behind bars might have the opposite of its intended effect. At first, Clear couldn't get anyone to publish it. He tried the major academic journals in his field and failed at all of them. No one believed him, except the corrections community. Clear says, "One of the little-known facts of my world is that corrections professionals, for the most part, don't think that what they are doing is going to make things better. They try to run humane prisons, do the best they can. But they watch what's going on, and they're right there. They know—they say things like 'My guards are mistreating people' or 'They aren't going to leave the prison feeling better' or 'We don't give them anything they need.' This is a real embitterment experience for them. So my paper was making the rounds, people were handing it to one another, and some guy at the Oklahoma Criminal Justice Research Consortium asked if he could publish it. I said sure. He published it. And for a long time, if you Googled me, that was the first thing that came up."

[†] In its simplest formation, Clear's thesis is as follows: "Cycling a large number of young men from a particular place through imprisonment, and then returning them to that place, is not healthy for the people who live in that place."

The damage she was trying to repair with her hugs and turkeys wasn't caused by an absence of law and order. It was caused by *too much* law and order: so many fathers and brothers and cousins in prison that people in the neighborhood had come to see the law as their enemy. Brownsville was on the right side of the inverted U. In California in 1989, there were seventy-six thousand people behind bars. Ten years later, largely because of Three Strikes, that number had more than doubled. On a per capita basis, by the turn of the twenty-first century, California had between *five and eight times* as many people in prison as did Canada or Western Europe. Don't you think it's possible that Three Strikes turned some neighborhoods in California into the equivalent of Brownsville?

Reynolds is convinced that his crusade saved six lives a day, because crime rates came tumbling down in California after Three Strikes was passed. But upon closer examination, it turns out that those reductions started before Three Strikes went into effect. And while crime rates came tumbling down in California in the 1990s, they also came tumbling down in many other parts of the United States in the same period, even in places that didn't crack down on crime at all. The more Three Strikes was studied, the more elusive its effects were seen to be. Some criminologists concluded that it did lower crime. Others said that it worked but that the money spent on locking criminals up would have been better spent elsewhere. One recent study says that Three Strikes brought down the overall level of crime but, paradoxically, increased the number of violent crimes. Perhaps the largest group of studies can find no effect at all, and there is even a set of studies that argue that Three Strikes *raised* crime rates.* The state of California conducted the greatest penal experiment in American history, and after twenty years and tens of billions of dollars, nobody could ascertain whether that experiment did any good.† In November of 2012, California finally gave up. In a state referendum, the law was radically scaled back.‡

4.

Wilma Derksen was at home, trying to clean up the family room in the basement, when her daughter Candace called. It was a Friday afternoon in November, a decade before Kimber Reynolds walked out of her parents' home for the last time. The Derksens lived in Winnipeg, Manitoba, on the prairies of central Canada, and at that time of year,

---

* For example, under the law, prosecutors can choose whether to ask for Three Strikes penalties in sentencing criminals. Some cities, like San Francisco, use it sparely. In some counties in California's Central Valley—near where Mike Reynolds was from—prosecutors have used it as many as twenty-five times more often. If Three Strikes really prevents crime, then there should be a connection between how often a county uses Three Strikes and how quickly its crime falls. There isn't. If Three Strikes really acts as a deterrent, then crime rates should drop faster for those offenses that qualify for the law's penalties than for those that don't—right? So did they? They didn't.

† In the 1980s, California spent 10 percent of its budget on higher education and 3 percent on prisons. After two decades of Three Strikes, the state was spending more than 10 percent of its budget on prisons—$50,000 a year for every man and woman behind bars—while education spending had fallen below 8 percent.

‡ In November 2012, 68.6 percent of Californian voters voted in favor of Proposition 36, which stated that in order to receive a twenty-five-years-to-life sentence, a repeat offender's third felony must be of a "serious or violent" nature. Proposition 36 also allows offenders previously sentenced under Three Strikes and currently serving a life sentence to appeal for resentencing if the third conviction was not serious.

the temperature outside was well below freezing. Candace was thirteen. She was giggling, flirting with a young boy from her school. She wanted her mother to come and pick her up. Wilma did a series of calculations in her head. The Derksens had one car. Wilma had to pick up her husband, Cliff, from work. But he wouldn't be finished for another hour. She had two other children—a two-year-old and a nine-year-old. She could hear them quarreling in the other room. She would have to bundle them up first, pick up Candace, then go and pick up her husband. It would be an hour in the car with three hungry children. There was a bus. Candace was thirteen, no longer a child. The house was a mess.

"Candace, do you have money for the bus?"

"Yup."

"I can't pick you up," her mother said.

Derksen returned to her vacuuming. She folded laundry. She bustled about. Then she stopped. Something seemed wrong. She looked at the clock. Candace should have been home by now. The weather outside had suddenly turned colder. It was snowing. She remembered that Candace hadn't dressed warmly. She began to pace between the window in the front of the house and the kitchen window in the back overlooking the alleyway. Candace might come in from either direction. The minutes passed. It was time to pick up her husband. She packed up her other two children, got in the car, and drove slowly along Talbot Avenue, the road that connected the Derksens' neighborhood to Candace's school. She peered inside the windows of the 7-Eleven, where her daughter sometimes lingered. She drove to the school. The doors were locked.

"Mom, where is she?" her nine-year-old daughter asked. They drove to Cliff's office.

"I can't find Candace," she said to her husband. "I'm worried."

The four of them went back home, watching each side of the street. They began calling her friends one by one. No one had seen her since that afternoon. Wilma Derksen drove to see the boy Candace had been flirting with before she called home. He said he had last seen her walking down Talbot Avenue. The Derksens called the police. At eleven that night, two officers knocked on their door. They sat at the dining room table and asked Wilma and her husband one question after another about whether Candace had been happy at home.

The Derksens formed a search committee, recruiting people from their church and Candace's school and whomever else they could think of. They put up "Have you seen Candace?" posters all over Winnipeg, mounting the largest civilian search in the city's history. They prayed. They cried. They did not sleep. A month passed. They took their two young children to see the movie *Pinocchio* as a distraction—until the movie got to the part where Geppetto is wandering heartbroken, looking for his lost son.

In January, seven weeks after Candace Derksen's disappearance, the Derksens were at their local police station when the two sergeants assigned to the case asked if they could speak to Cliff alone. After a few minutes, they took Wilma to the room where her husband was waiting and closed the door. He waited and then spoke.

"Wilma, they've found Candace."

Her body had been left in a shed a quarter of a mile

from the Derksens' house. Her hands and feet had been tied. She had frozen to death.

5.

The Derksens suffered the same blow as Mike Reynolds. The city of Winnipeg reacted to Candace's disappearance the same way that Fresno reacted to Kimber Reynolds's murder. The Derksens grieved, just as Mike Reynolds grieved. But there the two tragedies start to diverge.

When the Derksens came home from the police station, their house began to fill with friends and relatives. They stayed all day. By ten at night, only the Derksens and a few close friends were left. They sat in the kitchen, eating cherry pie. The doorbell rang.

"I remember thinking that somebody probably left some gloves or something," Derksen said. She was sitting in the backyard of her home in Winnipeg in a garden chair as we talked. She spoke haltingly and slowly, as she remembered the longest day of her life. She opened the door. There was a stranger standing there. "He just said, 'I'm a parent of a murdered child, too.'"

The man was in his fifties, a generation older than the Derksens. His daughter had been killed in a doughnut shop a few years earlier. It had been a high-profile case in Winnipeg. A suspect named Thomas Sophonow had been arrested for the killing and tried three times. He had served four years in prison before he was exonerated by an appeals court. The man sat in their kitchen. They gave him a slice of cherry pie—and he began to talk.

"We all sat around the table and just stared at him," Wilma Derksen said. "I remember him going through all the trials—all three. He had this little black book—very much like a reporter does. He went through every detail. He even had the bills he'd paid. He lined them all up. He talked about Sophonow, the impossibility of the trials, his anger that there was no justice, the inability of the system to pin the crime on anybody. He wanted something clear. This whole process had destroyed him. It had destroyed his family. He couldn't work anymore. His health. He went through the medications he was on—I thought he was going to have a heart attack right there. I don't think he divorced his wife, but the way he spoke, it was kind of like that was over. He didn't talk much about his daughter. It was just this huge absorption with getting justice. We could see it. He didn't even have to tell us. We could feel it." His constant refrain was, I'm telling you this to let you know what lies ahead. Finally, well after midnight, the man stopped. He looked at his watch. He had finished his story. He got up and left.

"It was a horrifying day," Derksen said. "You can imagine, we were just nuts. I mean, we were—I mean, I don't even know how to explain how—kind of numb. But yet having this experience sort of broke through that numbness, because it was so vivid. I had this feeling that this is important. I don't know how to explain it. It's kind of like, take notes, this is important to you. You know, you're going through a hard time, but pay attention here."

The stranger presented his own fate as inevitable. *I'm telling you this to let you know what lies ahead.* But to the Derksens, what the man was saying was not a prediction but a warning. This is what *could* lie ahead. They could lose their health and their sanity and each other if they allowed their daughter's murder to consume them.

"If he hadn't come at that point, it might have been different," Derksen said. "The way I look at it in hindsight, he forced us to consider another option. We said to each other, 'How do we get out of this?'"

The Derksens went to sleep—or tried to. The next day was Candace's funeral. Then the Derksens agreed to talk to the press. Virtually every news outlet in the province was there. Candace Derksen's disappearance had gripped the city.

"How do you feel about whoever did this to Candace?" a reporter asked the Derksens.

"We would like to know who the person or persons are so we could share, hopefully, a love that seems to be missing in these people's lives," Cliff said.

Wilma went next. "Our main concern was to find Candace. We've found her." She continued, "I can't say at this point I forgive this person," but the stress was on the phrase "at this point." "We have all done something dreadful in our lives, or have felt the urge to."

6.

Is Wilma Derksen more—or less—of a hero than Mike Reynolds? It is tempting to ask that question. But it is not right: Each acted out of the best of intentions and chose a deeply courageous path.

The difference between the two was that they felt differently about what could be accomplished through the use of power. The Derksens fought every instinct they had as parents to strike back because they were unsure of what that could accomplish. They were not convinced of the power of giants. They grew up in the Mennonite religious tradition. The Mennonites are pacifists and outsiders. Wilma's family emigrated from Russia, where many Mennonites settled in the eighteenth century. During the Russian Revolution and the Stalinist years, the Mennonites were persecuted—viciously and repeatedly. Entire Mennonite villages were wiped out. Hundreds of adult men were shipped off to Siberia. Their farms were looted and burned to the ground—and entire communities were forced to flee to the United States and Canada. Derksen showed me a picture of her great-aunt, taken years ago in Russia. She said she remembered her grandmother talking about her sister while looking at that same picture and weeping. Her great-aunt had been a Sunday school teacher—a woman whom children flocked to—and during the Revolution, armed men had come for her and the children and massacred them. Wilma talked about her grandfather waking up in the middle of the night with nightmares about what had happened in Russia, and then getting up in the morning and going to work. She remembered her father deciding not to sue someone who owed him a lot of money, choosing instead to walk away. "This is what I believe, and how we live," he would say.

Some religious movements have as their heroes great warriors or prophets. The Mennonites have Dirk Willems, who was arrested for his religious beliefs in the sixteenth century and held in a prison tower. With the aid of a rope made of knotted rags, he let himself down from the window and escaped across the castle's ice-covered moat. A guard gave chase. Willems made it safely to the other side. The guard did not, falling through the ice into the freezing water, and Willems stopped, went back, and pulled his pursuer to safety. For his act of compassion, he was taken back to prison, tortured, and then burned slowly at the stake as he repeated "Oh, my Lord, my God" seventy times over.[*]

"I was taught that there was an alternative way to deal with injustice," Derksen said. "I was taught it in school. We were taught the history of persecution. We had this picture of martyrdom that went right back to the sixteenth century. The whole Mennonite philosophy is that we forgive and we move on." To the Mennonites, forgiveness is a religious imperative: *Forgive those who trespass against you.* But it is also a very practical strategy based on the belief that there are profound limits to what the formal mechanisms of retribution can accomplish. The Mennonites believe in the inverted-U curve.

---

[*] In the book *Amish Grace,* there is a story of a young Amish mother whose five-year-old son was struck and critically injured by a speeding car. The Amish, like the Mennonites, are heirs to the tradition of Dirk Willems. They suffered alongside the Mennonites in the early years of their faith. In the Mennonite and Amish tradition, there are countless stories like this one:

> As the investigating officer placed the driver of the car in the police cruiser to take him for an alcohol test, the mother of the injured child approached the squad car to speak with the officer. With her young daughter tugging at her dress, the mother said, "Please take care of the boy." Assuming she meant her critically ill son, the officer replied, "The ambulance people and doctor will do the best they can. The rest is up to God." The mother pointed to the suspect in the back of the police car. "I mean the driver. We forgive him."

Mike Reynolds had none of that understanding of limits. He believed, as a matter of principle, that the state and the law could deliver justice for his daughter's death. At one point, Reynolds spoke of the infamous Jerry DeWayne Williams case, which involved a young man arrested for grabbing a slice of pizza from four children on the Redondo Beach pier just south of Los Angeles. Because Williams had five previous convictions, for everything from robbery to drug possession to violating parole, the pizza-slice theft counted as his third strike. He was sentenced to twenty-five years to life.[*] Williams had a longer sentence than his cellmate, who was a murderer.

In retrospect, the Williams case was the beginning of the end for Mike Reynolds's crusade. It highlighted everything that was wrong with Three Strikes. The law could not distinguish between pizza thieves and murderers. But Mike Reynolds never understood why the Williams case provoked so much public outrage. To him, Williams had violated a fundamental principle: he had repeatedly broken society's rules and thereby forfeited his right to freedom. It was as simple as that. "Look," Reynolds told me, "those that are actually going down on third strikes, they got there the old-fashioned way—they earned it." What mattered to him was that the law made an example of repeat offenders. "Every time the media has done a story on some idiot that steals a slice of pizza and it was his third strike," he went on, "that does more to stop crime than anything else in the state."

---

[*] Williams was released a few years later after a judge reduced his sentence, and his case became the rallying cry for the anti–Three Strikes movement.

The British acted from the same principle in the early days of the Troubles. People cannot be allowed to make bombs and harbor automatic weapons and shoot one another in broad daylight. No civil society can survive under those circumstances. General Freeland had every right to get tough with thugs and gunmen.

What Freeland did not understand, however, was the same thing that Reynolds did not understand: there comes a point where the best-intentioned application of power and authority begins to backfire. Searching the first house in the Lower Falls made sense. Ransacking the entire neighborhood only made things worse. By the mid-1970s, every Catholic household in Northern Ireland had been searched, on average, twice. In some neighborhoods, that number reached ten times or more. Between 1972 and 1977, *one in four* Catholic men in Northern Ireland between the ages of sixteen and forty-four were arrested at least once. Even if every one of those people had done something illegal, that level of severity cannot succeed.*

This final lesson about the limits of power is not easy to learn. It requires that those in positions of authority accept that what they thought of as their greatest advantage—the fact that they could search as many homes as they wanted and arrest as many people as they wanted and imprison people for as long as they wanted—has real constraints. Caroline Sacks faced a version of this when

---

* By the mid-1990s, the IRA was organizing daily bus trips to the prison outside Belfast, as if it were an amusement park. "Almost everyone in the Catholic ghettos has a father, brother, uncle, or cousin who has been in prison," the political scientist John Soule wrote at the height of the Troubles. "Young people in this atmosphere come to learn that prison is a badge of honor rather than a disgrace."

she realized that what she thought was an advantage actually put her at a disadvantage. But it is one thing to acknowledge the limitations of your own advantages if you are faced with the choice between a very good school and a very, very good school. It is quite another when you have held your daughter's hand as she lay dying in a hospital bed. "Daddy can fix everything, and when this happened to our daughter, it was something I couldn't fix," Reynolds said. What he promised his daughter was that he would stand up and say, Enough. He cannot be faulted for that. But the tragedy of Mike Reynolds was that in fulfilling that promise, he left California worse off than it had been before.

Over the years, many people have come to Fresno to speak to Reynolds about Three Strikes: the long drive up from Los Angeles into the flat fields of the Central Valley has become a kind of pilgrimage. It is Reynolds's habit to take his visitors to the Daily Planet—the restaurant where his daughter ate before she was killed across the street. I heard about one of those visits before I made the same journey. Reynolds had gotten into an argument with the restaurant's owner. She told him to stop bringing people around on tours. Reynolds was harming her business. "When will this be over?" she asked him. Reynolds was livid. "Sure, it's hurt her business," he said, "but it's wrecked our lives. I told her it will be over when my daughter comes back."

At the end of our interview, Reynolds said he wanted to show me where his daughter was murdered. I couldn't say yes. It was too much. So Reynolds reached across the table and placed his hand on my arm.

"Do you carry a wallet?" he said. He handed me a passport-size photo of his daughter. "That was taken a month before Kimber was murdered. Maybe set that in there and think about that when you open your wallet. Sometimes you need to put a face with something like this." Mike Reynolds would always be grieving. "That kid had everything to live for. To have something like this happen, to have somebody kill her in cold blood like that—that's bullshit. It's just gotta be stopped."

7.

In 2007, the Derksens got a call from the police. "I put them off for two months," Wilma Derksen said. What could it possibly be about? It had been twenty years since Candace's disappearance. They had tried to move on. What good could come from opening old wounds? Finally they responded. The police came. They said, "We've found the person who killed Candace."

The shed where Candace's body was found had been stored all those years in a police warehouse, and DNA from the scene had now been matched to a man named Mark Grant. He had been living not far from the Derksens. He had a history of sexual offenses and had spent most of his adult life behind bars. In January of 2011, Grant was brought to trial.

Derksen says that she was terrified. She didn't know how she would react. Her daughter's memory had been settled in her mind, and now everything was being dredged up. She sat in the courtroom. Grant was puffed up, pasty-looking. His hair was white. He looked unwell and diminished. "His anger toward us, his hostility, were so weird," she said. "I didn't know why he was angry with us, when we should have been angry with him. It probably wasn't until the very end of the preliminary hearing that I finally looked at him, you know, and said to myself, *You're the person who killed Candace.* I remember the two of us looking at each other and just the unbelief of it: *Who are you? How could you? How can you be like this?*

"The worst moment for me was when—I'm going to cry—was when I..." She stopped and apologized for her tears. "I realized that he had hog-tied Candace and what that meant. Sexuality takes on different forms, and I hadn't realized..." She stopped again. "I'm a naive Mennonite. And to realize that his pleasure came out of tying Candace up and watching her suffer, that he gained pleasure out of torturing her...I don't know if it makes any sense. To me, that's even worse than lust or rape, you know? It's inhuman. I can understand sexual desire gone awry. But this is Hitler. This is horrible. This is the worst."

It was one thing to forgive in the abstract. When Candace was killed, they didn't know her murderer: he was someone without a name or a face. But now they *knew.*

"How can you forgive somebody like that?" she went on. "My story was now much more complicated. I had to fight my way through all those feelings of *oh, why doesn't he just die? Why doesn't somebody just kill him?* That's not healthy. It's revenge. And in some way it would be torturing him, too, keeping his destiny in my hands.

"One day I sort of lost it a little bit in church. I was with a group of friends and I just railed against the sexual insanity of it. And then the next morning, one of them called me and said, 'Let's have breakfast.' Then she goes, 'No, we can't talk here. We've got to go to my apartment.' So I went to her apartment. And then she talked about her addiction to porn and sexual bondage and S and M. She had been in that world. So she understood it. She told me all about it. And then I remembered I loved her. We had worked in the ministry together. This whole dysfunction, this whole side to her, had been hidden from me."

Derksen had been talking for a long time, and the emotion had begun to take its toll. She was talking slowly and softly now. "She was very worried," Derksen went on. "She was so scared. She had seen my anger. And now would I stay locked in that anger and direct it to her? Would I reject her?" To forgive her friend, she realized, she had to forgive Grant. She could not carve out exceptions for the sake of her moral convenience.

"I fought against it," she went on. "I was reluctant. I'm not a saint. I'm not always forgiving. It's the last thing you want to do. It could have been so much easier to say"—she made a fist—"because I would have had many more people on my side. I probably would have been a huge advocate by now. I could have had a huge organization behind me."

Wilma Derksen could have been Mike Reynolds. She could have started her own version of Three Strikes. She chose not to. "It would have been easier in the beginning," she continued. "But then it would have gotten harder. I think I would have lost Cliff, I think I would have lost my children. In some ways I would be doing to others what he did to Candace."

A man employs the full power of the state in his grief and ends up plunging his government into a fruitless and costly experiment. A woman who walks away from the promise of power finds the strength to forgive—and saves her friendship, her marriage, and her sanity. The world is turned upside down.

CHAPTER NINE

André Trocmé

"WE FEEL OBLIGED TO TELL YOU
THAT THERE ARE AMONG US A
CERTAIN NUMBER OF JEWS."

1.

When France fell in June of 1940, the German Army allowed the French to set up a government in the city of Vichy. It was headed by the French World War One hero Marshal Philippe Pétain, who was granted the full powers of a dictator. Pétain cooperated actively with the Germans. He stripped Jews of their rights. He pushed them out of professions. Revoking laws against anti-Semitism, he rounded up French Jews and put them into internment camps and took a dozen other authoritarian steps, large and small, including instituting the requirement that every morning French schoolchildren honor the French flag with a full fascist salute—right arm outstretched, palm down. On the scale of the adjustments necessary under German occupation, saluting the flag each morning was a small matter. Most people complied. But not those living in the town of Le Chambon-sur-Lignon.

Le Chambon is one of a dozen villages on the Vivarais Plateau, a mountainous region not far from the Italian and Swiss borders in south-central France. The winters are snowy and harsh. The area is remote, and the closest large towns are well down the mountain, miles away. The region is heavily agricultural, with farms tucked away in and around piney woods. For several centuries, Le Chambon had been home to a variety of dissident Protestant sects, chief among them the Huguenots. The local Huguenot pastor was a man named André Trocmé. He was a pacifist. On the Sunday after France fell to the Germans, Trocmé preached a sermon at the Protestant temple of Le Chambon. "Loving, forgiving, and doing good to our adversaries is our duty," he said. "Yet we must do this without giving up, and without being cowardly. We shall resist whenever our adversaries demand of us obedience contrary to the orders of the Gospel. We shall do so without fear, but also without pride and without hate."

Giving the straight-armed fascist salute to the Vichy regime was, to Trocmé's mind, a very good example of "obedience contrary to the orders of the Gospel." He and his co-pastor, Édouard Theis, had started a school in Le Chambon several years earlier called the Collège Cévenol. They decided that there would be no flagpole and no fascist salutes at Cévenol.

Vichy's next step was to require all French teachers to sign loyalty oaths to the state. Trocmé, Theis, and the entire staff of Cévenol refused. Pétain asked for a portrait of himself to be placed in every French school. Trocmé and Theis rolled their eyes. On the one-year anniversary of the Vichy regime, Pétain ordered towns across the country to ring their church bells at noon on August 1. Trocmé told the church custodian, a woman named Amélie, not to bother. Two summer residents of the town came and complained. "The bell does not belong to the marshal, but to God," Amélie told them flatly. "It is rung for God—otherwise it is not rung."

Throughout the winter and spring of 1940, conditions for Jews across Europe grew progressively worse. A woman appeared at the Trocmés' door. She was terrified and trembling from the cold. She was Jewish, she said. Her life was in danger. She had heard Le Chambon was a welcoming place. "And I said, 'Come in,'" André Trocmé's wife, Magda, remembered years later. "And so it started."

Soon more and more Jewish refugees began showing up in Le Chambon. Trocmé took the train to Marseille to meet with a Quaker named Burns Chalmers. The Quakers provided humanitarian aid for the internment centers that had been set up in southern France. The camps were appalling places, overrun with rats, lice, and disease; at one camp alone, eleven hundred Jews died between 1940 and 1944. Many of those who survived were eventually shipped east and murdered in Nazi concentration camps. The Quakers could get people—especially children—out of the camps. But they had nowhere to send them. Trocmé volunteered Le Chambon. The trickle of Jews coming up the mountain suddenly became a flood.

In the summer of 1942, Georges Lamirand, the Vichy minister in charge of youth affairs, paid a state visit to Le Chambon. Pétain wanted him to set up youth camps around France patterned after the Hitler Youth camps in Germany.

Lamirand swept up the mountain with his entourage, resplendent in his marine-blue uniform. His agenda called for a banquet, then a march to the town's stadium for a meeting with the local youth, then a formal reception. But the banquet did not go well. The food was barely adequate. Trocmé's daughter "accidentally" spilled soup down the back of Lamirand's uniform. During the parade, the streets were deserted. At the stadium, nothing was arranged: the children milled around, jostling and gawking. At the reception, a townsperson got up and read from the New Testament Book of Romans, chapter 13, verse 8: "Owe no one anything except to love one another; for he who loves his neighbor has fulfilled the law."

Then a group of students walked up to Lamirand, and in front of the entire town presented him with a letter. It had been drafted with Trocmé's help. Earlier that summer, the Vichy police had rounded up twelve thousand Jews in Paris at the request of the Nazis. Those arrested were held in horrendous conditions at the Vélodrome d'Hiver south of Paris before being sent to the concentration camp at Auschwitz. Le Chambon, the children made it clear, wanted no part in any of this. "Mr. Minister," the letter began:

We have learned of the frightening scenes which took place three weeks ago in Paris, where the French police, on orders of the occupying power, arrested in their homes all the Jewish families in Paris to hold them in the Vél d'Hiv. The fathers were torn from their families and sent to Germany. The children torn from their mothers, who underwent the same fate as their husbands....We are afraid that the measures of deportation of the Jews will soon be applied in the southern zone.

We feel obliged to tell you that there are among us a certain number of Jews. But, we make no distinction between Jews and non-Jews. It is contrary to the Gospel teaching.

If our comrades, whose only fault is to be born in another religion, received the order to let themselves be deported, or even examined, they would disobey the order received, and we would try to hide them as best we could.

We have Jews. You're not getting them.

2.

Why didn't the Nazis come to Le Chambon and make an example of the residents? The enrollment at the school started by Trocmé and Theis rose from 18 pupils on the eve of the war to 350 by 1944. It didn't take any great powers of deduction to figure out who those extra 332 children were. Nor did the town make any great secret of what it was doing. *We feel obliged to tell you that there are among us a certain number of Jews.* One aid worker described coming up on the train from Lyon several times a month with a dozen or so Jewish children in tow. She would leave them at the Hotel May by the train station and then walk around town until she found homes for them all. In France, under the laws of Vichy, transporting and hiding Jewish refugees was plainly illegal. At other points during the war, the Nazis had demonstrated that they were not inclined to be conciliatory on the question of Jews. At one point, the Vichy police came and set up shop in Le Chambon for three weeks, searching the town and the surrounding countryside for Jewish refugees. All they could come up with were two arrests—one of whom they later released. Why didn't they just line up the whole town and ship them to Auschwitz?

Philip Hallie, who wrote the definitive history of Le Chambon, argues that the town was protected at the end of the war by Major Julius Schmehling, a senior Gestapo official in the region. There were also many sympathetic people in the local Vichy police. Sometimes André Trocmé would get a call in the middle of the night, warning him that a raid was coming the next day. Other times a local police contingent would arrive, following up on a tip about hidden refugees, and treat themselves to a long cup of coffee at the local café first, to give everyone in town ample warning of their intentions. The Germans had enough on their plate, particularly by 1943, when the war on the Eastern Front began to go sour for them. They might not have wanted to pick a fight with a group of disputatious and disagreeable mountain folk.

But the best answer is the one that *David and Goliath* has tried to make plain—that wiping out a town or a people or a movement is never as simple as it looks. The powerful are not as powerful as they seem—nor the weak as weak. The Huguenots of Le Chambon were descendants of France's original Protestant population, and the truth is that people had tried—and failed—to wipe them out before. The Huguenots broke away from the Catholic

Church during the Reformation, which made them outlaws in the eyes of the French state. One king after another tried to make them reunite with the Catholic Church. The Huguenot movement was banned. There were public roundups and massacres. Thousands of Huguenot men were sent to the gallows. Women were imprisoned for life. Children were put in Catholic foster homes in order to rid them of their faith. The reign of terror lasted more than a century. In the late seventeenth century, two hundred thousand Huguenots fled France for other countries in Europe and North America. Those few who remained were forced underground. They worshiped in secrecy, in remote forests. They retreated to high mountain villages on the Vivarais Plateau. They formed a seminary in Switzerland and smuggled clergy across the border. They learned the arts of evasion and disguise. They stayed and learned—as the Londoners did during the Blitz—that they were not really afraid. They were just afraid of being afraid.*

"The people in our village knew already what persecutions were," Magda Trocmé said. "They talked often about their ancestors. Many years went by and they forgot, but when the Germans came, they remembered and

---

* The historian Christine van der Zanden calls the area the Plateau of Hospitality. The region had a long history of taking in refugees. In 1790, the French Assembly declared that all Catholic clergy, under penalty of imprisonment, had to pledge an oath to the state, making the church subordinate to the government. Those who refused to sign the pledge fled for their lives. Where did many of them go? To the Vivarais Plateau, a community already well practiced in the arts of defiance. The number of dissenters grew. During the First World War, the people of the plateau took in refugees. During the Spanish Civil War, they took in people fleeing the fascist army of General Franco. They took in socialists and communists from Austria and Germany in the early days of the Nazi terror.

were able to understand the persecution of the Jews better perhaps than people in other villages, for they had already had a kind of preparation." When the first refugee appeared at her door, Magda Trocmé said it never occurred to her to say no. "I did not know that it would be dangerous. Nobody thought of that." *I did not know that it would be dangerous? Nobody thought of that?* In the rest of France, all people thought about was how dangerous life was. But the people of Le Chambon were past that. When the first Jewish refugees arrived, the townsfolk drew up false papers for them—not a difficult thing to do if your community has spent a century hiding its true beliefs from the government. They hid the Jews in the places they had been hiding refugees for generations and smuggled them across the border to Switzerland along the same trails they had used for three hundred years. Magda Trocmé went on: "Sometimes people ask me, 'How did you make a decision?' There was no decision to make. The issue was, Do you think we are all brothers or not? Do you think it is unjust to turn in the Jews or not? Then let us try to help!"

In attempting to wipe out the Huguenots, the French created instead a pocket in their own country that was all but impossible to wipe out.

As André Trocmé once said, "How could the Nazis ever get to the end of the resources of such a people?"

3.

André Trocmé was born in 1901. He was tall and solidly built and had a long nose and sharp blue eyes. He worked tirelessly, lumbering from one end of Le Chambon to the other. His daughter, Nelly, writes that "a sense of duty exuded from his pores." He called himself a pacifist, but there was nothing pacifist about him. He and his wife, Magda, were famous for their shouting matches. He was often described as *un violent vaincu par Dieu*—a violent man conquered by God. "A curse on him who begins in gentleness," he wrote in his journal. "He shall finish in insipidity and cowardice, and shall never set foot in the great liberating current of Christianity."

Six months after the visit from Minister Lamirand, Trocmé and Édouard Theis were arrested and imprisoned in an internment camp (where, according to Hallie, "personal possessions were taken from them, and noses were measured to ascertain whether or not they were Jewish"). After a month, the two were told they would be released—but only on the condition that they pledged to "obey without question orders given me by governmental authorities for the safety of France, and for the good of the National Revolution of Marshal Pétain." Trocmé and Theis refused. The director of the camp came up to them in disbelief. Most of the people in the camp would end up dead in a gas chamber. In exchange for signing their names on a piece of paper, to a bit of patriotic boilerplate, the two men were getting a free ticket home.

"What is this?" the camp director shouted at them. "This oath has nothing in it contrary to your conscience! The marshal wishes only the good of France!"

"On at least one point we disagree with the marshal," Trocmé replied. "He delivers the Jews to the Germans.... When we get home we shall certainly continue to be opposed, and we shall certainly continue to disobey orders from the government. How could we sign this now?"

Finally the prison officials gave up and sent them home.

Later in the war, when the Gestapo stepped up their scrutiny of Le Chambon, Trocmé and Theis were forced to flee. Theis joined up with the underground and spent the remainder of the war ferrying Jews across the Alps to the safety of Switzerland. ("It was not reasonable," he explained to Hallie of his decision. "But you know, I had to do it, anyway.") Trocmé moved from town to town, carrying false papers. Despite his precautions, he was arrested in a police roundup at the Lyon railway station. He was thrown into turmoil—not just at the prospect of discovery but also and more crucially at the question of what to do about his false papers. Hallie writes:

> His identity card gave his name as Béguet, and they would ask him if this was indeed true. Then he would have to lie in order to hide his identity. But he was not able to lie; lying, especially to save his own skin, was "sliding toward those compromises that God had not called upon me to make," he wrote in his autobiographical notes on this incident. Saving the lives of others—and even saving his own life—with false identity cards was one thing, but standing before another human being and speaking lies to him only for the sake of self-preservation was something different.

Is there really a moral difference between giving yourself a false name on your identity card and stating that false name to a police officer? Perhaps not. Trocmé, at the time, was traveling with one of his young sons. He was still actively engaged in the business of hiding refugees. He had plenty of extenuating circumstances, in other words, to justify a white lie.

But that is not the point. Trocmé was disagreeable in the same magnificent sense as Jay Freireich and Wyatt Walker and Fred Shuttlesworth. And the beauty of the disagreeable is that they do not make calculations like the rest of us. Walker and Shuttlesworth had nothing to lose. If your house has been bombed and the Klan has surrounded your car and pummeled you with their fists, how can things get any worse? Jay Freireich was told to stop what he was doing and warned that he was risking his career. He was heckled and abandoned by his peers. He held dying children in his arms and jabbed a thick needle into their shinbones. But he had been through worse. The Huguenots who put their own self-interest first had long ago converted to some other faith or given up or moved away. What was left was stubbornness and defiance.

The arresting officer, it turned out, never asked for Trocmé's papers. Trocmé talked the police into taking him back to the railway station, where he met up with his son and slipped out a side door. But had the police asked him if he was Béguet, he had already decided to tell the truth: "I am not Monsieur Béguet. I am Pastor André Trocmé." *He didn't care.* If you are Goliath, how on earth do you defeat someone who thinks like that? You could kill him, of course. But that is simply a variant of the same approach that backfired so spectacularly for the British in Northern Ireland and for the Three Strikes campaign in California. The excessive use of force creates legitimacy problems, and force without legitimacy leads to defiance, not submission. You could kill

André Trocmé. But in all likelihood, all that would mean is that another André Trocmé would rise in his place.

When Trocmé was ten years old, his family drove one day to their house in the country. He was in the backseat with his two brothers and a cousin. His parents were in the front. His father grew angry at a car driving too slowly in front of them and pulled out to pass. "Paul, Paul, not so fast. There's going to be an accident!" his mother cried out. The car spun out of control. The young André pushed himself away from the wreckage. His father and brothers and cousin were fine. His mother was not. He saw her lying lifeless thirty feet away. Confronting a Nazi officer paled in comparison with seeing your mother's body by the side of the road. As Trocmé wrote to his deceased mother, many years later:

> If I have sinned so much, if I have been, since then, so solitary, if my soul has taken such a swirling and solitary movement, if I have doubted everything, if I have been a fatalist, and have been a pessimistic child who awaits death every day, and who almost seeks it out, if I have opened myself slowly and late to happiness, and if I am still a somber man, incapable of laughing whole-heartedly, it is because you left me that June 24th upon that road.
>
> But if I have believed in eternal realities...if I have thrust myself toward them, it is also because I was alone, because you were no longer there to be my God, to fill my heart with your abundant and dominating life.

It was not the privileged and the fortunate who took in the Jews in France. It was the marginal and the damaged, which should remind us that there are real limits to what evil and misfortune can accomplish. If you take away the gift of reading, you create the gift of listening. If you bomb a city, you leave behind death and destruction. But you create a community of remote misses. If you take away a mother or a father, you cause suffering and despair. But one time in ten, out of that despair rises an indomitable force. You see the giant and the shepherd in the Valley of Elah and your eye is drawn to the man with the sword and shield and the glittering armor. But so much of what is beautiful and valuable in the world comes from the shepherd, who has more strength and purpose than we ever imagine.

The eldest son of Magda and André Trocmé was Jean-Pierre. He was a sensitive and gifted adolescent. André Trocmé was devoted to him. One evening near the end of the war, the family went to see a recital of Villon's poem "The Ballad of the Hanged Men." The next night, they came home from dinner and found Jean-Pierre hanging from a noose in the bathroom. Trocmé stumbled into the woods, crying out, "Jean-Pierre! Jean-Pierre!" Later, he wrote:

> Even today I carry a death within myself, the death of my son, and I am like a decapitated pine. Pine trees do not regenerate their tops. They stay twisted, crippled.

But surely he must have paused when he wrote those words, because everything that had happened in Le Chambon suggested that there was more to the story than that. Then he wrote:

> They grow in thickness, perhaps, and that is what I am doing.

Acknowledgments

David and Goliath has benefited greatly from the wisdom and generosity of many others: my parents; my agent, Tina Bennett; my *New Yorker* editor, Henry Finder; Geoff Shandler and Pamela Marshall and the whole team at Little, Brown; Helen Conford at Penguin in England; and too many of my friends to count. Among them: Charles Randolph, Sarah Lyall, Jacob Weisberg, the Lyntons, Terry Martin, Tali Farhadian, Emily Hunt, and Robert McCrum. Special thanks to my fact checkers, Jane Kim and Carey Dunne, and my theological consultant, Jim Loepp Thiessen of the Gathering Church in Kitchener, Ontario. And Bill Phillips, as always. You are the maestro.

Notes

INTRODUCTION: GOLIATH

The scholarly literature on the battle between David and Goliath is extensive. Here is one source: John A. Beck, "David and Goliath, a Story of Place: The Narrative-Geographical Shaping of 1 Samuel 17," *Westminster Theological Journal* 68 (2006): 321–30.

Claudius Quadrigarius's account of single combat is from Ross Cowan, *For the Glory of Rome* (Greenhill Books, 2007), 140. No one in ancient times would have doubted David's tactical advantage once it was known that he was an expert in slinging. Here is the Roman military historian Vegetius (*Military Matters*, Book I):

> Recruits are to be taught the art of throwing stones both with the hand and sling. The inhabitants of the Balearic Islands are said to have been the inventors of slings, and to have managed them with surprising dexterity, owing to the manner of bringing up their children. The children were not allowed to have their food by their mothers till they had first struck it with their sling. Soldiers, notwithstanding their defensive armor, are often more annoyed by the round stones from the sling than by all the arrows of the enemy. Stones kill without mangling the body, and the contusion is mortal without loss of blood. It is universally known the ancients employed slingers in all their engagements. There is the greater reason for instructing all troops, without exception, in this exercise, as the sling cannot be reckoned any encumbrance, and often is of the greatest service, especially when they are obliged to engage in stony places, to defend a mountain or an eminence, or to repulse an enemy at the attack of a castle or city.

Moshe Garsiel's chapter "The Valley of Elah Battle and the Duel of David with Goliath: Between History and Artistic Theological Historiography" appears in *Homeland and Exile* (Brill, 2009).

Baruch Halpern's discussion of the sling appears in *David's Secret Demons* (Eerdmans Publishing, 2001), 11.

For Eitan Hirsch's calculations, see Eitan Hirsch, Jaime Cuadros, and Joseph Backofen, "David's Choice: A Sling and Tactical Advantage," *International Symposium on Ballistics* (Jerusalem, May 21–24, 1995). Hirsch's paper is full of paragraphs like this:

> Experiments with cadavers and hybrid simulation models indicate that an impact energy of 72 joules is sufficient to perforate (but not exit) a cranium when it is impacted on the parietal portion of the skull with a 6.35 mm diameter steel projectile at 370 m/s. A pro-

jectile does not have to perforate the skull, but just crush a part of the frontal bone to produce a depressed skull fracture (at best), or a stunning blow to render a person unconscious. Such an impact produces strain in the blood vessels and brain tissues upon impact to the front of the skull…because the motion of the brain lags the motion of the skull. The impact energy required to achieve these two effects are much lower, on the order of 40 to 20 joules, respectively.

Hirsch presented his analysis at a scientific meeting. In an e-mail to me, he added:

> A day after the lecture was given an attendee came to me telling me that in the creek on the site where the duel took place one could find stones of Barium Sulphate which had a mass density of 4.2 grams/cc (compared to about 2.4 in usually found stones). If David chose one of those to use against Goliath it gave him significant advantage in addition to the calculated numbers brought in the tables.

Robert Dohrenwend's article "The Sling: Forgotten Firepower of Antiquity" (*Journal of Asian Martial Arts* 11, no. 2 [2002]) is a very good introduction to the power of the sling.

Moshe Dayan's essay about David and Goliath, "Spirit of the Fighters," appears in *Courageous Actions—Twenty Years of Independence* 11 (1968): 50–52.

The idea that Goliath suffered from acromegaly appears to have first been suggested in C. E. Jackson, P. C. Talbert, and H. D. Caylor, "Hereditary Hyperparathyroidism," *Journal of the Indiana State Medical Association* 53 (1960): 1313–16, and then by David Rabin and Pauline Rabin in a letter to the *New England Journal of Medicine* on October 20, 1983. Subsequently a number of other medical experts reached the same conclusion. In a letter to the journal *Radiology* (July 1990), Stanley Sprecher writes:

> Undoubtedly Goliath's great size was due to acromegaly secondary to a pituitary macroadenoma. This pituitary adenoma was apparently large enough to induce visual field deficits by its pressure on the optic chiasm, which made Goliath unable to follow the young David as he circled him. The stone entered Goliath's cranial vault through a markedly thinned frontal bone, which resulted from enlargement of the frontal paranasal sinus, a frequent feature of acromegaly. The stone lodged in Goliath's enlarged pituitary and caused a pituitary hemorrhage, resulting in transtentorial herniation and death.

The most complete account of Goliath's disability is by the Israeli neurologist Vladimir Berginer. It is Berginer who stresses the suspicious nature of Goliath's shield bearer. See Vladimir Berginer and Chaim Cohen, "The Nature of Goliath's Visual Disorder and the Actual Role of His Personal Bodyguard," *Ancient Near Eastern Studies* 43 (2006):

27–44. Berginer and Cohen write: "We thus surmise that the phrase 'shield bearer' was originally used by the Philistines as an honorable euphemistic title for the individual who served as Goliath's guide for the visually impaired so as not to denigrate the military reputation of the Philistine heroic warrior. They may well have even given him a shield to carry in order to camouflage his true function!"

CHAPTER ONE: VIVEK RANADIVÉ

Ivan Arreguín-Toft's book about underdog winners is *How the Weak Win Wars* (Cambridge University Press, 2006).

"We could not lightly draw water after dark" is from T. E. Lawrence, *Seven Pillars of Wisdom* (Wordsworth Editions, 1999).

William R. Polk's history of unconventional warfare is *Violent Politics: A History of Insurgency, Terrorism, and Guerrilla War, from the American Revolution to Iraq* (Harper, 2008).

CHAPTER TWO: TERESA DEBRITO

Perhaps the best-known study of the effects of class reduction was the Project STAR (Student-Teacher Achievement Ratio) in Tennessee in the 1980s. STAR took six thousand children and randomly assigned them to either a small or a large class and then followed them throughout elementary school. The study showed that the children in the smaller classes outperformed those children in the larger classes by a small but meaningful degree. The countries and U.S. states that subsequently spent billions of dollars on class-size reduction did so, in large part, because of the results of STAR. But STAR was far from perfect. There is strong evidence, for example, of an unusual amount of movement between the large- and small-class arms of the study. It seems that a large number of highly motivated parents might have succeeded in getting their children transferred into the small classrooms—and underperforming children may have been dropped from the same classes. More problematic is that the study wasn't blind. The teachers with the smaller classes *knew* that it was their classrooms that would be under scrutiny. Normally in science, the results of experiments that are "unblinded" are considered dubious. For a cogent critique of STAR, see Eric Hanushek, "Some Findings from an Independent Investigation of the Tennessee STAR Experiment and from Other Investigations of Class Size Effects," *Educational Evaluation and Policy Analysis* 21, no. 2 (summer 1999): 143–63. A "natural experiment" of the sort that Hoxby did is much more valuable. For what Hoxby found, see Caroline Hoxby, "The Effects of Class Size on Student Achievement: New Evidence from Population Variation," *Quarterly Journal of Economics* 115, no. 4 (November 2000): 1239–85. For more discussion of class size, see Eric Hanushek, *The Evidence on Class Size* (University of Rochester Press, 1998); Eric Hanushek and Alfred Lindseth, *Schoolhouses, Courthouses and Statehouses: Solving the Funding-Achievement Puzzle in America's Public Schools* (Princeton University Press, 2009), 272; and Ludger Wössmann and Martin R. West, "Class-Size Effects in School Systems Around the World: Evidence from Between-Grade Variation in TIMSS," *European Economic Review* (March 26, 2002).

For studies of money and happiness, see Daniel Kahneman and Angus Deaton, "High Income Improves Evaluation of Life but Not Emotional Well-Being," *Proceedings of the National Academy of Sciences* 107, no. 38 (August 2010): 107. Barry Schwartz and Adam Grant discuss happiness in terms of an inverted-U curve in "Too Much of a Good Thing: The Challenge and Opportunity of the Inverted U," *Perspectives on Psychological Science* 6, no. 1 (January 2011): 61–76.

In "Using Maimonides' Rule to Estimate the Effect of Class Size on Scholastic Achievement" (*Quarterly Journal of Economics* [May 1999]), Joshua Angrist and Victor Lavy acknowledge the possibility that what they are seeing is a left-side phenomenon: "It is also worth considering whether results for Israel are likely to be relevant for the United States or other developed countries. In addition to cultural and political differences, Israel has a lower standard of living and spends less on education per pupil than the United States and some OECD countries. And, as noted above, Israel also has larger class sizes than the United States, United Kingdom, and Canada. So the results presented here may be showing evidence of a marginal return for reductions in class size over a range of sizes that are not characteristic of most American schools."

For a discussion of the relationship between drinking and health as an inverted-U curve, see Augusto Di Castelnuovo et al., "Alcohol Dosing and Total Mortality in Men and Women: An Updated Meta-analysis of 34 Prospective Studies," *Archives of Internal Medicine* 166, no. 22 (2006): 2437–45.

Jesse Levin's research on class size and achievement is "For Whom the Reductions Count: A Quantile Regression Analysis of Class Size and Peer Effects on Scholastic Achievement," *Empirical Economics* 26 (2001): 221. The obsession with small class sizes has real consequences. The one thing that all educational researchers agree about is that teacher quality matters far more than the size of the class. A great teacher can teach your child a year and a half's material in one year. A below-average teacher might teach your child half a year's material in one year. That's a year's difference in learning, *in one year.* That suggests that there is much more to be gained by focusing on the person at the front of the classroom than on the number of people sitting in the classroom. The problem is that great teachers are rare. There simply aren't enough people with the specialized and complex set of skills necessary to inspire large groups of children year in, year out.

So what should we be doing? We should be firing bad teachers. Or coaching them in order to improve their performance. Or paying the best teachers more in exchange for taking more students. Or raising the profile of the teaching profession to try to attract more of the special kind of person who can excel in the classroom. The *last* thing we should do in response to the problem of there being too many poor teachers and not enough good teachers, though, is go out and hire more teachers. Yet that is precisely what many industrialized countries have done in recent years, as they have become obsessed with lowering class size. It is also worth pointing out that *nothing* costs more than reducing class size. It costs so much to hire extra teachers and build them classrooms in which to teach that there is precious little money left over to pay teachers. As a result, the salaries of teachers, relative to other professions, have steadily fallen over the past fifty years.

In the past generation, the American educational system has decided not to seek the very best teachers, give them lots of kids to teach, and pay them more—which would help children the most. It has decided to hire every teacher it can get its hands on and pay them less. (The growth in spending on public education over the course of the twentieth century in the United States was staggering: between 1890 and 1990, in constant dollars, the bill went from $2 billion to $187 billion, with that spending accelerating toward the end of the century. That money went, overwhelmingly, toward hiring more teachers in order to make classes smaller. Between 1970 and 1990, the pupil-staff ratio in American public schools fell from 20.5 to 15.4, and paying for all those extra teachers accounted for the lion's share of the tens of billions of dollars in extra educational spending in those years.

Why did this happen? One answer lies in the politics of the educational world—in the power of teachers and their unions, and in the peculiarities of the way schools are funded. But that is not an entirely satisfactory explanation. The American public—and the Canadian public and the British public and the French public and on and on—wasn't forced to spend all that money on lowering class size. They *wanted* smaller classes. Why? Because the people and countries who are wealthy enough to pay for things like really small classes have a hard time understanding that the things their wealth can buy might not always make them better off.

CHAPTER THREE: CAROLINE SACKS

The discussion of the Impressionists is based on several books, principally: John Rewald, *The History of Impressionism* (MOMA, 1973); Ross King, *The Judgment of Paris* (Walker Publishing, 2006), which has a marvelous description of the world of the Salon; Sue Roe, *The Private Lives of the Impressionists* (Harper Collins, 2006); and Harrison White and Cynthia White, *Canvases and Careers: Institutional Change in the French Painting World* (Wiley & Sons, 1965), 150.

The first academic paper to raise the issue of relative deprivation with respect to school choice was James Davis's "The Campus as Frog Pond: An Application of the Theory of Relative Deprivation to Career Decisions of College Men," *The American Journal of Sociology* 72, no. 1 (July 1966). Davis concludes:

> At the level of the individual, [my findings] challenge the notion that getting into the "best possible" school is the most efficient route to occupational mobility. Counselors and parents might well consider the drawbacks as well as the advantages of sending a boy to a "fine" college, if, when doing so, it is fairly certain he will end up in the bottom ranks of his graduating class. The aphorism "It is better to be a big frog in a small pond than a small frog in a big pond" is not perfect advice, but it is not trivial.

Stouffer's study (coauthored with Edward A. Suchman, Leland C. DeVinney, Shirley A. Star, and Robin M. Williams Jr.) appears in *The American Soldier: Adjustment During Army Life*, vol. 1 of *Studies in Social Psychology in World War II* (Princeton University Press, 1949), 251.

For studies of so-called happy countries, see Mary Daly, Andrew Oswald, Daniel Wilson, and Stephen Wu, "Dark Contrasts: The Paradox of High Rates of Suicide in Happy Places," *Journal of Economic Behavior and Organization* 80 (December 2011), and Carol Graham, *Happiness Around the World: The Paradox of Happy Peasants and Miserable Millionaires* (Oxford University Press, 2009).

Herbert Marsh teaches in the Department of Education at Oxford University. His academic output over the course of his career has been extraordinary. On the subject of "Big Fish/Little Pond" alone, he has written countless papers. A good place to start is H. Marsh, M. Seaton, et al., "The Big-Fish-Little-Pond-Effect Stands Up to Critical Scrutiny: Implications for Theory, Methodology, and Future Research," *Educational Psychology Review* 20 (2008): 319–50.

For statistics on STEM programs, see Rogers Elliott, A. Christopher Strenta, et al., "The Role of Ethnicity in Choosing and Leaving Science in Highly Selective Institutions," *Research in Higher Education* 37, no. 6 (December 1996), and Mitchell Chang, Oscar Cerna, et al., "The Contradictory Roles of Institutional Status in Retaining Underrepresented

Minorities in Biomedical and Behavioral Science Majors," *The Review of Higher Education* 31, no. 4 (summer 2008).

John P. Conley and Ali Sina Önder's breakdown of research papers appears in "An Empirical Guide to Hiring Assistant Professors in Economics," *Vanderbilt University Department of Economics Working Papers Series,* May 28, 2013.

The reference to Fred Glimp's "happy-bottom-quarter" policy comes from Jerome Karabel's fascinating book *The Chosen: The Hidden History of Admission and Exclusion at Harvard, Yale, and Princeton* (Mariner Books, 2006), 291. Karabel comments:

> Would it be better, [Glimp] implied, if the students at the bottom were content to be there? Thus the renowned (some would say notorious) Harvard admission practice known as the "happy-bottom-quarter policy" was born....Glimp's goal was to identify "the right bottom-quarter students—men who have the perspective, ego strength, or extracurricular outlets for maintaining their self-respect (or whatever) while making the most of their opportunities at a C-level."

The question of affirmative action is worth discussing in some detail. Take a look at the following table from the work of Richard Sander and Stuart Taylor, *Mismatch: How Affirmative Action Hurts Students It's Intended to Help, and Why Universities Won't Admit It* (Basic Books, 2012). It shows where African-Americans rank in their law school classes compared with white students. The class ranks run from 1 to 10, with 1 being the bottom tenth of the class and 10 being the top.

Rank	Black	White	Other
1.	51.6	5.6	14.8
2.	19.8	7.2	20.0
3.	11.1	9.2	13.4
4.	4.0	10.2	11.5
5.	5.6	10.6	8.9
6.	1.6	11.0	8.2
7.	1.6	11.5	6.2
8.	2.4	11.2	6.9
9.	0.8	11.8	4.9
10.	1.6	11.7	5.2

There are a lot of numbers in this table, but only two rows really matter—the first and second rows, showing the racial breakdown of the bottom of the average American law school class.

Rank	Black	White	Other
1.	51.6	5.6	14.8
2.	19.8	7.2	20.0

Here is the way that Sander and Taylor analyze the costs of this strategy. Imagine two black law school students with identical grades and identical test scores. Both are admitted to an elite law school under an affirmative-action program. One accepts and one declines. The one who declines chooses instead—for logistical or financial or family reasons—to attend his or her second choice, a less prestigious and less selective law school. Sander and Taylor looked at a large sample of these kinds of "matched pairs" and compared how well they did on four measures: law school graduation rate, passing the bar on their first attempt, ever passing the bar, and actually practicing law. The comparison is not even close. By every measure, black students who don't go to the "best" school they get into outperform those who do.

Career Success	White	Black	Black (Affirmative Action)
Percentage who graduate from law school	91.8	93.2	86.2
Percentage who pass bar first attempt	91.3	88.5	70.5
Percentage who ever pass bar	96.4	90.4	82.8
Percentage who practice law	82.5	75.9	66.5

Sander and Taylor argue very convincingly that if you are black and you really want to be a lawyer, you should do what the Impressionists did and steer clear of the Big Pond. Don't accept any offer from a school that wants to bump you up a notch. Go to the school you would have otherwise gone to. Sander and Taylor put it bluntly: "At any law school the bottom of the class is a lousy place to be."

By the way, those of you who read my book *Outliers*, where I also discussed affirmative action and law school, know that in the book I was interested in making a very different point—that the usefulness of IQ and intelligence starts to level off at a certain point, meaning that the kinds of distinctions among students made by elite institutions are not necessarily useful. In other words, it is wrong to assume that a lawyer admitted to a very good law school with lesser credentials will be a less able lawyer than those admitted with sterling credentials. To back this up, I used data from the University of Michigan Law School, which shows that their black law school affirmative-action graduates had careers every bit as distinguished as their white graduates.

Do I still believe this? Yes and no. I think the general point about the benefits of intelligence leveling off at the high end remains. But I now think the specific point made about law schools in *Outliers* was, in retrospect, naive. I was not familiar with relative deprivation theory at the time. I am now a good deal more skeptical of affirmative-action programs.

CHAPTER FOUR: DAVID BOIES

A good general introduction to the problem of dyslexia is Maryanne Wolf, *Proust and the Squid: The Story and Science of the Reading Brain* (Harper, 2007).

The Bjorks have written widely and brilliantly on the subject of desirable difficulty. Here's a good summary of their work: Elizabeth Bjork and Robert Bjork, "Making Things Hard on Yourself, But in a Good Way: Creating Desirable Difficulties to Enhance Learning," *Psychology and the Real World*, M. A. Gernsbacher et al., eds. (Worth Publishers, 2011), ch. 5.

The puzzles about the bat and ball and the widgets come from Shane Frederick, "Cognitive Reflection and Decision Making," *Journal of Economic Perspectives* 19, no. 4 (fall 2005). The results of Adam Alter and Daniel Oppenheimer's experiment with the CRT at Princeton are described in Adam Alter et al., "Overcoming Intuition: Metacognitive Difficulty Activates Analytic Reasoning," *Journal of Experimental Psychology: General* 136 (2007). Alter has a wonderful new book about this line of research called *Drunk Tank Pink* (Penguin, 2013).

Julie Logan's study of dyslexia among entrepreneurs is "Dyslexic Entrepreneurs: The Incidence; Their Coping Strategies and Their Business Skills," *Dyslexia* 15, no. 4 (2009): 328–46.

The best history of IKEA is Ingvar Kamprad and Bertil Torekull's *Leading by Design: The IKEA Story* (Collins, 1999). Incredibly, there is nothing in Torekull's interviews with Kamprad to suggest that Kamprad had even a moment's hesitation about doing business with a Communist country at the height of the Cold War. On the contrary, Kamprad seems almost blasé about it. "At first we did a bit of advance smuggling. Illegally, we took tools such as files, spare parts for machines, and even carbon paper for ancient typewriters."

CHAPTER FIVE: EMIL "JAY" FREIREICH

Sources for the London Blitz include Tom Harrisson, *Living Through the Blitz* (Collins, 1976). "Winston Churchill described London as 'the greatest target in the world,'" appears on page 22; "I lay there feeling indescribably happy and triumphant," page 81; and "What, and miss all this?" page 128. Other sources include Edgar Jones, Robin Woolven, et al., "Civilian Morale During the Second World War: Responses to Air-Raids Re-examined," *Social History of Medicine* 17, no. 3 (2004); and J. T. MacCurdy, *The Structure of Morale* (Cambridge University Press, 1943). "In October 1940 I had occasion to drive through South-East London" appears on page 16; "the morale of the community depends on the reaction of the survivors," pages 13–16; and "When the first siren sounded," page 10.

The informal survey of famous poets and writers is from Felix Brown, "Bereavement and Lack of a Parent in Childhood," in *Foundations of Child Psychiatry*, Emanuel Miller, ed. (Pergamon Press, 1968). "This is not an argument in favour of orphanhood" appears on page 444. J. Marvin Eisenstadt's study is detailed in "Parental Loss and Genius," *American Psychologist* (March 1978): 211. Lucille Iremonger's findings about the backgrounds of England's prime ministers can be found in *The Fiery Chariot: A Study of British Prime Ministers and the Search for Love* (Secker and Warburg, 1970), 4. Iremonger actually made an error in her calculations, which was corrected by the historian Hugh Berrington in the *British Journal of Political Science* 4 (July 1974): 345. The scientific literature on the association between parental loss and eminence is considerable. Among other studies are S. M. Silverman, "Parental Loss and Scientists," *Science Studies* 4 (1974); Robert S. Albert, *Genius and Eminence* (Pergamon Press, 1992); Colin Martindale, "Father's Absence, Psychopathology, and Poetic Eminence," *Psychological Reports* 31 (1972): 843; Dean Keith Simonton, "Genius and Giftedness: Parallels and Discrepancies," in *Talent Development: Proceedings from the 1993 Henry B. and Jocelyn Wallace National Research Symposium on Talent Development*, vol. 2, N. Colangelo, S. G. Assouline, and D. L. Ambroson, eds., 39–82 (Ohio Psychology Publishing).

Two excellent sources on the history of the fight against childhood leukemia are John Laszlo, *The Cure of Childhood Leukemia: Into the Age of Miracles* (Rutgers University Press, 1996), and Siddhartha Mukherjee, *The Emperor of All Maladies* (Scribner, 2011). "There was a senior hematologist" is quoted in Laszlo's book on page 183. Laszlo conducted a series of interviews with every key figure from that period—and each chapter of the book is a separate oral history.

Stanley Rachman's experiments with people with phobias are described in "The Overprediction and Underprediction of Pain," *Clinical Psychology Review* 11 (1991).

"A voice rose from the wreckage," appears on page 97 of Diane McWhorter's *Carry Me Home: Birmingham, Alabama; The Climactic Battle of the Civil Rights Revolution* (Touchstone, 2002); "Hell, yeah, we're going to ride," page 98; "To the child's disbelief," page 109; "Today is the second time within a year," page 110; and "Coke bottles shattered," page 215.

Eugen Kogon's memoir is *The Theory and Practice of Hell* (Berkley Windhover, 1975). "The more tender one's conscience, the more difficult it was to make such decisions" appears on page 278.

CHAPTER SIX: WYATT WALKER

The story of the photograph—and of all the iconic civil rights photographs—is brilliantly told by Martin Berger in *Seeing Through Race: A Reinterpretation of Civil Rights Photography* (University of California Press, 2011). Berger's book is the source for all the discussion of the photograph and the impact it caused. Berger's larger point—which is deeply thought-provoking—is that mainstream white Americans in the 1960s *needed* black activists to seem passive and "saintly." Their cause seemed more acceptable that way. The denunciation of King and Walker for the use of children in the protests is on pages 82–86. Gadsden's explanation of his actions ("I automatically threw my knee") is on page 37.

The single best account of King's Birmingham campaign—and the book to which this chapter is greatly indebted—is Diane McWhorter's *Carry Me Home: Birmingham, Alabama; The Climactic Battle of the Civil Rights Revolution* (Touchstone, 2002). If you think Walker's story is extraordinary, then you should read McWhorter's book. It is as good a work of history as I have ever read. "In Birmingham, it was held a fact of criminal science" appears in a footnote on page 340; "One of the attendees at the meeting was the president's wife," page 292; "A Jew is just a 'nigger turned inside out,'" page 292; "A black man in Chicago wakes up one morning," page 30; "They were astounded to watch King," page 277; "militant out of Dr. Seuss," page 359; "We got to use what we got," page 363; "The K-9 Corps," page 372; and "Sure, people got bit by the dogs," page 375. McWhorter's account of the showdown in Kelly Ingram Park is extraordinary. I have greatly condensed it.

King's mock eulogy appears in Taylor Branch's *Parting the Waters: America in the King Years 1954–63* (Simon and Schuster, 1988), 692. For Branch's description of Wyatt Walker ("he acquired dark-rimmed glasses"), see page 285. "As a general principle, Walker asserted that everything must build" is on page 689. King's words to the parents whose children had been arrested appear on pages 762–64.

"When I kissed my wife and children good-bye" is from an interview of Wyatt Walker by Andrew Manis at Canaan Baptist Church of Christ, New York City, April 20, 1989, page 6. A transcription of the interview is held at Birmingham Public Library, Birmingham, Alabama. From the same interview are: "This man must be out of his goddam mind," 14; and "They can only see...through white eyes," page 22.

"De rabbit is de slickest o' all de animals de Lawd" is cited in Lawrence Levine's *Black Culture and Black Consciousness: Afro-American Folk Thought from Slavery to Freedom* (Oxford University Press, 2007), 107. Also from Levine are: "The rabbit, like the slaves who wove tales about him," page 112; "painfully realistic stories," page 115; and "The records left by nineteenth-century observers of slavery," page 122. The story of the Terrapin is on page 115.

"I'm not hard to get along with, dahlin's" is from a Wyatt Walker interview with John Britton that is part of the Civil Rights Documentation Project, housed in the Moorland-Spingarn Research Center at Howard University. See page 35 of the transcript. Also from the interview are: "If you get in my way, I'll run smack dab over you," page 66; "If I'd had my razor," page 15; "At times I would accommodate or alter my morality," page 31; "Oh, man, it was a great time to be alive," page 63; "Tip his hand," page 59; "I called Dr. King," page 61; and "It was hot in Birmingham," page 62.

Robert Penn Warren conducted several interviews with civil rights activists and leaders as part of his research for his book *Who Speaks for the Negro?* These interviews are collected in the Robert Penn Warren Civil Rights Oral History Project and housed in the Louie B. Nunn Center for Oral History at the University of Kentucky. "Pure joy" comes from tape 1 of his interview with Wyatt Walker on March 18, 1964.

The argument that the trickster tales informed the civil rights movement has been made before. For example: Don McKinney, "Brer Rabbit and Brother Martin Luther King, Jr: The Folktale Background of the Birmingham Protest," *The Journal of Religious Thought* 46, no. 2 (winter-spring 1989–1990): 42–52. McKinney writes (page 50):

> Just as Brer Rabbit's cunning tricked Brer Tiger into doing exactly what the small animals wanted (i.e., he begged to be tied up), so the nonviolent techniques that issued from King and his cadre of shrewd advisors had a similar effect in getting Bull Connor to do what they wanted; namely, to imprison black protestors in such numbers that not only drew national attention, but also virtually immobilized the city of Birmingham.

See also Trudier Harris, *Martin Luther King, Jr., Heroism and African American Literature* (University of Alabama Press, forthcoming).

The detail from the conversation between Pritchett and King about Pritchett's wedding anniversary is cited in Howell Raines, *My Soul Is Rested: The Story of the Civil Rights Movement in the Deep South* (Penguin, 1983), 363–65.

Walker's explanation for why the movement needed Bull Connor's opposition ("There would be no movement, no publicity") is quoted in Michael Cooper Nichols, "Cities Are What Men Make Them: Birmingham, Alabama, Faces the Civil Rights Movement 1963," Senior Thesis, Brown University, 1974, page 286.

Walker's reaction to the use of K-9 units ("We've got a movement. We've got a movement") appears in James Forman, *The Making of Black Revolutionaries: A Personal Account* (Macmillan, 1972).

King's reprimand of the photographer from *Life* ("The world doesn't know this happened") is given in Gene Roberts and Hank Klibanoff, *The Race Beat: The Press, the Civil Rights Struggle, and the Awakening of a Nation* (Random House, 2006).

CHAPTER SEVEN: ROSEMARY LAWLOR

"For God's sake, bring me a large Scotch" is from Peter Taylor, *Brits* (Bloomsbury, 2002), page 48.

Nathan Leites and Charles Wolf Jr.'s report on how to deal with insurgencies is *Rebellion and Authority: An Analytic Essay on Insurgent Conflicts* (Markham Publishing Company, 1970). "Fundamental to our analysis" appears on page 30.

The description of Ian Freeland is by James Callaghan in *A House Divided: The Dilemma of Northern Ireland* (Harper Collins, 1973), page 50. Freeland and the officials and journalists being likened to "the British Raj on a tiger hunt" is from Peter Taylor, *Provos: The IRA and Sinn Fein* (Bloomsbury, 1998), page 83.

Seán MacStiofáin's quote about revolutions being caused by the stupidity and brutality of governments appears in Richard English, *Armed Struggle: The History of the IRA* (Oxford University Press, 2003), page 134.

The principle of legitimacy has been articulated by a number of scholars, but three deserve special mention: Tom Tyler, author of *Why People Obey the Law* (Princeton University Press, 2006); David Kennedy, author of *Deterrence and Crime Prevention* (Routledge, 2008); and Lawrence Sherman, coeditor of *Evidence-Based Crime Prevention* (Routledge, 2006). Here is another example of the same principle. The following is a list of developed-world countries ranked according to the percentage of their economy that is underground—that is, the amount that is deliberately concealed by their citizens in order to avoid taxes—in 2010. It's one of the best ways to compare the honesty of taxpayers in different countries.

U.S.A.	7.8	Finland	14.3
Switzerland	8.34	Denmark	14.4
Austria	8.67	Germany	14.7
Japan	9.7	Norway	15.4
New Zealand	9.9	Sweden	15.6
Netherlands	10.3	Belgium	17.9
United Kingdom	11.1	Portugal	19.7
Australia	11.1	Spain	19.8
France	11.7	Italy	22.2
Canada	12.7	Greece	25.2
Ireland	13.2		

The list is from Friedrich Schneider's "The Influence of the Economic Crisis on the Underground Economy in Germany and other OECD-countries in 2010" (unpublished paper, revised edition, January 2010). The list is not surprising. American, Swiss, and Japanese taxpayers are pretty honest. So are most of the other Western European democracies. Greece, Spain, and Italy are not. In fact, the level of tax evasion in Greece is such that the country's deficit—which is so large that Greece has teetered on the brink of outright bankruptcy for years—would all but disappear if Greek citizens obeyed the law and paid what they owed. Why is America so much more law-abiding when it comes to taxes than Greece?

Leites and Wolf would attribute that to the fact that the costs of tax evasion in the United States are much greater than the benefits: that if Americans cheat, there's a good chance they'll get caught and punished. But that's completely untrue. In the United States, a little more than 1 percent of tax returns are audited every year. That's tiny. And if they get caught underreporting their income, the most common penalty is simply paying back taxes plus a relatively modest fine. Jail time is rare. If American taxpayers behaved rationally—according to Leites and Wolf's definition of the word—tax evasion in America should be rampant. As the tax economist James Alm puts it:

> In countries with effective audit rates of one percent, you *should* observe cheating levels of 90 percent or above. If you declare one more dollar of income, you would pay 30, 40 cents in tax. If you don't declare that dollar, then you keep all of it and there is some chance you will get caught. But it's .01 or less. And if you are detected then the IRS has to determine whether it is intentional. If it is not, you pay back taxes plus about ten percent. If you are audited and you are found to be fraudulent you pay back taxes plus about 75 percent. So the ex-

pected cost of getting caught is just not that large. The calculus is tilted very, very heavily in favor of cheating.

So why don't Americans cheat? *Because they think that their system is legitimate.* People accept authority when they see that it treats everyone equally, when it is possible to speak up and be heard, and when there are rules in place that assure you that tomorrow you won't be treated radically different from how you are treated today. Legitimacy is based on fairness, voice, and predictability, and the U.S. government, as much as Americans like to grumble about it, does a pretty good job of meeting all three standards.

In Greece, the underground economy is three times larger in relative terms than that of the United States. But that's not because Greeks are somehow less honest than Americans. It's because the Greek system is less legitimate than the American system. Greece is one of the most corrupt countries in all of Europe. Its tax code is a mess. Wealthy people get special insider deals, and if you and I lived in a country where the tax system was so blatantly illegitimate—where nothing seemed fair, and where our voices weren't heard, and where the rules changed from one day to the next—we wouldn't pay our taxes either.

The discussion of parades in marching season in Ireland comes from Dominic Bryan, *Orange Parades: The Politics of Ritual, Tradition and Control* (Pluto Press, 2000).

Desmond Hamill's account of the British Army in Northern Ireland is *Pig in the Middle: The Army in Northern Ireland 1969–1984* (Methuen, 1985). The ditty that begins "On the 15th of August" appears on page 18. "The [IRA] retaliated" is on page 32.

The statistics on deaths and violence in 1969 Northern Ireland are from John Soule's "Problems in Applying Counterterrorism to Prevent Terrorism: Two Decades of Violence in Northern Ireland Reconsidered," *Terrorism* 12 (1989): 33.

The account of when General Freeland descended on the Lower Falls is told by Seán MacStiofáin in Seán Óg Ó Fearghaíl's *Law (?) and Orders: The Story of the Belfast Curfew* (Central Citizens' Defense Committee, 1970). The details about Patrick Elliman's death appear on page 14. A good source on the curfew is Taylor's *Provos*. The detail about the man in his pajamas comes from Nicky Curtis, *Faith and Duty: The True Story of a Soldier's War in Northern Ireland* (André Deutsch, 1998).

CHAPTER EIGHT: WILMA DERKSEN

The account of the history of Three Strikes relies on several sources, chief among them: Mike Reynolds, Bill Jones, and Dan Evans, *Three Strikes and You're Out! The Chronicle of America's Toughest Anti-Crime Law*

(Quill Driver Books/Word Dancer Press, 1996); Joe Domanick, *Cruel Justice: Three Strikes and the Politics of Crime in America's Golden State* (University of California Press, 2004); Franklin Zimring, Gordon Hawkins, and Sam Kamin, *Punishment and Democracy: Three Strikes and You're Out in California* (Oxford, 2001); and George Skelton, "A Father's Crusade Born from Pain," *Los Angeles Times,* December 9, 1993.

Richard Wright and Scott Decker's interviews of convicted armed robbers appear in *Armed Robbers in Action: Stickups and Street Culture* (Northeastern University Press, 1997). The comments cited are on page 120. Wright and Decker's book is fascinating. Here's a bit more from them on the psychology of criminality:

> Some of the armed robbers also tried not to think about getting caught because such thoughts generated an uncomfortably high level of mental anguish. They believed that the best way to prevent this from happening was to forget about the risk and leave matters to fate. One of them put it this way. "I don't really trip off getting caught, man, 'cause you'll just worry yourself like that." Given that almost all of these offenders perceived themselves not only as being under pressure to obtain money quickly but also as having no lawful means of doing so, this makes sense. Where no viable alternative to crime exists, there clearly is little point in dwelling on the potentially negative consequences of offending. It should come as no surprise, then, to learn that the offenders usually preferred to ignore the possible risk and concentrate instead on the anticipated reward: "The way I think about [the threat of being apprehended] is this: I would rather take a chance on getting caught and getting locked up than running around out here broke and not taking a chance on even trying to get no money."

David Kennedy's discussion of criminal motivations appears in his book *Deterrence and Crime Prevention* (Routledge, 2008). Anthony Doob and Cheryl Webster's analysis of punishment studies is "Sentence Severity and Crime: Accepting the Null Hypothesis," *Crime and Justice* 30 (2003): 143.

The charts showing the relationship between age and criminality are from Alfred Blumstein, "Prisons: A Policy Challenge," in *Crime: Public Policies for Crime Control,* James Q. Wilson and Joan Petersilia, eds. (ICS Press, 2002), 451–82.

Todd Clear's book on the effects of mass incarceration on poor places is *Imprisoning Communities: How Mass Incarceration Makes Disadvantaged Neighborhoods Worse* (Oxford University Press, 2007). You can find Clear's hard-to-get-published paper "Backfire: When Incarceration Increases Crime" in the *Journal of the Oklahoma Criminal Justice Research Consortium* 3 (1996): 1–10.

There is an entire library of studies on the effects of Three Strikes on California's crime rate. The best book-length academic work is Zimring's *Punishment and Democracy,* mentioned above. Here is a sample from one of the most recent scholarly examinations of the law. It's from Elsa Chen's "Impacts of 'Three Strikes and You're Out' on Crime Trends in California and Throughout the United States," *Journal of Contemporary Criminal Justice* 24 (November 2008): 345–70:

> The impacts of Three Strikes on crime in California and throughout the United States are analyzed using cross-sectional time series analysis of state-level data from 1986 to 2005. The model measures both deterrence and incapacitation effects, controlling for preexisting crime trends and economic, demographic, and policy factors. Despite limited use outside California, the presence of a Three Strikes law appears to be associated with slightly but significantly faster rates of decline in robbery, burglary, larceny, and motor vehicle theft nationwide. Three Strikes also is associated with slower declines in murder rates. Although California's law is the broadest and most frequently used Three Strikes policy, it has not produced greater incapacitation effects on crime than other states' far more limited laws. The analyses indicate that the toughest sentencing policy is not necessarily the most effective option.

There are two excellent accounts of the Candace Derksen case: Wilma Derksen, *Have You Seen Candace?* (Tyndale House Publishers, 1992); and Mike McIntyre, *Journey for Justice: How Project Angel Cracked the Candace Derksen Case* (Great Plains Publications, 2011). The story of the Amish mother whose son was critically injured by a car is told in Donald B. Kraybill, Steven Nolt, and David Weaver-Zercher's *Amish Grace: How Forgiveness Transcended Tragedy* (Jossey-Bass, 2010), 71.

On the British use of power and authority in Northern Ireland during the Troubles, see Paul Dixon, "Hearts and Minds: British Counter-Insurgency Strategy in Northern Ireland," *Journal of Strategic Studies* 32, no. 3 (June 2009): 445–75. Dixon says (page 456):

> Paddy Hillyard estimates that one in four Catholic men between the ages of 16 and 44 had been arrested at least once between 1972 and 1977. On average, every Catholic household in Northern Ireland had been searched twice, but since many homes would not be under suspicion, some houses in certain districts would have been searched "perhaps as many as ten or more times." One account claims the Army conducted routine four monthly checks on the occupants of certain houses in selected areas. "It has been estimated that by mid-1974 the Army had details on between 34 and 40 percent of the adult and juvenile population of Northern Ireland." Between 1 April 1973 and 1 April 1974 four million vehicles were stopped and searched.

John Soule's paper written at the height of the Troubles is "Problems in Applying Counterterrorism to Prevent Terrorism: Two Decades of

Violence in Northern Ireland Reconsidered," *Terrorism* 12, no. 1 (1989). I read about Reynolds's taking visitors to the Daily Planet in Joe Domanick's *Cruel Justice*, 167.

CHAPTER NINE: ANDRÉ TROCMÉ

For an excellent overview of the village of Le Chambon-sur-Lignon and its culture, see Christine E. van der Zanden, *The Plateau of Hospitality: Jewish Refugee Life on the Plateau Vivarais-Lignon* (unpublished thesis, Clark University, 2003). For books about the Trocmés, see Krishana Oxenford Suckau, *Christian Witness on the Plateau Vivarais-Lignon: Narrative, Nonviolence and the Formation of Character* (unpublished dissertation, Boston University School of Theology, 2011); Philip Hallie, *Lest Innocent Blood Be Shed: The Story of the Village of Le Chambon and How Goodness Happened There* (Harper, 1994); and Carol Rittner and Sondra Myers, eds., *The Courage to Care: Rescuers of Jews During the Holocaust* (New York University Press, 2012).

"Loving, forgiving, and doing good to our adversaries" is from *Christian Witness*, 6.

From *Lest Innocent Blood Be Shed:* "'The bell does not belong to the marshal,'" 96; "Lamirand swept up the mountain," 99; "A sense of duty exuded from his pores," 146; "A curse on him who begins in gentleness," 266; "What is this?" 39; "'It was not reasonable,'" 233; "His identity card gave his name as Béguet," 226; "When Trocmé was ten years old," 51; and "'Jean-Pierre! Jean-Pierre!'" 257.

From *The Courage to Care:* "And I said, 'Come in,'" 101; "'The people in our village knew already,'" 101.

Trocmé's question "How could the Nazis ever get to the end...?" is cited in Garret Keizer's *Help: The Original Human Dilemma* (HarperOne, 2005), 151.

Index

Note: Italic page numbers refer to illustrations.

297

About the Author

Malcolm Gladwell has been a staff writer at *The New Yorker* since 1996. Prior to that, he was a reporter at the *Washington Post*. Gladwell was born in England and grew up in rural Ontario. He lives in New York.